WALKING
IN ANDALUCÍA

The Best Walks in Southern Spain's Natural Parks

SEVENTH EDITION

Guy Hunter-Watts

SANTANA BOOKS

WALKING IN ANDALUCÍA (7th Edition)

Published by Ediciones Santana, S.L.
Apartado 41
29650 Mijas-Pueblo (Málaga)
Spain

Tel: (0034) 952 48 58 38
E-Mail: info@santanabooks.com
www.santanabooks.com

Photos by Guy Hunter-Watts

Cartography:
1:50000 Maps for Alpujarras, Aracena, Cazorla, Grazalema and Los Alcornocales reproduced with permission of Instituto Geográfico Nacional

Cartografía Original: Instituto Geográfico Nacional

1:50000 Maps L Series for La Axarquía reproduced with thanks to Servicio Geográfico del Ejercito

Designed by: Cheryl Gatward

Printed in Spain by Industrias Gráficas Solprint, S.L.

ISBN: 978-84-89954-92-2
Depósito Legal: MA 2005 - 2011

Acknowledgements

I'd like to extend sincere thanks to all those who have helped over the many years of this guide's existence with a special *gracias* this time round to Sam and Jeannie Chesterton in Aracena and Julie Holliday in Capileira.

Many walkers have emailed letting me know when there have been changes to the routes described: your help, too, has been much appreciated.

I also owe heaps of gratitude to Peter Jones and Martin Jacoby for providing the check lists for birds and plants which are a new addition to the book. More of the same is due to Cheryl Gatward of New Image for her creative nouse when it came to the design and layout of this latest edition.

And humongous thanks, as always, to Tiki for your patience and support.

Photography
All photographic images by the author apart from cover image by Tiki Kyte and ornithological images courtesy of Spanish Nature.

This edition is dedicated to the many walkers who participated in The Andalucían Coast to Coast Walk for Children in Nepal *as well as to those who supported the walk through their generous sponsorship.*

Contents

Foreword

My first experience of inland Spain came at the age of twenty one when I rode an old sit-up-and-beg bike across inland Andalucía, from Huelva in the West to Murcía in the East. What most excited me were the vast, open spaces through which I was travelling. Coming from southern England the small number of cars and the sparsely populated landscape seemed as exotic a sight as the palm trees and bougainvillea which gave nearly every remote *cortijo* such a heady allure.

Many years later I returned. This time I exchanged two wheels for two leather boots and headed for the mountains south of Ronda. Again I was inspired and moved by the huge expanse of wild and rugged mountains. The landscape felt unbridled compared with the more domesticated countryside that I had left behind.

Rewalking the routes in this book for this seventh edition has again been inspirational and although almost thirty years have passed since my first foray into the Sierras of the south the mountains have lost none of their appeal. It hardly seems credible that in covering almost 500kms of trail I met with less than half that number of walkers and often found myself on footpaths from where no villages nor even remote farms were visible.

It's this sense of space which makes walking in Andalucía so special. More people are walking Spain's southern Sierras yet the vast majority of the routes within these pages remain blissfully undiscovered. If you decide to head for the hills with this guide you can be sure of two things: you'll be walking through areas of great natural beauty and will meet with few other walkers. There's nothing to detract from the sheer pleasure of simply going out for a walk.

'That something exists outside ourselves and our preoccupations, so near, so readily available, is our greatest blessing'

'There are things we will never see, unless we walk to them'

'Walking is egalitarian and democratic; we do not become experts at walking and one side of the road is as good as another'

Thomas A. Clark on Walking

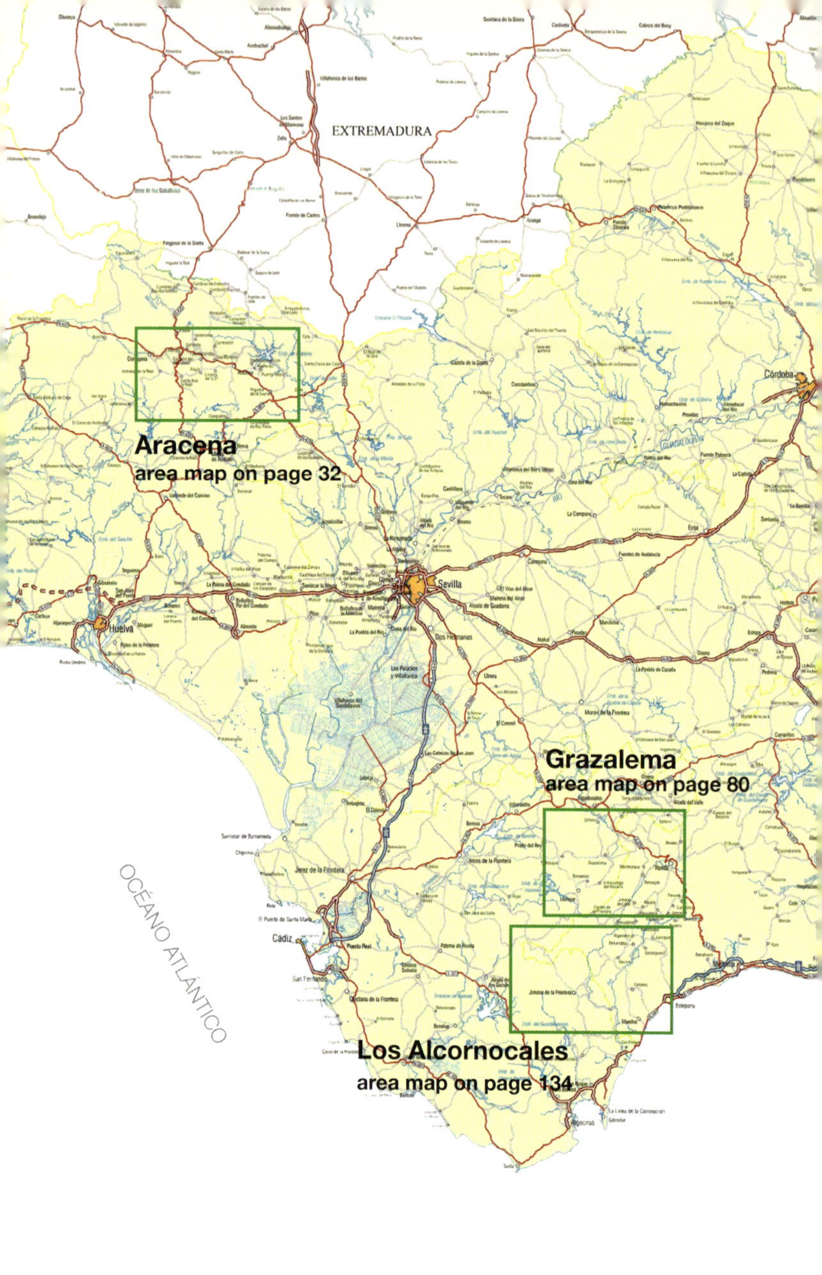
EXTREMADURA
Aracena
area map on page 32
Grazalema
area map on page 80
Los Alcornocales
area map on page 134
OCÉANO ATLÁNTICO
Sevilla
Huelva
Córdoba
Cádiz
Dos Hermanas
San Fernando
Algeciras
Estepona

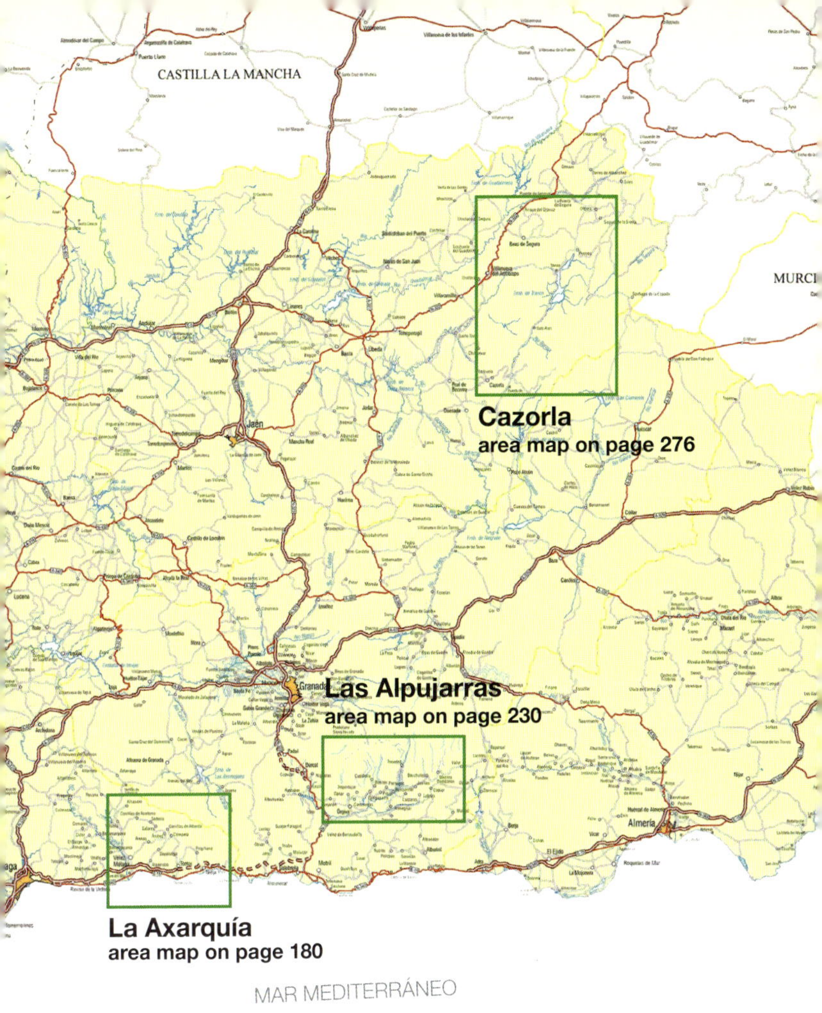

Andalucía and the Natural Parks described in this guide

Introduction

The mountains and villages of Andalucía

Few people are aware that Spain, after Switzerland, is the most mountainous country in Europe or that the walking here can be as good as anywhere on the Continent. Perhaps it's because people have long associated holidays here, especially in Andalucía, with sun, sand and sea. Inland Spain has always been seen as a little too raw, too different, by the package tourists who prefer the familiarity of their beachside hotels.

Yet the coastal belt represents just a tiny part of the rich fabric of Spain. Travel a few kilometres inland and you'll find any number of pretty villages where there is scarcely a foreign resident and where the idea of *pueblo* (it means both *village* and *people*) remains as vibrant and as strong as it has for centuries. Not to visit these villages is, in a sense, not to visit Spain. Ask a Spaniard where she or he is from and rather than replying '*España*' they invariably give you the name of their home village. Ask one of Andalucía's many emigrant workers what they miss most and they'll probably tell you that, after their family and friends, it's their annual village fiesta.

Many of these villages are wrapped into the fabric of the great belt of the Cordillera Bética mountains which run from east to west across Andalucía. This vast range includes mainland Spain's highest peak, the Mulhacén which, in spite of its southerly position, will sometimes have snow on its upper reaches for nine months of the year. And within this mighty, rumpled chain of mountains there are no fewer than twenty Natural Parks, each of them with a character all of its own.

The aim of this walking book is two-fold. It is not only to

introduce you to the most beautiful of Andalucía's Natural Parks but also to lead you to their most attractive villages and small towns. To this end, all walks described here (with just a couple of exceptions) either link two villages or are circular routes departing and ending in villages which are not only worth visiting but also where good accommodation and food is available. Surely the greatest pleasures after a long walk are to tuck into a delicious meal then slump into a comfortable bed?

The good news is that over the last decade or so there's been a silent revolution taking place in the hills of Southern Spain. Paths are being cleared, routes waymarked and groups of walkers, mostly from northern Europe, are extending the season of many a rural hotel. What began with pots of Brussels money, and initiatives like the creation of the G.R.7 Long Distance Footpath, is now beginning to take root. It was gratifying when rewalking the 36 routes for this edition to come across several new walking guides in English and Spanish to the different parks. Spain badly needs this type of sustainable tourism and all the signs are that this is a sector that will continue to grow in future years.

If you're looking for purpose-built trails of the sort that you find, say, in the Parks of the U.S.A., then the walking in Andalucía will probably not be for you. Many of these walks follow old drovers' paths which have seen scant use since the coming of the roads. They can be rough or loose underfoot and where waymarking exists, it can sometimes be confusing. But that's the whole point of this guide and none of the walks I describe will pit you against Nature. They are, I believe, all beautiful, all different and all within the capabilities of anyone who walks on a regular basis.

When to walk in Andalucía

As a general rule the best time to walk in Andalucía is from late April through to early June and from mid September to the end of October when you're likely to encounter mild, sunny weather: warm enough to picnic yet not so hot as to make temperature an additional challenge. Wild flowers tend to be at their best in late April/early May and this is the time when many walking companies plan their walks. The months most walkers avoid are July and August when temperatures are just too high to make walking easy or pleasant. If you limit yourself to shorter circuits, get going early and take plenty of water you can still enjoy walking in summer. But you should be in good physical shape.

If you're prepared to risk rain then winter is a wonderful time to be out walking, especially from December to February when rainfall is generally less than in November, March and April. *Generally* means exactly that: rainfall statistics for the past century confirm the above but the past decades, with the prolonged drought of the nineteen-nineties, followed by some unusually wet winters, and now another run of dry winters, provides no steady yardstick against which to base your predictions.

The exception to the above is the Cazorla Park which is further north than the other Parks included in this book. Here the Mediterranean influence is less marked and there may well be snow and ice on the higher routes from November onwards. On the other hand the Alpujarras, although higher than Cazorla, rarely have snow settling beneath 1200m and to walk with a snowy Sierra Nevada as a backdrop makes for truly memorable experience. But you'll need to be well equipped and ready for brusque changes in temperature.

The routes

For each of the six regions I've included a mixture of half day and full day walks which will:

- introduce you to the most attractive area of each Park
- lead you to the most interesting villages in the area

The introduction to each walk should give you a feel for what any given itinerary involves whilst the walking notes and maps will give a good idea of the distance and the differences in height that you'll encounter.

How to use the walking notes

The walking notes, together with the individual route map, should allow you to follow these walks without difficulty. But I recommend that you always have a compass and the recommended map of the area, in addition to the one that we provide in this book.

Distance: Self explanatory

Rating: Walks are graded in three brackets:

Easy – shorter walks with little height gain

Medium – mid-length walks with some steep up and downhill sections

Difficult – longer routes with a number of steep up and downhill sections.

If you're reasonably fit then you should experience no difficulty with any of these routes. For walks classed as *Difficult* the most important thing is to allow yourself plenty of time and take a good supply of water. The very longest walk described is 19km (12 miles). But remember what can be an easy walk in cooler weather becomes a much more difficult challenge in the heat.

I've based my rating system on walking in cooler weather, of the sort you're likely to encounter in Spring or Autumn in Andalucía.

Time required

This is my estimate of how long you should allow to get the most out of any particular walk, allowing for rest stops and lunch breaks. **This is different to the bracketed timings of the route notes** which are my timings for walking a route, without breaks, at an *average* walking pace.

If your pace is slower or faster than mine, don't worry. These timings are intended to give an idea of how far into any particular walk you might be. You could simply ignore them: it will be fairly clear from the map how far you have to go.

Map

Lists the best map to have along with you on any particular walk. I sometimes suggest an alternative.

Water

For each itinerary I've listed the springs you pass with a W symbol. Be aware that in dry years these springs can slow to little more than a trickle or dry up altogether so always carry plenty of your own water. For obvious reasons avoid plastic water bottles: Sigg-style bottles are durable and keep water much cooler. I'd also recommend having water purification tablets in your day pack: you never know when you might need them.

G.P.S. References

For this edition of the book I've added G.P.S. references for each walk. These are provided in U.T.M. European 1950 format as used on all the I.N.G. maps in this guide. These references will be available as free G.P.X. downloads from my website. www.walkinginandalucia.es

By using a programme such as Garmin's BaseCamp you

can download the files to your desktop, import them into the programme then transfer them to your G.P.S. handheld device.

You can download the Basecamp programme for Mac and P.C. at: www.garmin.com/garmin/cms/us/onthetrail/basecamp

I provide all G.P.S. references in good faith but can accept no responsibility for their accuracy. Your first point of reference should always be the walking notes themselves.

Definition of terms

I've tried to make notes as unambiguous as possible. When describing the walks I've used *track* for any thoroughfare wide enough to permit vehicle access and *path* to describe one that is wide enough only for pedestrians and animals.

G.R. & P.R.

You'll see references in many walks to G.R. and P.R..

G.R. stands for *Gran Recorrido* or Long Distance footpath and these routes are marked with red and white waymarking.

P.R. stands for *Pequeño Recorrido* or Short Distance footpath and these routes are marked with yellow and white waymarking.

Walking check list

The two most important things to have along when you walk in Andalucía are:

- **Water:** carry a minimum of 1 litre and preferably more. During the warmer months the greatest potential danger facing you is heat exhaustion and dehydration. Wear loose-fitting clothing, a hat and keep drinking
- **Comfortable, broken-in walking boots:** no walk is enjoyable with blisters

You should also remember the following (this list compiled with maximum safety in mind):

- **Water bottle** (*Sigg* bottles are excellent)
- **Hat & sun block**
- **Map & compass**
- **Swiss army knife** or similar
- **Torch & whistle**
- **Mobile phone:** coverage is patchy in the mountains but if you have a mobile phone it would be silly not to take it along
- **Waterproofs** according to season
- **Fleece or jumper:** temperatures can drop rapidly at the top of the higher passes
- **Picnic**
- **First aid kit** to include antihistamine cream, plasters, bandage, plastic skin etc for blisters
- **Water purifying tablets**
- **Walking stick(s):** many hikers are now using light weight aluminium walking sticks, the best of which have shock-absorbing tips. Evidence shows that they reduce the possibility of injury whilst conserving energy
- **Chocolate/sweets** or glucose tablets

Things to remember when walking in Andalucía

- **Close all gates** You'll come across some extraordinary gate closing devices. They can take time, patience and effort to open and to close.

- **Ganado Bravo** Watch out for this sign: it designates an area where you could find bulls. Signs for *Coto* or *Coto Privado de Caza* designates an area where hunting is permitted in season: it doesn't mean that you're entering on private property. *Cotos* are normally marked by a small rectangular sign divided into a white and black triangle.

- **Fire** In the dry months the hillsides of the South become a vast tinder box. Be very careful if you smoke or use camping stoves.

- **Rubbish** Take yours and – why not? – other people's back with you.

Safety when walking

When heading off on any walk you should always let at least one person know where you are headed and the time you expect to return.

Emergency telephone numbers that you should have in your mobile:

- 112 Emergency services: general number
- 062 *Guardía Civil*
- 061 Medical emergencies
- 080 Fire Brigade

Maps

Under each general section I've recommended the best map available for the area. And at the back of this book I've included a bilingual order form which will make the process of ordering easier within Spain. All places listed in Spain will send maps *contra reembolso* i.e. you pay when the maps are delivered to you by the delivery company.

In Andalucía the best places to buy maps are:

L.T.C. – Avenida Menéndez Pelayo 42-44, Sevilla.
Tel: 954 425 964 Fax: 954 423 451
e-mail: ltc@ltcideas.com www.ltcideas.com

or

Mapas y Compañia – Calle Compañia 33, Málaga
Tel: 952 608 815
e-mail: info@mapasycia.es www.mapasycia.es

In Madrid the best places to order maps are:

La Tienda Verde – Calle Maudes 23 & 38, 28003 Madrid.
Tel: 91 533 0791 Fax: 91 533 6454
e-mail: info@tiendaverde.org www.tiendaverde.org

or

Centro Nacional de Información Geográfica
General Ibánez de Ibero 3, 28010 Madrid
Tel: 91 597 9453 Fax: 91 553 2913
e-mail: consulta@cnig.es www.cnig.es

In the UK the best place for maps, which can be ordered on line, is:

Stanfords – 12-14 Long Acre, London, WC1
Tel: 0207 836 1321 Fax: 0207 836 0189
Email: sales@stanfords.co.uk www.stanfords.co.uk

Bibliography of Fauna and Flora

Ornithology

The species check list at the end of this book was kindly provided by Peter Jones of the Andalucía Bird Society who organise birding excursions in Spain and in several other parts of the world (see check list for Peter's contact details).

The classic field guides are:

A Field Guide to the Birds of Britain & Europe
Peterson, Mountfort & Hollom (ISBN 0-00-219900-9).

Bird Guide
Mullarney, Svennsson, Zetterström & Grant (ISBN 0-00-219728-6).

Where to Watch Birds in Southern Spain
García & Paterson (ISBN 0-7136.3859-1).

An interesting reference book but too large for the field is:
Birds of Iberia
Finlayson & Tomlinson (ISBN 84-88127-08-1).

Botany

The plant list at the end of this guide was kindly provided by Martin Jacoby. Recently retired, Martin continues to be involved in conservation in Andalucía and is a leading expert on the Doñana National Park. References quoted in his plant list correspond to the classic field guide:

Wildflowers of the Mediterranean
Marjorie Blamey & Christopher Grey-Wilson (ISBN 0-7136-7015-0)

Other recommended flower guides:
Flowers of Southwest Europe: A Field Guide
Oleg, Polunin & Smythies (ISBN: 0-19-288178-7). Very

comprehensive: this is a classic botanical *must-have*.

Wildflowers of Southern Spain.
Betty Molesworth Allen (ISBN 84-88127-06-5). The book not only gives you the botanical information but also describes medicinal and culinary uses of the plants. It also lists the common Spanish names.

A Field Guide to the Wild Flowers of Southern Europe
Davies & Gibbons (ISBN 1-85223-659-0). A more comprehensive work than the above and of manageable size

Accommodation

I've included my favourite hotels, hostals and B&Bs in the villages where walks begin or end. All places included have one thing in common: they are clean and welcoming. Nearly all offer breakfast and most can prepare an evening meal. Some can prepare picnics if you let the owners know the night before.

Under **Best Eats** I've listed other good local eateries when there's no food available or when there's a particularly memorable restaurant close by.

Prices quoted are a guideline. You may get a lower price out of season and there may also have been slight increases so always check when you book. Be aware that a few of the smaller places listed don't accept credit cards.

Hotels in Andalucía often make extensive use of marble which is a perfect material for the searing heat of the summer. But in winter floors can be icy cold: packing a pair of slippers can be a Godsend. Remember that some cheaper hostals don't provide soap and when sleeping in budget options during the colder months it's always a good idea to ring ahead to ask the owners if they'd mind switching on the heating before your arrive.

In the Grazalema general section you'll find details of my two village houses, El Tejar and Dar Hajra. The houses (one sleeps 2-4, the other up to 8) could be a great base if you plan to spend a week exploring the area and prefer to self cater. We have masses of maps and information on walking in the Grazalema/Zahara/Montecorto area including route descriptions of several walks in addition to those listed in this guide. See www.rondatejar.com

Eating in Southern Spain

The Spanish eat much later than is the custom in northern Europe and the USA. Lunch is not generally available until 2pm, few people sit down to dinner before 9pm and dining rooms rarely open before 8.30pm. Bear in mind that there's nearly always a *menú del día* available even if waiters assume you'll want to eat *à la carte*. It is often marvellous value.

A common lament amongst walkers is that breakfast is often not served until 9am which can mean not setting out on your walks until close on 10am. If you're keen to make an earlier start take a thermos along: most places will willingly fill it with tea or coffee the night before.

Updates by Email

I've tried to be as accurate as possible in describing all routes and have checked each itinerary for this edition. But paths change fast, especially now that the fencing of farms is becoming a national obsession. I'd be grateful for feedback on any changes you encounter via info@rondatejar.com

Any significant changes to the descriptions of walks in this book are added to a Facebook Group, *Walking in Andalucía*. The page also serves as a forum for adding suggestions and feedback about walks described in this book. I look forward to receiving your feedback! **Many thanks – and happy walking!**

Aracena

La Nava
Valdelarco
Cortelazor
Carboneras
Cala
Arroyo
Galaroza
Castaño del Robledo
Almonaster la Real
Aracena
Corteconcepción
Santa Ana la Real
Alajar
Linares de la Sierra
Higuera de la Sierra
Zufre
A-461
Campofrío
La Granada de Río-Tinto
N-435
N-433
El Campillo
NERVA
Castillo

AREA MAP

ARACENA

THE AREA

The Natural Park of the Sierra de Aracena y Los Picos de Aroche lies an hour and a half by car to the northwest of Seville and encompasses an impressive 184,000 hectares of the province of Huelva. The range forms the western-most tip of the Sierra Morena, the mountainous belt which forms a natural divide between Spain's central Meseta and the Guadalquivir valley to the south. The massif gradually loses height as it cuts sabre-like across Andalusia, with its last foothills reaching out and across the border into Portugal.

All of the walks described in this chapter lie within the Sierra of Aracena, one of the park's three mountain ranges, which stretches west from the delightful town of the same name. Within the *sierra* are a string of attractive villages which, until just 50 years ago, were connected to one another by an elaborate network of drovers' paths. These century-old thoroughfares cut out from the villages by way of cultivated *huertas* (see glossary) where small groves of citrus alternate with carefully tended vegetable plots. Most walks described follow these ancient paths. In many places the original cobbling remains intact and there are long sections of path which run between old stone-walls, covered in mosses and lichens. There are few walkers, gradients are for the most part not too steep and the itineraries are generally easy to follow.

The area gets surprisingly heavy rainfall considering its southerly position: the Atlantic weather systems cross Portugal unhindered before being forced upwards by this last spur of the Iberian massif which rises to a height of nearly 1000 metres in little more than a dozen miles. In spite of the predominantly impervious subsoil, substantial ground cover ensures that much of this rainfall is retained. This fact, along with a relative absence of the use of pesticides, ensures that the wildflowers here are spectacular in all but the summer months.

The most singular feature of the area is the extensive *dehesa* system of woodland management (see glossary) whose persistence has ensured that a staggering 90% of the area of the Park remains forested. The trees most characteristic of the *dehesa* are holm and cork oaks. They provide rich and sustainable grazing for the much-prized Iberian pigs which are so much a feature of the Aracena hills: you'll see them scuttling away from you beneath the oaks on all of these walks. No trip to the Sierra would be complete without tasting the Jabugo ham, the region's most famous culinary delicacy.

The hillsides are also characterised by large swathes of chestnut groves. These became an important part of the local economy after being introduced in the period following the Reconquest. They have flourished in the unusually warm and damp conditions of the Sierra. The trees are at their most impressive in the autumn when the leaves are on the turn, whilst in winter their heavily coppiced forms look almost baobab-like when the leaves are down. To see them cloaked in winter mists is a sight never to be forgotten.

But the Park, particularly at its periphery, also encompasses extensive stands of eucalyptus and pine. Most of this forest mass owes its origin to the deforestation which followed the passing of the charcoal burners. When it came to replanting, indigenous species were abandoned in favour of those which could be quickly harvested. The routes in this book avoid these areas whenever possible: the impoverished subsoil provides little of interest as far as flora and fauna are concerned and in many places denuded hillsides have suffered severe erosion.

Although the scenery here is less wild or rugged than in other mountain ranges of the South – you are always aware that the hand of man has been instrumental in fashioning the landscape – there are few areas which offer more enchanting walking than the Aracena Park. Both long and short-distance paths have recently been waymarked and the region is bound to attract a growing number of visitors. So visit as soon as possible.

If you plan to stay for a number of days be sure to stay at least one night in Aracena and then, perhaps, move on to Linares, Alájar, or Almonaster. All three villages have a beauty all of their own and are worth a second or third night. My personal favourite is Alájar. It has a reliable small *posada*, good restaurants and bars, and the extraordinary Peña de Arias Montero towers above the village.

Other Walks

Several waymarked routes criss-cross the park. The small guide *Los Senderos de la Sierra de Aracena y Picos de Aroche*, available from the Aracena tourist office, describes these routes, allbeit with very scant detail: don't attempt to follow the routes without a map and there's no English translation as yet. To the North of the N433 road leading from Aracena to Portugal are two parallel, long-distance paths: the G.R.41 and the G.R.48. Both cut east-west across the park. The scenery is not as pretty as that of the centre of the Park and you are also skirting round the eucalyptus belt. The G.R.41.3 runs too close to the N433 for my personal liking. Much more attractive is the G.R.42.1 which cuts a lovely loop out from Galaroza via Jabugo and Almonaster then on to Aroche at the Western end of the Park.

Maps

The best maps are the IGN 1:50000 maps. 98% of walks described in this section are covered by Aracena (917) whilst a tiny part of the walk east from Aracena to Corteconcepción and back spills over onto Santa Olalla del Cala (918).

BEST PLACES TO SLEEP & EAT

ARACENA

Hotel Sierra de Aracena

Tel: 959 126 175 Email: hsierraaracena@terra.es

Reliable and attractive mid-range hotel just a couple of minutes walk from the main square. No evening meals but you are close to several restaurants. €50-€65 + 7% VAT. (Taxis: Jorge Canterla 689 649 145 or Vicente Garzón 617 422 003). **Best Eats:** Restaurante José Vicente, Bar El Porvenir, Bar Sirlache for plenty of local favour (setas) or for a treat Manolo Rivera Manolo Rivera ('Manzano').

Hotel Casa Noble

Tel: 959 127 778 Email: enquiries@lacasanoble.net

A colourful, upmarket (and expensive!) option in the town centre with masses of the original turn-of-century décor still in place, and with a lively wine bar right next door. €185 excluding breakfast. **Best Eats:** Tapas in your suite or on the terrace, Bar Sirlache for trad' Spanish cuisine or Manolo Rivera for a splurge.

LOS MARINES (just north of Linares de la Sierra)

Finca Buen Vino

Tel: 959 124 034 Email: availability@fincabuenvino.com

My personal favourite in the Sierra and well worth those extra euros. Sam and Jeannie Chesterton have created a supremely congenial house-party atmosphere at Buen Vino. €100-€140 + 7% VAT incl. breakfast. (Taxi: Sam will arrange). **Best Eats:** Here. Jeannie is a *cordon bleu* trained and her cooking is fantastic.

ALMONASTER LA REAL

Casa Garcia Tel: 959 143 109 Email: casagarcia@ozu.es

An attractive small hotel at the entrance to the village which has been refurbished. Excellent food great value. €65 + 7% VAT. (Taxi: Alfonso 959 143 130) **Best Eats:** Here or Rincón de Curro for superb *cocina andaluza*.

ALÁJAR

La Posada Tel: 959 125 712 Email: info@laposadadealajar.com

Just yards from the pretty main square. Small rooms and a tiny dining room where breakfasts and evening meals are served. €60 + 7% VAT. (Taxi: Angel 959 125 709 or 689 648 925). **Best Eats:** Simple meals available here or El Padrino (weekends), El Molino or La Bótica.

CORTECONCEPCIÓN

La Casa del Cura Tel: 959 120 120

Worth paying a little extra for one of the four top floor rooms which have balconies with great views out to the mountains to the north and the Aracena reservoir. Good food available in downstairs restaurant at weekends. €50-€60 + 7% VAT. **Best Eats:** Here, although the restaurant is only open at weekends: there are cheap and cheerful bars and restaurants in the village

LINARES DE LA SIERRA

Finca La Fronda

Tel: 959 501 247 Email: info@fincalafronda.com

A gorgeous hideaway close to Linares with beautiful bedrooms and suites, scrumptious breakfasts and *tapas* style meals if you prefer to eat at home. Excellent value given the level of comfort. €90-€105 **Best Eats:** Here or see Aracena listings.

ARACENA CIRCUIT

Distance: 10 kms **Duration:** 4/4.5 hours **Rating:** Easy

Map: IGN 1:50000 Aracena (917/10-37) & Santa Olalla del Calá (918/11-37)

W Water: In any of the bars in Corteconcepción @ 1 hr 25 mins

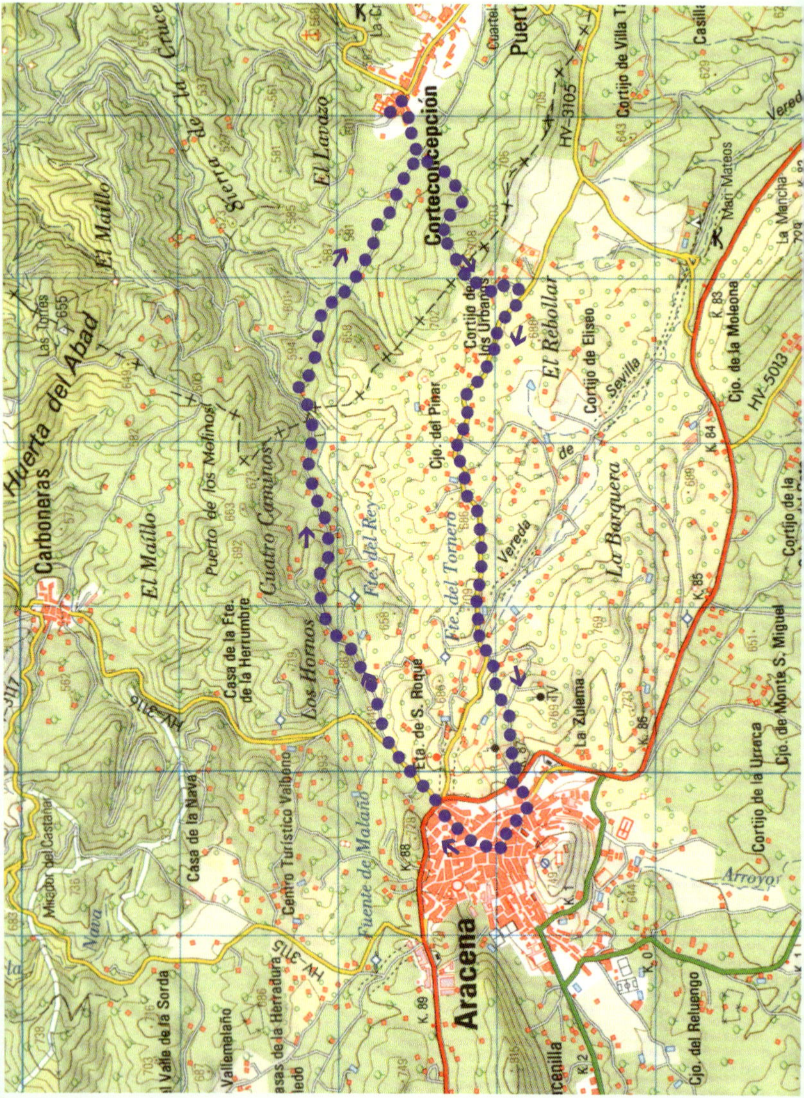

1 The Walk of the Virgin & the Pigs

This is an easy half day walk, much of which is along ancient muleteer's paths with wonderfully preserved sections of their original cobbling. You first follow a fertile valley out from Aracena before climbing up through groves of olives and stands of cork oak beneath which you'll see the region's prized Iberian pigs grubbing for acorns. If you visit Corteconcepción, a half hour diversion, you'll need to double back for a short distance but it would be a great shame to miss this sleepy village: the views from its *mirador* (glossary) next to the church of La Asunción are splendid and this makes a great spot for a picnic. The return journey takes you along a beautiful section of cobbled path before you meet with a broad farm track which runs back towards Aracena along the top of a ridge: you get great views both to the North and South. The variety of the terrain and abundance of fruit trees and hedgerows means there's a great variety of birdlife and the open terrain of the cork oak *dehesas* (glossary) means that they're pretty easy to spot.

The Route

The walk begins outside the Bar Manzano in Aracena's main square, *Plaza Marquesa de Aracena*. (1) From here head diagonally across the square to El Casino and climb up Calle Mesones. Just after passing La Iglesia del Carmen bear right and at the end of this next street turn sharp left and climb to the Ermita de San Roque. (2) Keep to the left of the chapel, pass under two bridges, go straight across at a roundabout, then follow a quiet road downhill. After 350m fork right onto a track: there's waymarking and a sign for *Corteconcepción*. (3)

You arrive at a small shrine dedicated to the *Virgen del Carmen*. (4) Bear right here and drop down through olive and almond groves. Passing a number of farmsteads the track runs past by La Fuente del Rey 5 and then an information board on the valley's *huertas* or irrigated market gardens. A few metres past the sign the track swings left then descends through olive groves and stands of cork oak. You shortly pass the entrance of the Tierna Esperanza Rehab' Centre and, a little further on, the gates of Finca La Postura. 6

Continue down through well-watered groves: agave, pomegranate and prickly pears lend an exotic hue. After passing a row of young eucalyptus trees the track divides **(40 mins)**. 7 Here bear right (there's a marker post), descend, cross the (dry) river via stepping stones and climb up past a farmhouse just to the right of your track which soon narrows to become a footpath. After climbing steadily upwards the path levels and you reach a bench 8 by a metal gate where the path angles right. You'll see white and yellow P.R. waymarking. After passing a number of mostly green gates to the right and left of the path you reach a junction. Here take the right option and continue on to another junction where your path meets with two others, one branching left, the other right, known locally as *Tres Caminos* **(1 hr 15 mins)**. 9

Turn left here, following the direction indicated by a ceramic tile set in the wall. Shortly before the village you come to a four-way junction. 10 Here turn left and you soon arrive at the first of the village houses. Head along Calle Montesina then angle left across a pretty cobbled square: there's a bar at its far, left hand corner where you could stop for a drink and replenish water supplies. Just beyond the bar 11 angle left and head up Calle Iglesias past La Casa del Cura to the Mirador Los Portales at the eastern end of the church **(1 hr 25 mins)**. 12 From here there's a huge sweep of vista to the northeast towards the Aracena reservoir. After taking in the views retrace your footseps back to waypoint 10.

Arriving once again at the four-way junction head straight on and climb a narrow cobbled track which immediately passes by a rather rickety shed made from wood and corrugated iron. After climbing steadily upwards you pass by a grey metal gate ⑬ after which the path becomes more overgrown. Climbing still it angles hard left, then slightly left again: fence-topped walls now run both to the left and right of the path. Angling back right the path runs up to merge with a broad track next to the gates of Finca La Rejoya. ⑭ Head straight on along a broad track which runs on past several farms through an area of *dehesa* (glossary) where there are enormous cork oaks. 50m after passing a long low brick shed the path divides. ⑮ Take the narrower, right hand option which shortly runs up to meet with a broad farm track by a 40kmph speed sign **(2 hrs 10 mins)**. ⑯

Bear right along the track: you'll be following it for some 20-25 minutes so can forget the route notes at this stage and abandon yourself to the views to both sides of the track. You pass a stone building and a memorial plaque ⑰ to a young Englishman, Joseph Thomson, who lived part of his short life in the house. Continue along the track past Villa Salud and, a little further on, past another shrine to the *Virgen del Rosario*. ⑱

The track now begins to climb then levels and passes yet another shrine to the Virgin, this one dedicated to *La Divina Pastora.* ⑲The track gradually descends until it runs up to a fork ⑳ by a large pylon. To your right is a poultry farm: your nose will let you know when you've reached this spot **(2 hrs 35 mins)**.

Here cut left off the track and after just 20m angle right and climb steeply up a concreted section of narrow track: a row of grey metal posts runs just to your right. After a steep pull you reach the top of the rise ㉑ where the track narrows down to become a footpath which now begins to descend between two stone walls, rather uneven and eroded at this point. Soon you

pass by the gate of Finca La Era, topped by twin ploughs which look wierdly bird-like. As you descend the castle above Aracena comes into view as the track arcs round to the right then meets with a concreted track. Bearing left and descending you reach the main road round Aracena, the N433. 22

Take care as you cross the road then hop over the crash barrier and turn left. After just 70m cut right at a No Entry sign 23 and head down hill towards a huge church, La Iglesia de la Asunción. At the next junction head straight over a tarmac road then at the bottom of the street turn right. You soon pass by Aracena's unusual Neo-Mudéjar *Ayuntamiento* (Town Hall). Immediately past this building angle left and head on down to the bottom of a narrower cobled street until you reach a junction. Here cut right along Calle Constitución to arrive back at Bar Manzano and the main square **(3 hrs 5 mins)**. 1

ARACENA CIRCUIT

Distance: 12.5 kms **Duration:** 4/4.5 hours **Rating:** Medium

Map: 1:50000 Aracena (917)

Water: Spring and bars in Linares @ 1 hr 25 mins

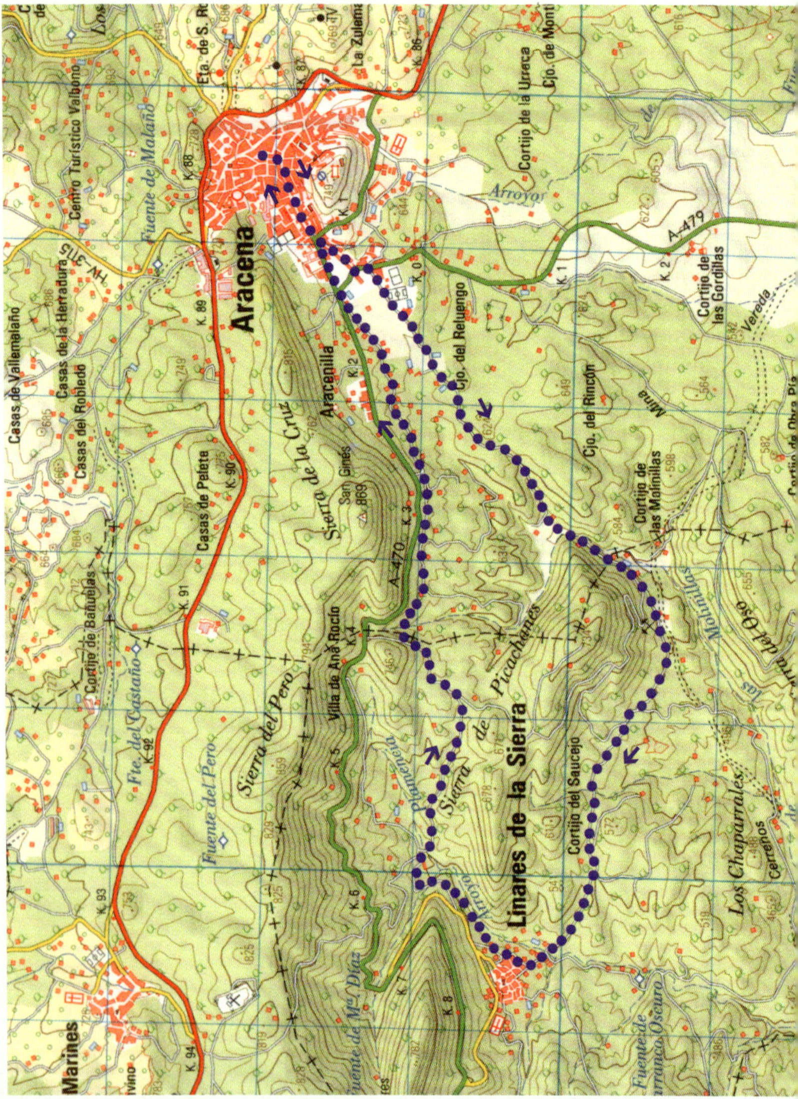

2 The Walk of the Bountiful Dehesa

This circuit could make for a good first shortish walk in the Aracena Sierra. The route begins in the town centre but you quickly leave traffic and the city's expanding suburbs behind you. The scenery you encounter along the way is terrifically varied: the walk takes you along narrow cobbled paths past irrigated orchards, and broader tracks which cut through an attractive swathe of *dehesa* (glossary). And the exceptionally pretty village of Linares lies half way through the walk. Gradients are for the most part gentle with one section of steeper climbing of about 25 minutes on the return leg. Take time to visit the centre of Linares and its unique *plaza de toros*. Nearly all of the houses in the village have intricate cobbled thresh-holds which are unique in the Sierra. There's a good restaurant in the village centre, *Los Arrieros*, and three cheap-and-cheerful bars in the *plaza de toros*.

The Route

The walk begins at Café Bar Manzano on Aracena's pretty main square. (1) Turn right out of the bar, cross the street and go past the Cajasol bank. At the end of this street turn right. Continue all the way down this street, passing by Hotel Los Castaños, until you reach a square lined with palm trees where there are a number of contemporary sculptures. (2) At the end of the square bear left along a one way street past an old wash house to your left. Head straight across at a mini roundabout then pass to the right of the municipal sport's ground, *El Estadio Municipal San Jerónimo*, then continue on past *Conservas Jabugo*. The tarmac road becomes a dirt track. (3)

You now drop down an ancient track which runs between old dry-stone walls. Pass Hacienda Boca de Oro and continue

on through a swathe of *dehesa* (glossary). Keep to main track and just before you reach a gate, just past a metal pylon, (4) cut right and descend through gorse and oaks on a broad, sandy path **(25 mins)**. You should spot faint P.R. yellow and white waymarking.

The track descends, bears right, then crosses a concrete bridge, (5) before bearing left. Climb for a short distance with the stream down to your left and at the point where you reach a brown metal gate cut right off the track onto a narrow path. Soon the path merges with a track (6) where you bear left, then right, and pass just above two farms: the second of them has a large pool. Just beyond the second farm your track merges with another, by a wooden gate with posts of dressed stone, at a point where it arcs up the hill **(50 mins)**. (7)

Here turn left and descend: you'll again see faint yellow and white P.R. waymarking. Soon you come to a pretty farm to the left of the track with a water tank. Just before reaching the farm the track bears right and runs up to a gate. Go through the gate and continue along a more indistinct track. It runs to the right of a wall, then a fenced enclosure, then passes through a second gate. (8) Continue on your same course: the sandy track narrows down and you shortly pass beneath a ruin.

The track runs on between fences then meets a better defined track. (9) Here turn right and climb between high stone walls. You shortly reach a fork; here keep left sticking to the track which will lead you all the way to Linares. Soon the track merges with another which comes in from your left, after which it becomes cobbled. You're now following the ancient drovers' path of *Las*

Dehasillas which once was one of the principal livestock routes across southwestern Spain. You pass just right of an ancient cobbled bridge then after crossing another bridge reach the outskirts of Linares at a junction **(1 hr 20 mins)**. 10

Turn right and climb up a cobbled track towards the village and the church following a line of black lamp posts. When you reach a junction by a palm tree turn right 11 along Calle Ramón y Cajal. (Or head on straight into the village centre where there are bars, and a spring. W) The cobbled street soon arcs left, passes Hacienda La Salud, then angles left and runs up to an unrendered brick tower festooned in bignonia. Here cut right and climb up to a junction and a map of your return leg 12 which tells you that you have a 5km walk to Aracena. You now follow a pretty section of cobbled track eastwards, running more or less parallel to the Aracena/Linares road which is above you, to your left.

You pass by a series of cultivated terraces and small farms. The track narrows to become a path, then widens again just beyond a stables, before it merges with another track. Continue on your same course. Soon you pass Cortijo La Herreria, to your right. At the next fork 13 swing right, descend past Hacienda La Herreria, then cross the river. Soon you reach a fork by a marker post, approx. 5m before you reach a ceramic sign depicting Christ, The Father and the Holy Spirit. Here cut right across a second bridge. 14 The track angles left and begins to climb, concreted at this stage. After climbing more steeply you pass a shrine to the Virgin. 15 The path levels for a short while then resumes its ascent. You reach a sign explaining what constitutes a *dehesa* (glossary) and a broad track **(2 hrs 15 mins)**. 16

Head straight over the track along a narrow footpath which descends through olive groves and cork oaks. After climbing once more the path merges with a track 17 where, bearing

left, you continue to climb before reaching a junction. 18 Here ignore the turning to the left, which leads up to road, but rather head straight on along an attractive final section of track. As you gradually descend the castle above Aracena comes into view. You reach the outskirts of the town where an ugly housing development is under construction. **(2 hrs 50 mins)**. 19

Here turn left and then at a *Give Way* sign bear right along the Aracena/Linares road. After 500m you pass the town's swimming pool then come to a roundabout. Heading straight on along a street with a *No Entry* sign, passing the Feria ground, you arrive back at the pretty square you passed at the beginning of the walk. Here cut left into Calle Chopos, then take the second right and head along to the end of Calle Alberca. At the end of an arched walkway cut left up some steps to reach a small square. Here take the first right and head up a broad street past the Hotel Sierra de Aracena. At the end of this street turn left to arrive back retrace in the main square **(3 hrs 15 mins)**. 1

ALÁJAR CIRCUIT

Distance: 11 kms **Duration:** 4/4.5 hours **Rating:** Medium

Map: 1:50000 Aracena (917) & Santa Olalla del Calá (918)

Ⓦ **Water:** In Linares at bars and spring @ 1 hr 30 mins

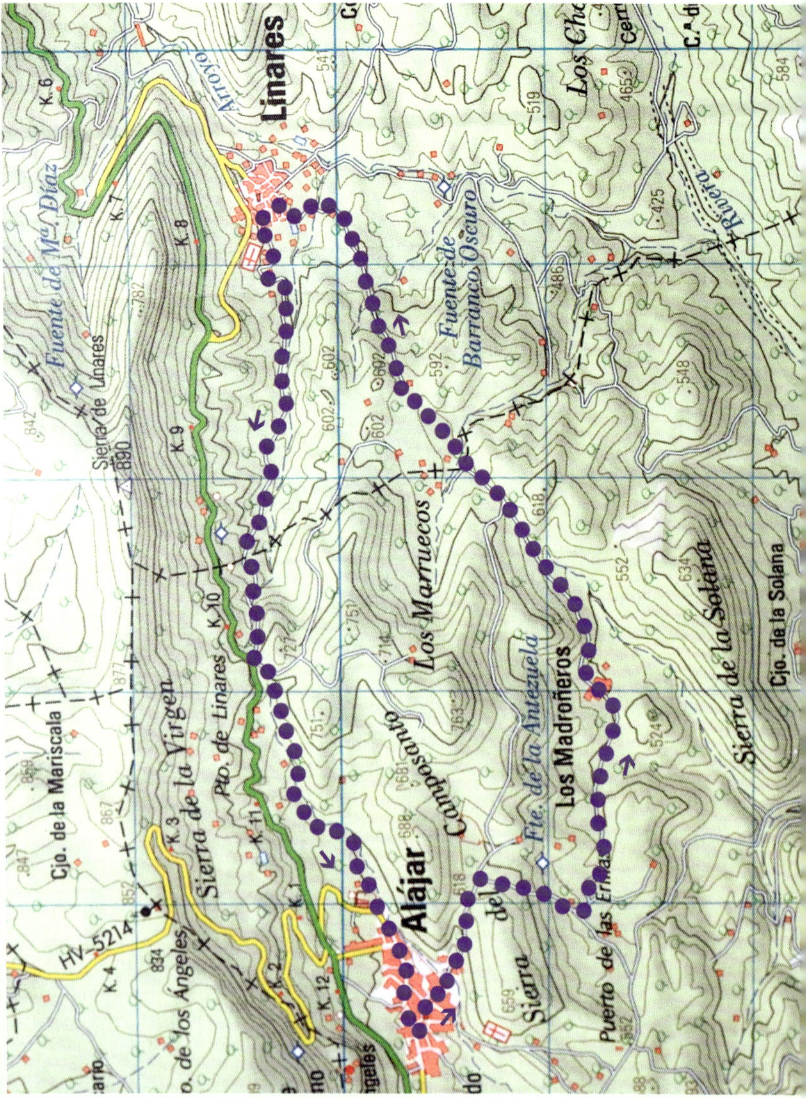

3 The Walk of the Forgotten Hamlet

This is one of the loveliest walks in the Sierra. It links two exceptionally pretty villages, is easy to follow and there's just one steep climb. The long sections of cobbled path, the abandoned hamlet of Los Madroñeros, and the peacefulness of the walk all contribute to make this a very favourite excursion. It's a walk to be savoured and is best combined with a leisurely picnic beneath one of the old oak or olive trees which you pass by before reaching Linares de la Sierra or you could treat yourself to lunch at the excellent Mesón Arrieros in the village centre. Be prepared for a fairly overgrown and rough section of path from Los Madroñeros up to Linares.

The Route

The walk begins in the main square of Alájar by a fountain with a statue of a girl with a water pitcher. 1 Leave the square on its south side via Calle San Bartolomé passing the Cajasol bank. When you reach a church turn left into Calle San Marcos. The road soon bears right, passes the small Plaza de Miguel Moya then drops down Calle Pintor Antonio Milla. At the end of the street you climb, bear right, then reach a sign for *Sendero Los Madroñeros.* 2

At this sign turn left and climb up a steep track that is at first concreted. Soon, descending between old stone walls, you reach a fork by a sign pointing left for *Caracol de Los M*, and right for *Los Madroñeros.* 3 Take the right fork, continuing straight on along a lovely cobbled section of path. Views open out to the south and the small hamlet of Los Madroñeros comes into sight, up ahead in the distance. Soon you reach the first houses of the abandoned hamlet **(30 mins)**. 4

Skirt around the southern side of the houses then cut bear left past the church to the village's central 'square' with a single mulberry tree at its midst. Its solitary form seems symbolic of the hamlet: it once had a population of 150 but is now disinhabited apart from the last Sunday in August when a pilgrimage takes place in honour of *Nuestra Señora de la Salud Venerada.* Go directly across this open area and at its top side cut right between two houses along up a path that runs on between ancient stone walls: there's faded P.R. waymarking. Crossing a (dry) stream the path winds on between evergreen and cork oaks then passes through a wire-and-post gate which is often left open **(45 mins)**. 5

Beyond the gate the path climbs gently upwards. Passing by Cortijo Mailozana 6 it descends then crosses the poplar-lined course of the Barranco de los Madroñeros. 7 Careful! Immediately beyond the stream angle left and pass through a gap in a tumbledown wall. The path is narrow and overgrown as it passes behind a ruin, then cuts along just to the left of a wall. The wall at the side has collapsed in several places and you're obliged to cut right into the ruined farm's enclosure before cutting back left and continuing along the path. Soon you pass by a number of metal-fenced corrals in a field to your left then, still fairly overgrown, the path cuts hard left and then once more right. 8 You pass by the gate of the leading to the farm of María Lozana. 9 The path continues to contour round the hillside towards Linares, deeply eroded in parts, and rough underfoot.

Linares comes into sight as the path drops down an eroded gulley. You wind down on a final steep, cobbled section of path, cross a stream via a footbridge then follow a narrow path which runs up hill between two high walls then loops right and reaches the outskirts of the village which you enter past a large, chocolate-coloured building (currently being converted into holiday accommodation). Here you reach a map of the walk that you have just followed **(1 hr 30 mins)**. 10

MAILOZANA

Here bear sharp left (*unless you plan to visit the village in which case head straight on up into the village* W) then immediately left again along a narrow path which runs between high walls with citrus groves to either side. You reach a wooden gate where, bearing right then left, you continue along the narrow path which now follows the course of a narrow water channel. Where the path ends you reach a cobbled track and another map, this one indicating the route that you'll now follow back to Alájar. 11

Turn left. Passing the village cemetery an oleander-filled stream soon runs to the left of your path. Continuing up along this track you pass a sign extolling the merits of the *Cerdo Ibérico* (free range pigs raised beneath the oaks) then a picnic site 12 before beginning a long, steep ascent. As the countryside opens out you occasionally catch sight of the Linares to Alájar road which is up above you, to your right. The track narrows, becomes a path, and continues to climb up through the oaks and cistus, cobbled in parts. Eventually the path runs up to the Alájar-Linares road **(2 hrs 30 mins)**. 13

Just before reaching the road turn left, climb a short flight of wooden posted steps, pass a bench, then descend a second flight of steps to a track. Head straight across the track to a marker post and a sign prohibiting the passage of quads and motorbikes. Here cut hard left and descend. After just 100m bear slightly left past a gate leading to a farm and continue your descent. The path at first hugs the left bank of the stream then crosses to its opposite bank. 14

The path reverts to track and continues descending. Having merged with another track it reaches the first houses of Alájar where it runs past another map of the walk you've just undertaken. 15 Just past the sign the track meets with a road. Here bear left along Calle Rafael Montesinos. Bear left again just past a telephone booth and continue along Calle Virgen de la Salud. At the end of this street bear right to reach the church of San Marco then follow along its northern wall then turn right, descend past the Cajasol bank, to return to the main square of Alájar **(3 hrs 15 mins)**. 1

ALÁJAR CIRCUIT

Distance: 17 kms **Duration:** 6.5/7 hours **Rating:** Medium/Difficult

Map: IGN 1:50000 Aracena (917/10-37)

W Water: spring @ 25 mins and in bars in Castaño del Robledo @ 3 hrs

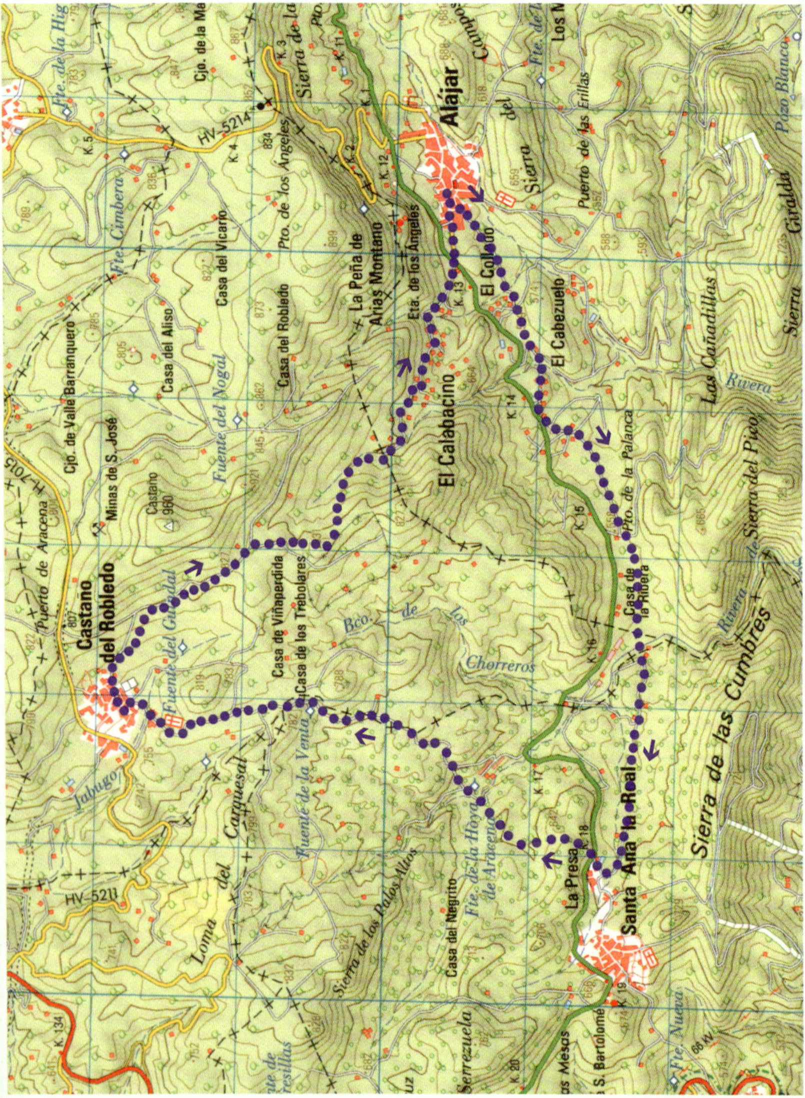

4 The Walk of the Sensible Hippy

This longish walk links three of the prettiest of the Sierra's villages and makes for a tremendously varied excursion. It takes you through groves of olive and cork oak, pine forest and *dehesa* (see glossary) and you constantly switch between narrow paths and farm tracks. An exquisite final section of cobbled path leads back to Alájar passing through a remote hamlet where a number of young folk in search of the Good Life have set up home in farms, yurts, tipis and caravans in amongst the thickly wooded hillside. The lovely section of cobbled track which descends past the chapel of comes as a fitting reward for the steep climb you will have tackled earlier in the day up through the pines between Santa Ana and Castaño del Robledo. The path is occasionally rough underfoot, especially on the final section of the walk, and can be slippery after rain.

The Route

The walk begins in the pretty main square of Alájar in front of the *Ayuntamiento*. 1 At the bottom of the square turn right into Calle Médico Emilio González. Take the first turning to the left opposite Hotel La Posada and head down Calle Constitución. Take the next right into Calle Talero then take the first turning to your left. 2

After a few metres you reach a fork. Bear right and descend along a cobbled path which runs between stone walls. Soon you come to a junction by a farm with a white water tank hoisted up on its roof: here head straight on. The path widens to become a track which merges with a broader track then runs up to meet with a tarmac road. 3

Turn right along the road after just 70m cut left down a narrow path which passes through a stand of cork oaks. The path merges with a track. 4 Here bear right, now climbing slightly. You begin to see yellow and white P.R. waymarking. After 60m the track forks again. Here go left past a gate marked *Año 1984* with a ceramic sign *Rdo de Alájar* then descend, cross a stream and climb up to a farm house 5 where, to your left, you'll see a spring (with a tap) to your right. W

Here, bearing right, you arrive at the tiny hamlet of El Cabezuelo. You pass a tiny *humilladero* (glossary) dedicated to *La Esperanza de Triana*. 6 40m past the shrine swing left down a concreted track **(25 mins)**. After a short descent the track levels then climbs up towards the road and passes a pretty spring. W Here, angling left, you pass above a house with a water tank then meet with a another track. Head straight and you soon reach a junction another track. 7 Here bear left and follow the track steeply down to the farm's entrance gates; they are normally left open. Head straight through the yard of a farm (it is a public Right of Way) ignoring a track which angles right **(30 mins)**.

Continue descending through a large swathe of *dehesa* (glossary). Soon you cross a (dry) stream then, bearing right, follow a pretty section of broad path which runs on between high walls. You'll see faded P.R. yellow and white waymarking. The path, cobbled in parts, sticks to a similar course as it runs between two wire fences: a few lone pines look rather incongruous amongst the cork oaks. At the next fork 8 angle away from the track along a narrower path which runs on in the same direction.

The path merges with a track which runs up to meet a second track which cuts in towards Finca El Manantial. Here head straight on. The track soon passes beneath two newly built houses and a pen for loading cattle. 9 After some 300m you reach another fork. 10 Here cut right, descend, and cross a (dry)

stream. A pretty section of path runs on between stone walls passing a number of magnificent cork oaks. Soon the path again descends down to the (dry) river of La Ribera de Santa Ana La Real which you cross via stepping stones **(1 hr)**. 11

Just beyond the stream bear right past a low farm building. Keeping to your same course head on up the hill passing by a first set of gates to Finca El Molino. Soon you pick up waymarking once again. The path runs on through rather more open countryside and passes another set of gates of Finca El Molino. Here the path widens, passes a third set of gates to El Molino, then runs past an unmarked green metal gate 12 to the right of the track next to an enormous cork oak before narrowing down to become a path.

You wind uphill between old cork oaks: some sections of the path are cobbled. You reach the first *huertas* (small patches of cultivated land) of the village and pass a spring, Fuente La Gancha 13 which you can reach via a wooden bridge.

Continue past the spring for some 100m then cut right along concrete track. 14 After cutting right then left you reach the hamlet of La Presa and the cobbled area at its centre. 15 Here cut right and climb up to the tarmac road which runs above the hamlet. Go straight across the road where you should now continue along a broad track which cuts steeply upwards **(1 hr 40 mins)**. Look for yellow and white P.R.waymarking.

After climbing the track cuts left, levels, then passes between two green gates before dropping gently down between chestnut groves: walls run to both sides of the path which has now narrowed down. You reach a junction by wooden marker post for *Camino de Santa Ana a Castaño de Robledo.* 16 Here turn right. The path soon angles hard right then left and you reach the valley floor 17 where you'll see a farm ahead of you. Here the track divides. Angle left, cross a footbridge, then climb 150m to a point where the track again divides. 18 Here branch right and climb up into the pines on an eroded and steep section of path.

(* You could take the left fork up to the waterfall called Los Chorros de Hoyarancón, a good place for a picnic: it takes about half an hour to get up and down).

Careful! 100m after this fork you should cut right on a narrower, deeply eroded path which runs parallel to a fence. Soon the path widens to become a track where you bear right. Climbing steeply up towards the top of the ridge you reach an area of sparser vegetation 19 where a tangerine coloured building comes into sight, over to your right. Continuing along the track

you pass its entrance gates at a point where the track reaches a more open swathe of ground **(2 hrs 15 mins)**.

The track soon resumes its ascent as the pine forest thickens once again, now following a line of pylons upwards. Passing another wooden sign for *Camino de Santa Ana a Castaño de Robledo* you reach the highest point of your climb. 20 The track, concreted in sections, descends to reach the cemetery of Castaño del Robledo 21 then leads past a small chapel **(3 hrs)**.

Just past the chapel bear right and drop down a concrete road to the tarmac road leading in to Castaño. Here bear right and head up into the village. You reach a small square, Plaza Muñiz Pablo. Here bear right into Calle Real then right again and, passing by Posada del Castaño, climb Calle José Sánchez Calvo to reach the church and the main square, La Plaza del Álamo. A recommended stop for refreshments is the bar directly beneath the Town Hall. 22

From the square go up Calle Arias Montano and, shortly before the street levels, opposite no.11, turn right. After 10m you reach a sign and marker post for *Rodeo al Cerro del Castaño*. 23 Here swing left onto a narrow cobbled path. Quite overgrown in parts, it climbs in a series of long steps then, passing a metal gate, runs on parallel to a track which runs just above you to your left before running up to a marker post next to a green gate.

Bear left at the marker post and continue on the same course along a narrow path which soon runs parallel to the track once again. After descending the path, sandier now, runs in to merge the track which runs over the top of a rise then descends to reach a marker post 24 pointing to the left. Ignore this! Here cut right and descend, immediately passing a sign prohibiting the passage of motorbikes and quads, along a broad track which descends through stands of chestnut, pine and cork oak. Soon you'll spot a thick black plastic water pipe running just to the left of the track. Continuing straight on down the track eventually reaches a gate with a damaged ceramic sign marking 'Cer Ignaci Navarro'. 25 Here angle left then after 80m bear right: you should see a tree with yellow and white P.R. waymarking. You now drop steeply down a narrow path, overgrown in parts, which follows the course of a (dry) stream bed. The path soon improves as it runs on downhill with walls to either side and becomes cobbled again. Soon it runs past a farm gate with white posts and a ceramic tile marked *Rdo de Alájar* **(4 hrs)**. 26

After passing the gate the path soon merges with a wider path 27 and continues to descend: ignore a branch which soon cuts away to the right. The broad cobble path zigzags down past the Ermita de la Virgen de Los Angeles 28 then passes by a number of houses inhabited by a friendly bunch of hippies: part of the attraction must surely be that there's no vehicle access at this point and there's no denying that they've chosen a delectable spot to live. The cobbled path continues on down, passes a spring, W then crosses a newly built footbridge. Bearing right you reach a track which leads down to meet with the tarmac road. Head straight across and soon you return to the village square **(4 hrs 30 mins)**. 1

GALAROZA CIRCUIT

Distance: 12.5 kms **Duration:** 3.5/4 hours **Rating:** Easy/Medium

Map: IGN 1:50000 Aracena (917/10-37)

Ⓦ **Water:** bars in Castaño del Robledo @ 1 hr 15 mins

5 The Walk of the Sylvan Valley

This exceptionally pretty circuit leads through oak and chestnut forests from Galaroza to the tiny village of Castaño del Robledo. The river valley of the Jabugo teems with birdlife, the walk is an aural as well as a visual feast and the paths that you follow on both legs of the walk are simply beautiful. It would be tempting to linger along the way and perhaps picnic in the shade of an oak somewhere along the return leg, beyond the Capilla de Cristo. And from the high path that you follow back to Galaroza you're treated to wonderful views west towards Portugal. Put time aside to explore both villages which have excellent bars, restaurants and some good lodgings, too.

The Route

The walk begins in the main square of Galaroza, La Plaza de la Constitución, next to the fountain. 1 With your back to the town hall turn left then, bearing left again, head away from the square past the Toribio restaurant. Soon you pass by a small supermarket, descend past Bar La Fuente, and pass a pretty palm-fringed square before coming to the main road leading from Aracena to Portugal, the N-433. 2 Cross the road, turn left in front of Café bar Venezia, and head along the main road towards Aracena. After just 80m you reach a sign marking the beginning of the path *La Ribera de Jabugo* – the Jabugo river valley walk. 3

Turn right here and drop down a narrow path. It soon becomes cobbled, bears left, and just 80m from the road you reach a junction. Here cut right. The narrow path runs on between two walls, crosses a water channel, then reaches another junction at an open tract of ground. **(10 mins)**. 4

Here bear sharply left and descend, following a sign for

Galaroza. You shortly cross the Múrtigas stream via a small stone bridge then pass a sign explaining the eco-system of the valley. The path widens to become a broad, sandy track which cuts through stands of oak, pine and chestnut whilst beneath you in the river valley are thick stands of poplar, ash and willow. The track narrows again to become a path as it passes behind a stone hut, 5 running more or less parallel to the River Jabugo's left bank. You pass a wooden bench then the path runs past a group of white buildings, Las Casas del Tortero, where it merges with a broader track **(30 mins)**. 6

The track runs past a number of farm buildings then merges with a broader, better surfaced track. Soon it descends, passes a pylon, runs close to the river, then crosses a small concrete bridge to the right bank. 7 Beyond the bridge the track bears left. At the next junction, just past an ivy-covered building, bear left and after passing an information board listing the edible mushrooms that are to be found in the valley *(Setas comestibles)* you cross the river once again. 8 You soon pass the entrance gates to the farm of El Tortero, continuing along the left bank of the river. This is a particularly verdant, leafy section of the walk.

After angling left away from the river on a pretty, narrow path which is cobbled in sections you reach a farm with a water butt on a metal platform. 9 Here bear hard left, picking up a broader track which runs past a number of smallholdings. There are cobbled and concreted sections. Passing by a cross you reach the outskirts of the village by a marker post and a newly built picnic area where there is tap water W **(1 hr 10 mins)**. 10

Here, bearing slightly left then hard right, follow Calle Soledad around the edge of the village. It soon runs up to meet with the main road next to a bar and a ham shop. 11 (If visiting the village centre, head straight across. There are a couple of small bars where you could break for refreshments W). Turning left on the main road you pass a bus stop then a ham warehouse and the *Señorio de Encinas* restaurant. Climbing for another 125m be ready to cut left away from the road 12 along a track which leads in to a picnic area next to a small shrine, *La Capilla del Cristo*.

Pass the chapel to its right and head up a broad track which climbs up through the forest. Views soon open out over to the left towards Jabugo and, beyond, to the mountains of Portugal. The track heads on up through groves of chestnut and reaches a junction. 13 Ignore the track which cuts left cuts towards two sets of farm gates: you should bear right, sticking to the main track. You occasionally will see faint yellow and white P.R. waymarking. The track soon descends, narrower now, then reaches a junction with a broad track **(1 hr 45 mins)**. 14

Here head straight across: you'll see P.R. markings and a sign for *Galaroza*. After 50m you reach a fork: here bear right. The path widens and continues its descent. Shortly you reach a point where the track divides: take the left path and, continuing to descend, you reach another junction where it splits three ways. 15 Take the middle path. Pines give way to oaks and, after passing two new houses and an older one to your right, you pass the farm Finca La Farruca whose shed walls have been adorned with a number of wierd sculptures. 16 The cobbled track passes a number of small farms, running on between stone walls.

Soon you cross the Múrtigas stream for the second time in the walk, via a small concrete bridge. 17 You climb a final steep section of cobbled track which bears right, then left, before

running up to meet with the main road, the N433. 18 Bear left and follow the road along to the outskirts of the village.

Just past a small shop which sells touristy paraphernalia turn right off the N433 at a sign for *Consultorio*. Follow this street past Bar Avenida then at its far end turn left at a sign for *Centro Población* and head up Calle Fernando Marquéz Tirado which soon becomes Calle Vitoria. Following Calle Vitoria to its far end, keeping right at a *No Entry* sign, you should then cut left down Calle San Sebastian. You pass a public phone booth then, sticking to your same course, come to a church and a large square. From here keep on in the same direction passing the Cajasol bank. After angling left past a large brick building continue along Calle Don Gumersindo Marquez to arrive back to your point of departure, la Plaza de la Constitución **(2 hrs 25 mins)**. 1

Add 30-45 minutes to all timings if you plan to visit Castaño de Robledo.

ALMONASTER CIRCUIT

Distance: 9 kms **Duration:** 4/4.5 hours **Rating:** Medium

Map: IGN 1:50000 Aracena (917/10-37)

Water: no springs, can fill water bottles in bars in Arroyo and Los Acebuches

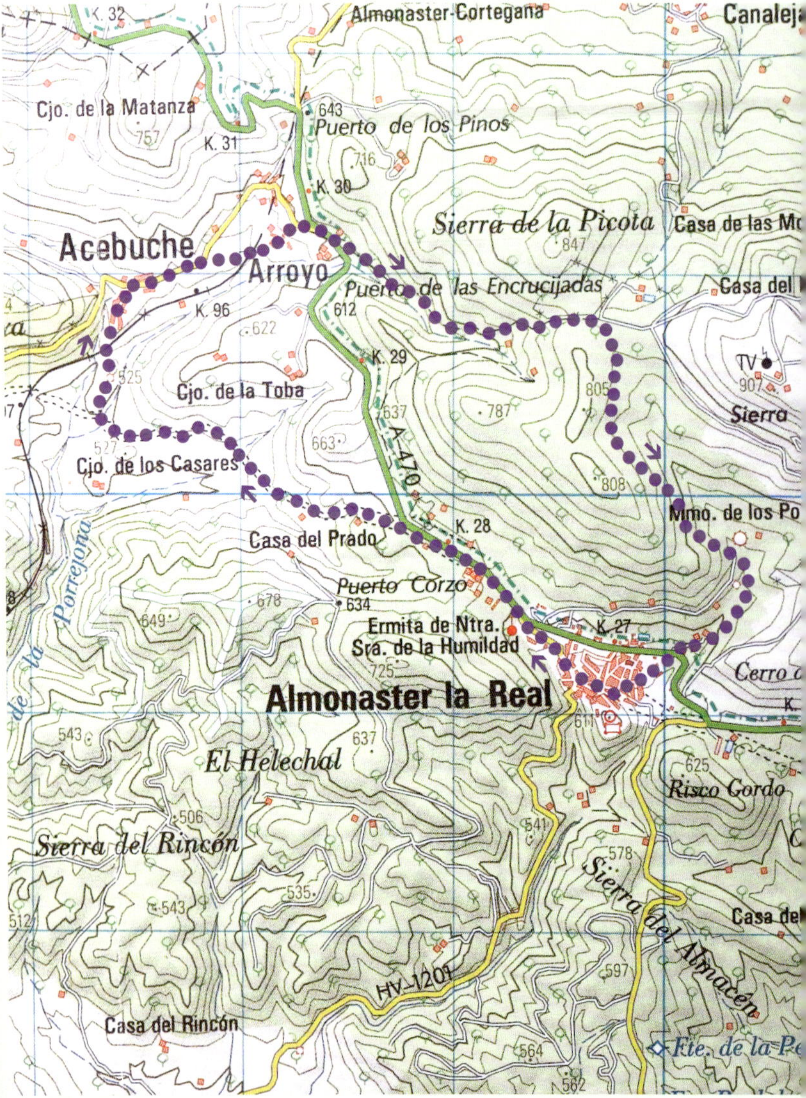

6 The Walk of Patience & Humility

This walk is a little shorter than some of the other Aracena itineraries but makes for a surprisingly varied half day walk and the steep climb that comes half way through makes it an enjoyable challenge. Your point of departure, Almonaster, is one of the Sierra's most attractive villages and the paths you encounter are as pretty as any in the *Sierra*. The reward for the steep climb up from Arroyo is a gorgeous final section of path which loops steeply down to the Almonaster past two ancient flour mills. No visit to the village would be complete without climbing up to its castle citadel and its beautiful wafer brick Mezquita.

The Route

The walk begins in the pretty main square of Almonaster la Real in front of the *Ayuntamiento*. 1 Cross the square towards the tobacconist then head down Calle El Pino. At the bottom of the street cut right into Calle Cristo and climb gently up towards the road leading to Cortegana. Just a few metres past the ham factory of Romero Martín cut left along a narrow path that runs past the chapel dedicated to *Nuestra Señora de la Humildad y Paciencia*. 2 The path bears right then meets the road by a builder's yard. 3 Following along the tarmac you passing the *butano* (gas) depot, the village cemetery then a farm, El Prao, which is to the left of the road.

100m past El Prao turn left 4 off the road onto a track. You immediately pass a sign for *Fin de Sendero* and a P.R./G.R. waymarking post. The track narrows to become a cobbled path which, after descending steeply, runs past a farm with solar pannels. 5 The path continues its descent through the cork oaks then crosses a (dry) stream. 6 Here the path winds right and climbs for a short distance with a wall running just to its left.

The path widens and reverts to track and runs on with fences to either side. You pass between two sets of look-alike grey metal gates 7 and continue on down. Again the path narrows, bears sharply to the right, 8 becomes cobbled then descends and crosses a (dry) stream **(45 mins)**. 9

Just beyond the stream the path angles hard left and after just 10m reaches a junction. Turn sharp right along a narrower path that climbs gently upwards: the stream is now down to your right. After angling left, and then once more right, you pass a rusting level crossing sign then come to a railway line. 10 Cross the track, angle left then right, and climb on the same course. The path becomes better defined and once again becomes cobbled. You reach the outskirts of the small village of Los Acebuches where the path merges with the first of its streets **(50 mins)**. 11

Head all the way up this street until you reach the main road that runs above the village. 12 Here turn right and follow the road. Soon you pass the Km 1 sign and, 350m further on, just beyond a point where pylons cross above you, turn right 13 off the road onto a narrow path. At the first fork in the path go left, cross a (dry) stream and climb.

The path, cobbled in parts, leads up to the tiny hamlet of Arroyo where you take the first street to the left 14 and climb steeply up to the road above the hamlet. Turning right here you meet the road from Cortegana to Almonaster. 15 Here turn right down the hill. Immediately past a bus stop cut left off the road. Pass just beneath a modern house then bear left up a broad cobbled track which climbs steeply up through an area of small, cultivated *huertas* (glossary).

The path heads on up, more or less parallel to the left bank of a tributary of the Acebuches stream which you crossed earlier

in the walk. After a steep climb the path eventually levels as you reach the highest point on the walk. 16 Descending slightly and passing by a metal gate you come to a more open, sandy area and a broad track by a small white electrical hut **(1 hr 45 mins)**. 17

Cut right in the direction indicated by a metal sign with twin arrows indicating the course you should follow down to Almonaster. The track cuts down through a chestnut grove. Soon a black plastic water pipe runs just to your left and then a rickety run of fence. The path narrows as it passes through a gate. 18 Marker posts and cairns help guide you down. Soon you pass a wooden bench 19 to the side of the path: at any fork stick to the most prominent path. Eventually the path, still descending, describes a series of cobbled loops, passes an information board explaining the geology of the San Cristobal mountain, then angles right and after about 200m meets with a track. 20 Here bear right and after just 150m, opposite a huge agave, 21 cut left and drop down another cobbled section of path. This was part of the old drovers' route that lead all the way to Mérida.

The path drops steeply down towards Almonaster and you are treated to a fine view of its old Mezquita that dominates the village. Just before you reach the river, bearing right you pass left of a couple of funky sculptures of birds then descend past two ancient old flour mills before coming to the road which leads from Almonaster to Alájar. 22

Pass under the road through a tunnel and follow a beautiful narrow path to the village. Here you pass by Restaurante La Cruz and then, at the end of a small square, cut up Calle Francisco Montero. At the top of the street turn left, pass bar Almonaster and then a *farmacia*, to arrive back in the main square of the village and the Town Hall **(2 hrs 45 mins)**. 1

Grazalema

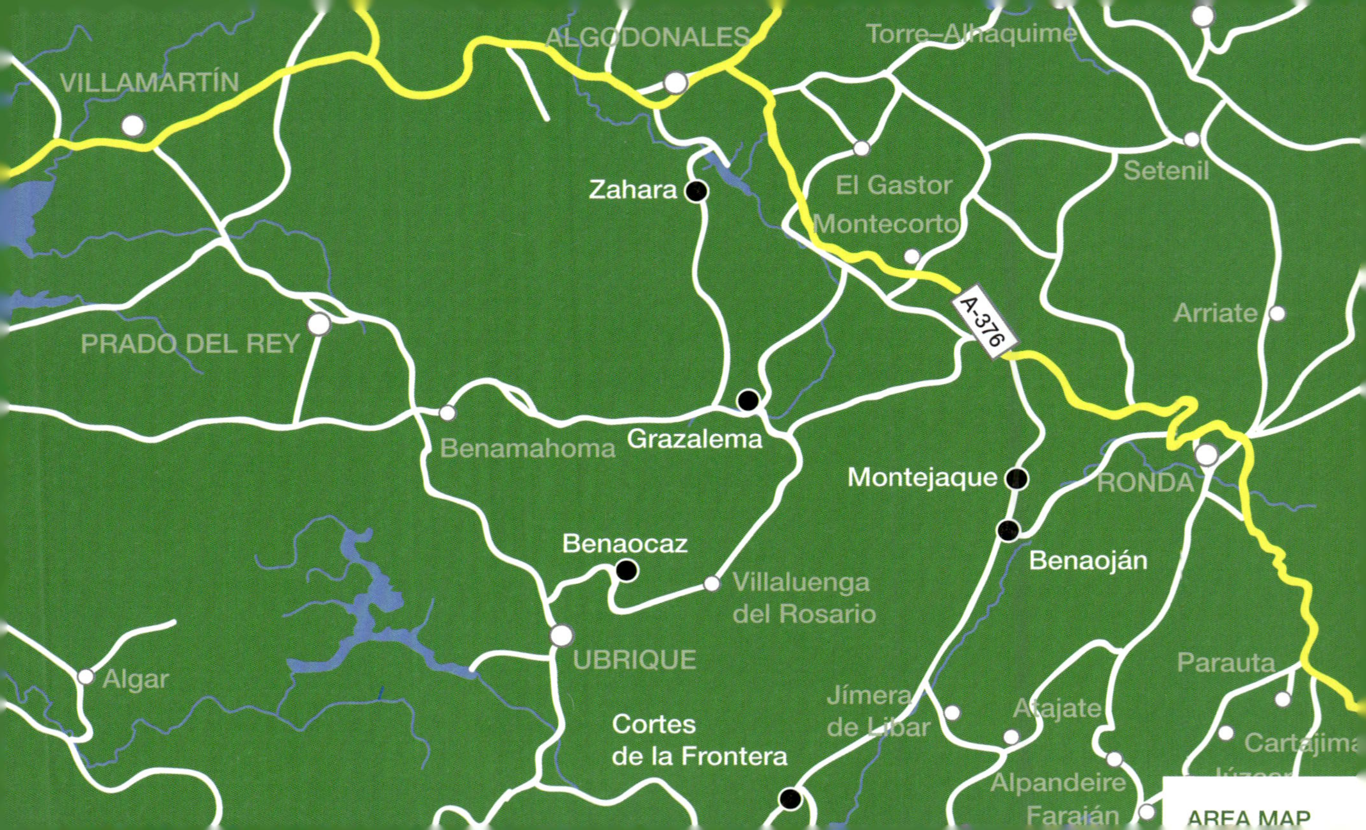
VILLAMARTÍN
ALGODONALES
Torre-Alhaquime
Setenil
Zahara
El Gastor
Montecorto
A-376
Arriate
PRADO DEL REY
Grazalema
Benamahoma
Montejaque
RONDA
Benaoján
Benaocaz
Villaluenga
del Rosario
UBRIQUE
Algar
Parauta
Jímera
de Líbar
Atajate
Cartajima
Cortes
de la Frontera
Alpandeire
Faraján

GRAZALEMA

THE AREA

The Grazalema Natural Park straddles the provinces of Cádiz and Málaga and encompasses the the tail-end of the Cordillera Bética, the most south-westerly mountain range in Europe. This rugged massif, predominantly composed of limestone and dolomite, rises dramatically up from the rolling farmlands around Jérez to a height of nearly 2000 metres. Although the park is comparatively small compared to others in Andalusia – it covers an area of just over 500 square kilometres – its terrain is extraordinarily varied. Jagged formations of karst give way to poplar-lined valleys, thick stands of cork and evergreen oaks alternate with old groves of olives and almonds and with fields of wheat and barley. The scenery changes with every turn in the path and the wildflowers here are as good as anywhere in Europe.

The extraordinary botanical variety – you'll find more than a third of the Spain's plants within this small area – is the result of unusually complex climatic conditions. Continental, Mediterranean and Atlantic influences are all present and the village of Grazalema, plum in the centre of the park, receives more rainfall per square centimetre than anywhere else in Spain. It is a remarkable micro climate: villages just half a dozen kilometres from Grazalema receive a quarter of the rainfall. But don't let this put you off coming to walk. The rainfall is markedly seasonal – November, April and May tend to be the wettest months – and at other times of the year the chances are the weather will be good. This abundant rainfall also means that the area is remarkably green by Andalusian standards and explains the existence of the large stand of pinsapo pines (*Abies Pinsapo Boiss*) on the northern slopes of the Sierra del Pinar.

The Park is an ornithological wonderland. You are bound to see hoopoes, wheatears, oriol, warblers, shrikes, rock thrushes, choughs and a whole lot more besides. But most notable are the raptors. Eagles (booted, short-toed and golden) are easily spotted and it's not unusual to see 100 or more griffon vultures on the wing: the largest colony in Europe inhabits the rocky ledges of the Garganta Verde close to Zahara de la Sierra (there are exceptional views of the gorge on the Zahara circular walk). Here, as in other parts of Spain, numbers are being maintained thanks to various feeding sites in the high Sierra. And one of the major migratory roots between Europe and Africa runs along the western flank of the park.

What makes the park a double treat are not only the walks but also the *Pueblos Blancos* or white villages. All the walks described in this book begin in one of them. These villages, nearly all of which are of Moorish origin, contain some of Spain's most distinctive architecture. Narrow streets of whitewashed houses, most of them with wrought iron *rejas* (window grills), drop steeply down the hillsides. Often just walking from the bottom to the top of a village is a hike in itself. Their abrupt mountain perches are testimony to their having been built with defence in mind: this was the area of the ever-changing frontier or *frontera* between Moslem and Christian Spain and it was only in the period following the Reconquest that villages moved down into the valley floors.

Grazalema, plum at the centre of the park and one of the very prettiest villages in the area, has long been a popular destination for walking groups from the UK and also with the Spanish from Sevilla and Cádiz who flock in at the weekends. So book ahead unless you're staying out of season, on a weekday. Better still, stay in one of the quieter villages at the edge of the Park like Zahara, Benaoján, Estación de Cortes or Montejaque.

Other Walks

El Pinsapar

The classic Grazalema itinerary takes you through the heart of the Pinsapo forest. This full-day excursion begins to the left of the road leading from Grazalema to Zahara. After a stiff climb of nearly 350m, a broad path leads through a large stand of pinsapos, one of the few remaining stands of these exceptionally beautiful pine trees (*abies pinsapo Boiss*). You need a permit to do the walk (see below). Get going early to avoid school parties and other groups. The walk takes approximately 4 hours.

Garganta Verde

Another spectacular walk for which a permit is required (see below). The walk begins about 3 kms from Zahara, to the right of the road marking leading to Grazalema. Access is limited because of the large colony of griffon vultures which nest in the gorge. You need approximately 3.5 hours to go down and back.

Torreón Ascent

The views from the top of the Park's highest peak are amazing. The walk begins a few kilometer beyond the Boyar pass to the right of the road leading to El Bosque. Allow about 4 hours for getting up and down. Again, a permit is required because of the proximity of the *pinsapo* forest (see below).

Permits are issued by the main Park Office in El Bosque (open Monday-Saturday 10h-14h and 16h-18h). If you don't want to drive to El Bosque you can call to reserve permits (956 727 079) quoting your passport number, the itinerary, number of walkers and the day you wish to walk. Your permit can then be faxed to either the Zahara or Grazalema tourist offices for collection. So long as you avoid weekends and public holidays permits are generally available.

Accompanied walks The author of this book is sometimes

available to lead guided walks in the area. Tel: 616 057 184
Email: info@rondatejar.com

In Grazalema Jo Carter accompanies full and half day walks.
Tel: 627 705 125

Maps

The best map of the whole area is the1:50000 mapa/guía of the Junta de Andalucía/Instituto Geográfico Nacional. You can normally find it at the Grazalema newsagent and the Park Offices in either El Bosque or Grazalema. The map covers all 6 itineraries listed here. The next best alternative are the standard IGN 1:50000 maps: you'll need Ubrique 1050, Olvera 1036, Cortes de la Frontera 1064. The Alpina 1:40000 map is also good to have as a second point of reference: it includes some footpaths which aren't marked on the IGN map but, somewhat mysteriously, others are missing.

BEST PLACES TO SLEEP & EAT

MONTECORTO

El Tejar & Dar Hajra

Tel: 616 057 184

Email: info@rondatejar.com

Self-catering accommodation perfect for small groups of walkers and couples wishing to do a full week of walking in the area: the two houses are rented on a weekly basis (by the author of this guide). Masses of information on local walks, extensive collection of maps, and gorgeous mountain views. For prices see www.rondatejar.com (Taxi: Esteban 606 986 666). **Best Eats:** several cheap and cheerful local restaurants.

MONTEJAQUE

El Elefante Amarillo

Tel: 952 167 252 Email: stay@elefanteamarillo

An attractive small hotel on the main square of Montejaque which has recently been given a through refurb under friendly British management. Approx €58-€75 + 7% VAT. (Alonso 607 919 352) **Best Eats:** here or good tapas in and around the square.

La Posada del Fresno

Tel: 952 167 544 Email: posadadelfresno@terra.es

A friendly inn with just 4 small rooms close to the main square and friendly Spanish owners. €60 + 7% VAT. (Alonso 607 919 352) **Best Eats:** here.

Cortijo Las Piletas

Tel: 605 080 295 Email: info@cortijodelaspiletas.com

A converted farm between Ronda and Montejaque with friendly young owners and excellent home cooking. €84-€90 + 7% VAT. (Taxi: Luis 649 362 437) **Best Eats:** here.

GRAZALEMA

La Mejorana Tel/Fax: 956 132 327 Email: info@lamejorana.net

Small, family run B&B at the centre of Grazalema. €52 incl. breakfast and VAT. (Taxi: Rafael 627 415 047). **Best Eats:** El Simancón or El Pinsapar.

ZAHARA

Al Lago Tel: 956 123 032 or 666 052 553 email: info@al-lago.es

Four lovely bedrooms looking out across the Zahara reservoir, and first class food prepared by chef-owner Stefan Crites. Chic, comfortable and worth the euros. €75-€100 + 7% VAT. (Taxi: Diego 600 328 845). **Best Eats:** here.

Hotel Arco de la Villa
Tel: 956 123 254 Email: arco-de-la-villa@tugasa.com

A small hotel close to the castle with views across the Zahara reservoir. Approx. €70 + 7% VAT. (Taxi: Diego 600 328 845). **Best Eats:** here, down the hill at Bar Los Estribos or Al Lago.

BENAOJÁN ESTACIÓN

Hotel Molino del Santo
Tel: 952 167 151 Email: info@molinodelsanto.com

Pleasant river-side hotel with a predominantly British clientèle and well used to walkers and their ways. Good food with plenty of veggie possibilities. €90-€190 + 7% VAT. (Alonso 607 919 352) **Best Eats:** here.

NEAR TO RONDA

Hotel La Fuente de la Higuera
Tel: 952 114 355 Email: info@hotellafuente.com

A stylishly converted olive mill just outside of Ronda. €148-€210 + 7% VAT. (Taxi: Luis 649 362 437). **Best Eats:** here or in Ronda.

FROM BENAOJÁN ESTACIÓN TO JIMERA DE LIBAR

Distance: 9 kms **Duration:** 2.5/3 hours **Rating:** Easy

Map: 1:50000 Ubrique (1050/14-44) & Cortes de la Frontera (1064/14-45)

W Water: no springs along the way so take plenty

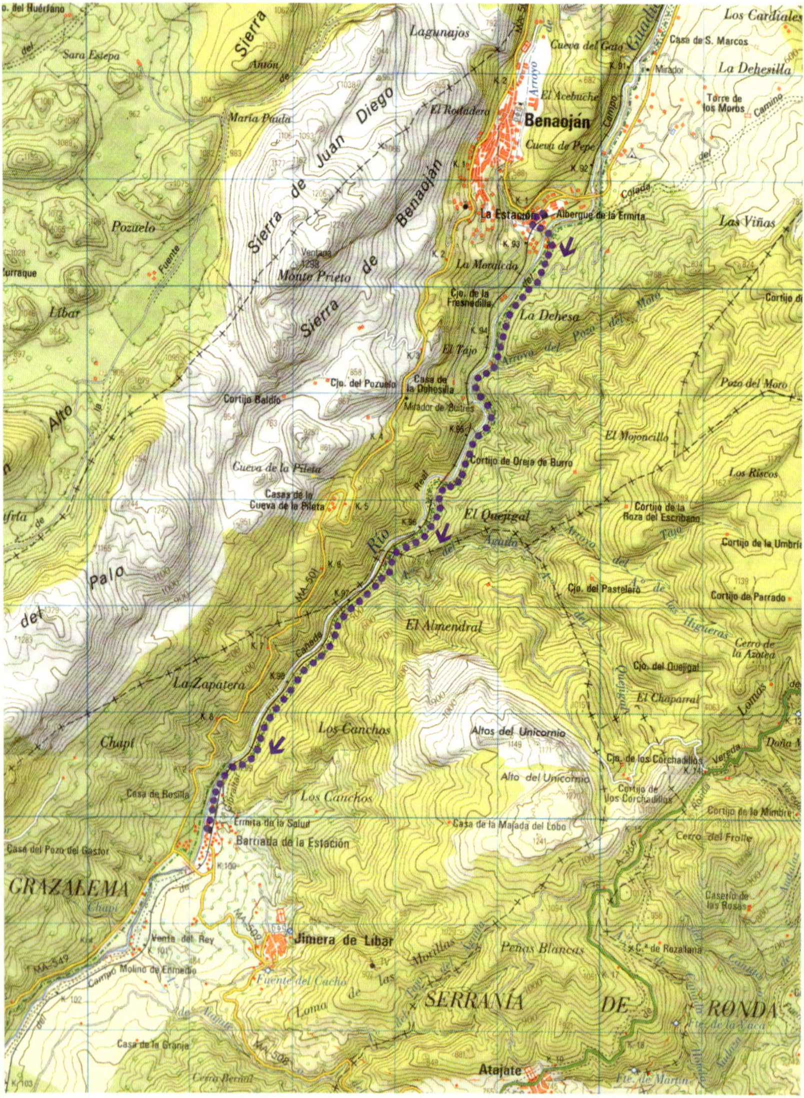

1 The Walk of Mr. Henderson's Railway

This short and easy walk follows a delightful riverside path which links the sleepy village of Benaoján Estación with the sleepier-still hamlet of Jimera de Líbar Estación. What makes it such a great half-day walk is that you can set off late in the morning, dawdle along the way, have a long lazy lunch in the excellent Quercus restaurant in Jimera de Líbar Estación (closed on Mondays) then return by train to your car. Departures from Jimera back to Benaoján are at 13.38, 17.03 and 20.04 (check for slight seasonal variations), arriving at Benaoján Estación just 7 minutes later. You could turn this into a longer walk by simply retracing your footsteps back along the Guadalete valley from Jimera.

The Route

The walk begins on the platform of the Estación de Benaoján. 1 From here head south along the platform, then drop down to the road. Continue past Bar Stop. After 75m turn left and cross over a level crossing. 2

The road drops down, passes between two garish modern houses, crosses the river Guadiaro and you reach a sign marking the beginning of the walk to Jimera. 3 Here turn right onto a track which runs along the left bank of the river. Soon you pass an abandoned farm with 3 magnificent old palm trees. The track narrows to become a path which shortly crosses a small wooden bridge 4 then bears right and passes a ruined farm **(10 mins)**.

Shortly after the farm the path divides. Take the left fork which leads slightly away from the river. The path leads through a gate and shortly afterwards you'll see that the railway is now on your side of the river. Don't deviate from this path.

You eventually drop down, cross a (dry) stream via a small wooden bridge 5 and after a short distance a concrete water channel runs to the left of the path. Soon you pass a rusting black and white sign *Ojo al Tren* then come to a sign for *Via Pecuaria*: you are on the old drover's path that lead from Cortes to Ronda. **(1 hr 15 mins)**.

Careful! Here a yellow and white PR post directs you hard round to the right towards the railway line. 6 You have a choice:

In dry weather follow the PR directions by looping hard right, crossing the railway line, then bearing left and following a narrow path between a fence on the left and brambles on the right. The path meets with a dirt track which in turn soon meets a concrete road. Here turn left 7 and you arrive at the Quercus restaurant (in a converted railway shed). From here the station platform of Jimera de Líbar is just 100m along the track **(1 hr 35 mins)**.

In wet weather (when the path beyond the track can be waterlogged) don't cross the tracks. Continue on your same course, sticking to the east side of the tracks. The path passes just to the left of a goat farm, then meets a broader track. Here bear left. Just past a ramshackle fence made of railway sleepers and all manner of junk the track crosses a bridge and comes to a fork. Bearing right you pass a number of modern houses then reach the east side of Jimera station **(1 hr 35 mins)**.

If planning to lunch at the Quercus restaurant, you need to cross the tracks and turn right. After lunch, either return by this same route or take the train. It is just a seven minute ride back to Benaoján Estación along Mr Henderson's railway line.

FROM BENAOJÁN TO CORTES DE LA FRONTERA

Distance: 16.5 kms **Duration:** 6/6.5 hours **Rating:** Medium/Difficult

Map: 1:50000 Ubrique (1050/14-44) & Cortes de la Frontera (1064/14-45)

Ⓦ **Water:** two springs in the Líbar valley @ approx. 2 hrs and 3 hrs and another beyond the final pass on your descent to Cortes @ approx 3 hrs 45 mins

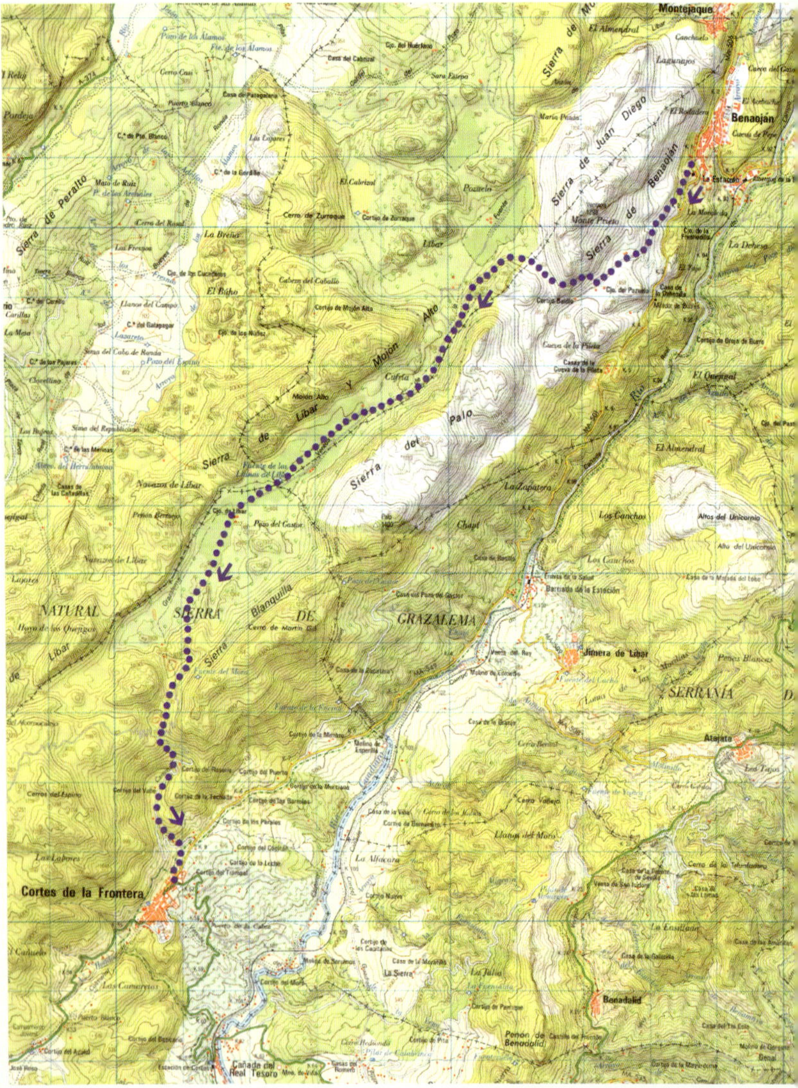

2 The Walk of the Bandoleros

This is one of the great walks in the Grazalema Park, allbeit a fairly demanding one. The route begins on the south side of Benaoján where you pick up the old drover's path which once led from Ronda to the villages south of Grazalema. After a steady climb up to an area of spectacular limestone crags and remote farmsteads you pick up the amazing Moorish path of *La Escalereta*, a cobbled footpath which snakes its way round the flank of the Sierra de Benaoján from where there are great views back towards Ronda and the Sierra de las Nieves. Beyond the pass you drop down another lovely section of footpath before heading all away along to the end of the Líbar valley via a broad track which runs between some of the Park's most ancient stands of oak trees. From here you climb once again through spectacular, rocky terrain before dropping steeply down to Cortes. It's easy to see how 19th century *bandoleros* and later persecuted Republicans were able to give the authorities the slip in this wild and rugged terrain. A short and inexpensive taxi ride brings you back from Cortes to your point of departure. **You could set out from Benaoján Estación and follow the path that leads behind Molino del Santo up to Benaoján and then, arriving in Cortes, cut down an old footpath to the Estación from where you can return to your point of departure by train. This means adding an extra couple of hours to the timings quoted.*

The Route

The walk begins at the far end of Benaoján, to one side of the road leading to Cortes de la Frontera on the south side of the village. Just beyond the last houses of the village you'll see an information board marking the beginning of the walk: *Sendero Benaoján-Llanos de Líbar.* (1) There's plenty of space on the other side of the road to park. Head up a broad track immediately beyond the sign which brings you to a flattish area where there's a metal well cover. Here bear hard right and climb up to a brick hut where you should arc left and continue climbing. Soon the path loops once more left then right as it passes by a long rectangular building, formerly a pig shed. 2

The path merges with a track then reaches a metal gate 3 which you should pass carefully by to its left: there's a steep drop to one side. Continue along the track for 80m then just before it arcs hard left, cut right and go through a metal gate. 4 Beyond the gate bear slighly left and follow a line of cairns which mark the best path for the next hour or so. After running parallel to the road the path gradually angles away to the right as it climbs up the flank of the Sierra de Benaoján. After passing across a swathe of open, shaley terrain the path reaches a track **(40 mins)**. 5 Bear right and follow the broad track on upwards. It soon loops right then left as it passes well to the left of two farm buildings then runs on south through the farm's almond grove. At a point where the track arcs right cut the corner via a narrow path. This path soon meets the track once again. Here head straight across the track along an indistinct path which soon runs along the left side of a grove of olives. At the far end of the grove the path drops down just before it reaches a quarried area. Here, angling slightly right, you reach a gate. 6

Go through the gate and follow a track which immediately passes above an ancient well and two troughs carved out of solid rock. Careful! Almost exactly 200m after passing the well look for a cairn just to the right of the track. 7 Here you should cut right and pick up a narrow footpath. After zigzagging steeply upwards you reach the beginning of a beautiful section of cobbled footpath which locals refer to as *La Escalareta* (the staircase): you'll soon see why. At a point where the cobbling suddenly becomes less distinct the path divides. 8 Here you

should cut left. The path is less distinct now as it levels and runs straight towards a rocky outcrop. Shortly before you reach the outcrop angle hard right 9 and continue on up, always looking for the most obvious path and keeping an eye open for cairns (please add to the existing ones).

The path runs up to a flat, open area. 10 Head straight across to its far left hand corner and continue climbing on roughly your same course. You soon reach a second swathe of flat, open land. Here head along its right hand side and continue following cairns on up to the highest point of the pass 11 which is marked by a cairn. Descending through the rocks you'll soon spot a wall up ahead, and a gate at its left end. Following cairns along the clearest path you soon reach the gate 12 and, just beyond it, angle left and follow a lovely path down into the Líbar valley where a final loop brings you down to a broad dirt track **(1 hr 40 mins)**. 13

Bearing left along the valley floor the track soon passes a by spring W with a drinking trough, over to your right, then runs between 2 ruins. At this stage you may prefer walk to parallel to the track, just to its right, where the going is softer underfoot. Continuing on your same course you pass by two tracks which angle left towards a gate in a stone wall. Stick to the main track which arcs right, crosses a cattle grid and reaches a metal gate. 14 Go through the gate then turn left along the track following a sign for *Cortes 9km* (the right turning leads up to the Refugio de Líbar, a mountain refuge which is rarely open). Head on along the broad valley with a fence now running just to the left of the track. Some 800m beyond the gate the track angles right away from the fence. Here you should stick to your same course and follow a less distinct track which runs just to the right of the fence. Soon it runs past a pond then reaches a metal gate 15 with two signs for *Zona de Seguridad* and *Prohibido el Paso* (the latter isn't true: you're on a public footpath that the owner of the

farm would prefer to have to himself!) **(2 hrs 30 mins)**.

Beyond the gate head on between two rows of recently planted trees along a faint track. It soon angles left then right between a parallel row of trees where it becomes better defined then merges with a broader track which leads to the farm buildings of El Cortijo de Líbar. 16 Where the track angles left you should head on up the valley along an indistinct footpath which runs to the left of a (dry) stream bed (by angling right here you would reach the farm's spring W). Following the most obvious path head down to the far end of the valley. Sticking to the valley's left hand side you reach a gate in the wall that runs across it southern end. 17 Go through the gate and head straight on. After 15m you cross a footpath then head up into the rocks: look for cairns and yellow and white P.R. waymarking. Sticking to the most clearly defined path, which cuts across two flat areas amongst the rocks as you climb gradually up to the top of the pass **(3 hrs 5 mins)**. 18 Beyond the pass the path contours round a deep flat-bottomed depression in the limestone which is down to your right. It shortly merges with a track 19 which you should follow gently upwards for some 200m then cut right 20 along a path which skirts round another deep depression, also over to your right, before it runs up to reach a wire-and-post gate. 21

On the other side of the gate, continuing straight ahead, you reach a track. Head straight along the track to a huge cairn. 5m beyond the cairn cut hard left then after just 10m 22 cut once more right, away from the track, and pick up a footpath which zigzags down between the rocks to meet with the track once more. 23 Turn right and drop down a concreted section, immediately passing beneath a spring and a long water trough. W After looping right then left you should again cut right down another section of footpath: it cuts off another big loop in the track. When you meet the track once again 24 turn right and

follow it along the valley floor. Careful! At a point where it begins to descend be ready to cut left after just 30m 25 along a narrow path which drops down through the broom. After looping right then left it meets with a track just beneath a brown metal gate. 26 Head straight across and continue along a narrow path which runs above an olive grove then reaches the first of the village's house, an ugly group of blocks of flats. Just beyond the third of them cut left by a wooden sign then take the first right, then the first left, to reach a *Stop* sign **(4 hrs 15 mins)**. 27

* A good rendezvous with your taxi driver (taxi in Cortes: Juan 600 219 795) would be Bar Los Alcornocales which has great food as well as excellent coffee and cakes. To get there turn left at the Stop sign and head along the road for approx. 150m. Or, to reach the taxi rank, turn right at the Stop sign and head towards the village centre and the bull ring. The rank is to the right of the road after approximately 250m.

MONTEJAQUE CIRCUIT

Distance: 16.5 kms **Duration:** 6/6.5 hours **Rating:** Medium/Difficult

Map: IGN 1:50000 Ubrique (1050/14-44)

Ⓦ **Water:** spring @ approx 3hrs 30 mins though difficult to access (see text)

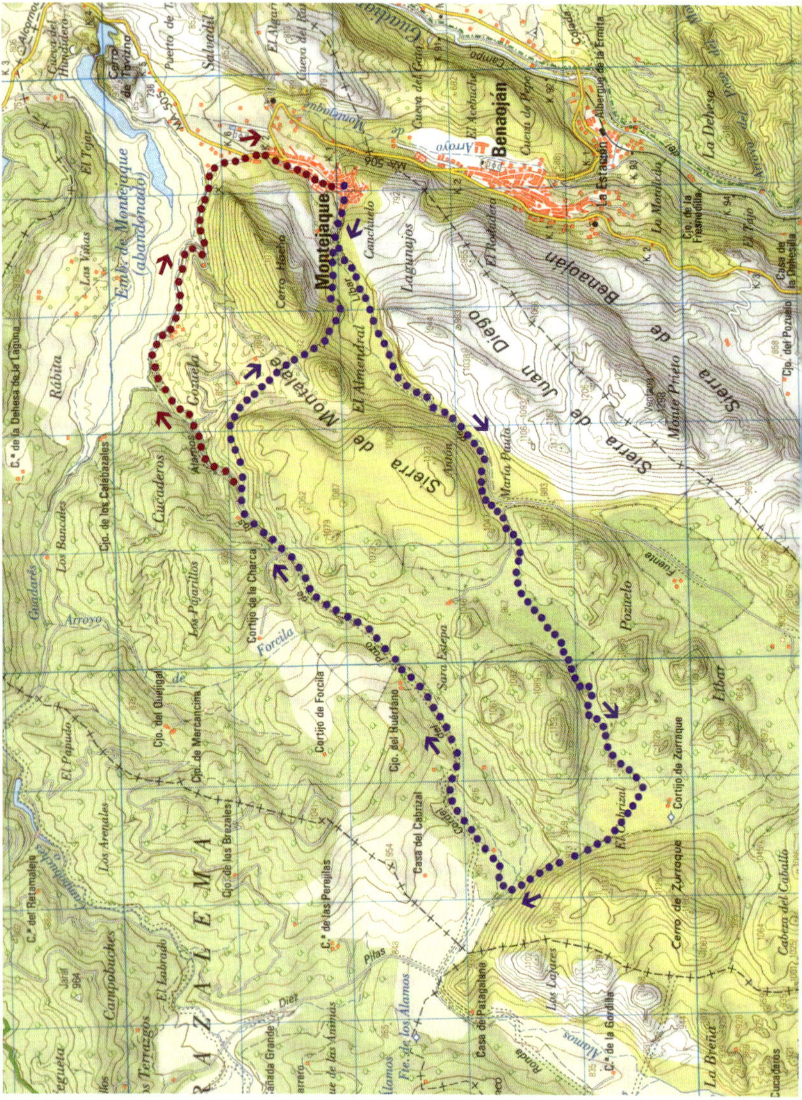

3 The Walk of the Hidden Valley

This is without doubt one of the Sierra's most special walks. It leads you to the heart of the Grazalema park, to an area with some of the most spectacular karst formations in Andalucía. There's a longish climb up and out of Montejaque first thing, along a broad track that cuts up to the top of the rocky Líbar valley. At the top of the pass the terrain changes in nature: it levels and you cross a broad, flat-bottomed valley before cutting down through some of the most beautiful rock formations in the park. The footpath leads on across more flat-bottomed valleys, between stands of ancient oak, before you eventually begin to descend back towards the village. The final section of the walk is less distinct but provided that you keep an eye open for for cairns you will easily find the way. Allow a full day to get the most out of this stunning itinerary.

The Route

The walk begins in the main square in Montejaque, in front of Hotel Elefante Amarillo. 1 Cross the square, head along the left side of the church under a row of palm trees then go right into Calle Nueva. After just 20m go left into Calle Santa Cruz. Follow this road all the way up through the village. You eventually leave the last houses behind then pass by a number of kennels built in amongst the rocks. The road that you have been following meets with a track by a G.R. marker post **(15 mins)**. 2

Continue on this track straight up the valley between the Sierra de Juan Diego and the Sierra de Benaoján. Nearing the top of the pass you cross a cattle grid. Continue for 300m then cut right, off the track, and go through a green gate in a stone wall **(55 mins)**. 3

Bear left up a narrow cobbled path. Pass right of a stone ruin then to the right of an old corral. You come to a wall and a black gate which is often left open. 4 The path, indistinct, leads beneath a clump of low oaks then crosses open ground before merging with a track. Bear right along the track and shortly, at a point where you reach a rectangular red sign on an oak tree to the left of the track, cut left on a stony footpath. 5 After about 60m the path arcs right: look for cairns which guide you through a stand of low oaks. Eventually, after angling right the path drops down to a stone wall. Go through a gap in the wall 6 and your path merges with a track which you follow across a vast, walled field. Having passed two bull-dozed watering holes the track runs up to gap in a stone wall. Bear right just before you reach the wall and, just beyond a large oak, go through a metal gate **(1 hr 25 mins)**. 7

Bear left on a narrow path, following the stone wall along. Soon the path climbs, bears left and reaches a small, flat, grassy area. Bear sharply right, looking for cairns, following a narrow path which threads between the rocks and descends. After dropping down for about 15 minutes you pass to the left of a ruined stone hut then go through a rickety old gate whose opening is sometimes closed with brush. 8 Following cairns, and making sure not to climb at any point, you eventually reach another vast, flat field similar in size to the one you traversed earlier **(1 hr 55 mins)**. 9

Careful! Look for a large stone arrow on the ground at the field's edge which gives you a bearing across the field (you need to angle about 45° right in a NNW direction). Cut all the way across the field, to a point where a wall, which runs across the mountainside to your west, drops down to meet with the field. As you traverse the field you pass a group of three huge oaks whose trunks all meet at the base. Beyond the oaks, at the far side of the field, look for cairns, and a second stone arrow, marking the point where you leave the field. 10 Follow an

indistinct path that climbs up across the rocks. It soon becomes clearer and you'll see a fence to your left. You reach a hollow with a stone-walled corral built against a cliff face **(2 hrs 25 mins)**.

Keep left here, contouring high round the hollow. The path leads over a ridge and the countryside opens out. At this point look for a small farm ahead of you: you will later be passing it by. The path descends, goes through a gate, then angles down across the hillside to a low stone wall and a fence. Follow the stone wall along, to its left, to a wire-and-post gate. 11 Open the gate with care – it has barbed wire along the top – then cross a (dry) stream. Continue straight ahead (there is no path) for 125m, climbing over a low ridge beyond which you meet with a track which cuts up towards the farm that you could see earlier. Soon you reach a fork. Here take the left hand option (**2 hrs 50 mins)**. 12

Soon you'll spot the farm and its corrals over to your right. Continue straight along the track until you reach a gate in a wall where the ground is sometimes churned up by cattle. Go through the gate and after just 10m bear left on a narrow path which shortly passes to the left of a chain and you arrive at a more open patch of ground. Bear right along its lower edge then enter a wooded area. The path is indistinct: look for cairns and don't climb too high! The path twists through the forest, crosses a stream then climbs an eroded bank to another gate. 13 Beyond the gate the path climbs then angles right and crosses a (dry) stream. The landscape again opens out and you reach a low stone wall. Ahead is another vast field. Bearing left, keeping to the same side of the field (just to the right of the trees to your left), continue to its far end and a boundary wall (you'll see cairns) where you pass through a rusting metal gate **(3 hrs 20 mins)**. 14

Bearing slightly right, you cross a (dry) stream then bear left again and cross back to the other side. Continuing up the middle of the enclosure you pass a metal drinking trough (* if you follow its black plastic pipe up hill it leads to a well surrounded by a wire fence: it is possible to climb down in to the well to refill your water bottle though extreme care should be taken). Soon the path runs just to the left of a wall and leads to the far end of the field. Here, go through a metal gate. 15 After just 10m the path merges with a track which you follow downwards. Soon you pass a white stone monument just to the left of the track which marks the place where a landowner was shot during the Civil War. Approximately 250m past the monument the track bears right and begins to climb slowly up and up: brace yourself for the steepest part of the walk. After passing a cattle grid 16 eventually the track reaches the top of the rise. 17 Just beyond it goes through a gap in a wall then merges with a second broad track **(3 hrs 50 mins)**.

Here bear right and descend steeply. Soon the track loops hard right, then left. Still descending steeply be ready to cut right off the track 18 on another track which angles steeply up to your right: look for cairns. (but see ** opposite). Where this track loops hard right cut left at a cairn and follow an indistinct path down to, then through, a black metal gate **(4 hrs)**. 19

Beyond the gate the path becomes clearer as it runs between olive groves, then becomes more overgrown. Twice you are forced to cut right and continue parallel to the path through the olives. You rejoin the path and soon it loops across a (dry) stream. 20 Beyond the stream (careful not to lose height) continue just to the right of a line of olives and oaks. Look for cairns! The line of the path, which has been ploughed into the grove in parts, is soon visible once again, running up to a brown metal sign which you pass to its right. 21 The path improves then merges with a track. Continuing along this track you soon

reach a wire-and-post gate **(4 hrs 25 mins)**.

Go through the gate. The track arcs right, levels, then loops down into the valley that you walked up earlier in the day. Sticking to the track you eventually pass by gates (and a fine threshing platform) to the left of the track then come to a junction. Here go right, then first left, 2 and retrace your footsteps back to the square in Montejaque **(4 hrs 55 mins)**. 1

** Alternative ending to the walk:

The route described from waypoint 18 can be heavy going after heavy rain. An easier option is to continue on down the track (ie don't branch right) to the bottom of the valley. Here turn right and follow a broader track along the side of the dry reservoir of Montejaque to the MA-505. Here turn right and when you reach a water trough angle right. Head all the way along to the very end of this street then turn left and retrace your footsteps back to the square.

FROM GRAZALEMA TO BENAOCÁZ

Distance: 11 or 14.5 kms **Duration:** 4/4.5 or 5.5/6 hrs **Rating:** Medium or Medium/Difficult **Map:** IGN 1:50000 Ubrique (1050/14-44)

W Water: about 200m to one side of the path @ approx. 45 minutes

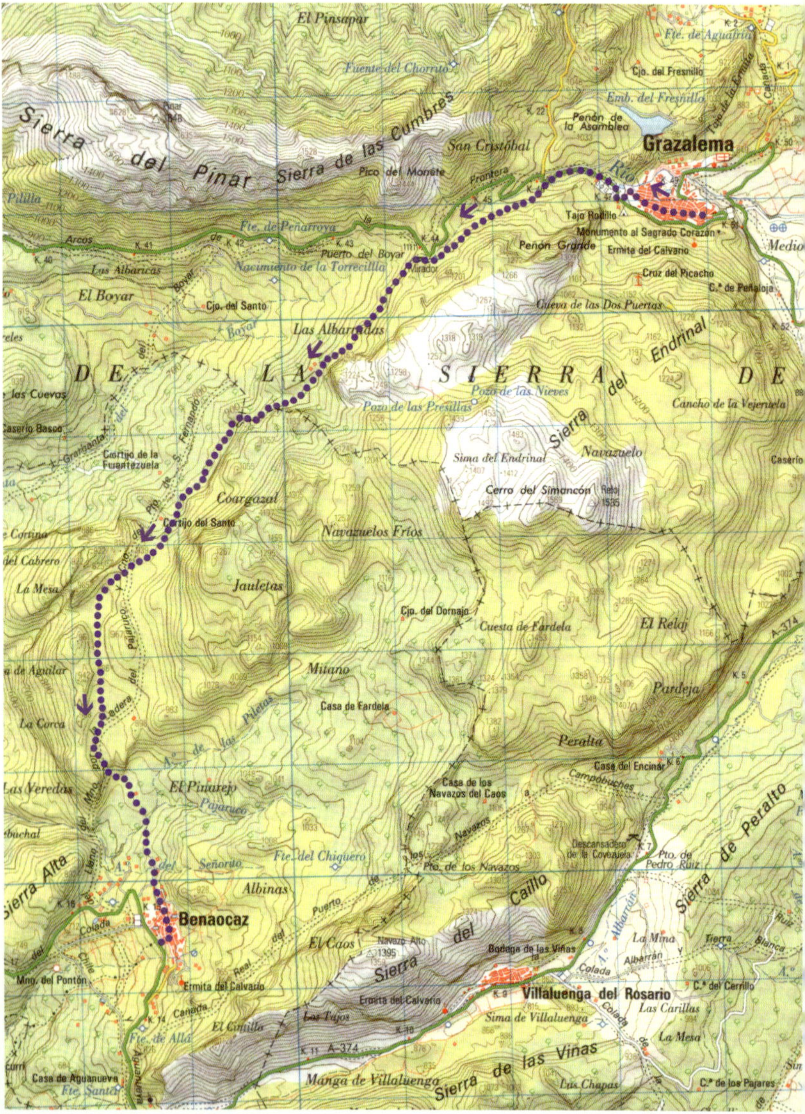

4 The Walk of the Goatherd's Leap

This is one of the Sierra's better-known walks – a linear route between two villages, returning to your point of departure by bus or by taxi – and fully deserves its reputation as a classic itinerary. There are constant changes of terrain and wonderful views to the west out across the *campiña* (glossary) of Jeréz and, on clear days, all the way to the Atlantic. Stands of ancient holm oaks, extraordinary karst formations, exceptional flora and good raptor-spotting possibilities make this a truly special full day excursion. You have a steep climb if you leave from Grazalema (long version). Or you can taxi to the top of the pass if you prefer a more leisurely walk (call Rafael 617 315 765 or arrange at Hostal Las Piedras in the village). From the Puerto del Boyar to Benaocáz there's just one short section of climbing. The popularity of the itinerary means that it is best undertaken on a weekday. If opting for the long version get going by 9.30h to allow plenty of time for a picnic along the way and to make the 15.40h bus from Benaocáz back to Grazalema (daily except Bank Holidays). In Benaocáz Bar Las Vegas serves a good food and has great views, too.

The Long Route

The long version starts from the square in Grazalema in front of the town hall, the *Ayuntamiento*. 1 Leave the village square by passing between the Unicaja bank and the *Ayuntamiento* along Calle José María Jiménez. Bear left at the end of the street and climb to the top of Calle Doctor Mateos Gago. Here turn left into Calle Portal then take the next right and Calle Nueva, passing a spring, to the top of the village. Here bear left at a sign *Quesos Frescos de Grazalema* 2 pass the Fromandal cheese factory, then turn right onto the Grazalema – El Bosque road.

Follow the right hand edge of the road. Soon you pass car parks to both sides of the road. From the one on the right there are great views across the rooftops of Grazalema.

Just before reaching a bridge cross the road and, just beyond a sign with a map of the first part of your walk, head for a sign *Camino Peatonal*. 3 Just beyond you cross a wooden footbridge then climb along a sandy footpath. After an unremitting climb through an area of young pines you pass a *calera* (glossary) and arrive at the carpark at the top of the pass, el Puerto del Boyar, where there is a sign *Merendero El Boyar*. 4 Walk straight ahead following green arrows to a rusting *Peligro de Incendio* sign next to a newer one with a map of the walk. Then pick up the itinerary below **(55 mins)**.

The Short Route

Take a taxi (or drive if leaving car here) to the top of the pass, El Puerto del Boyar, the highest point of the road between Grazalema and El Bosque. Here park just left of the road at the *Merendero El Boyar.* Care is needed as you pull off the road due to a high kerb (you could opt for an easier parking area some 70m further on).

To the right of the parking area is a *Peligro de Incendio* sign and a map of the route to the Salto del Cabrero. 4 Just beyond the signs is a large gate with a smaller green gate to its left. Go through the smaller gate and follow a track gently downwards. Soon you go through a large, metal gate. Ahead you'll see an isolated farm and, beyond in the distance, the spectacular cliffs of the *Salto del Cabrero* (Goatherd's Leap). Note that you'll later pass just to the left of the *Salto*. Just before reaching the farm the track arcs sharply to the right. Here cut left between two posts (there is a green arrow) 5 and, after dropping down, go through a wooden gate with a sign *Salto del Cabrero* **(20 mins)**.

A few metres further on you cross a wooden footbridge, go through a second gate, then cross a large flat area with magnificent old oaks. At the far end you pass between a tumbledown wall by a marker post. The path winds on through thicker undergrowth before running closer to the cliff face to your left. It soon swings sharply right (look for green arrows) and descends, running just to the right of a wall and a fence. After about 50m go through a large metal gate 6 in the wall and continue your descent through the thick undergrowth.

Take care at this stage not to drop too far to the right. If in doubt, keep left at any branch in the path, close to the base of the cliff. At times you see the *Salto* formation up ahead. You come up to another gate, sometimes left open, with a faint white walker symbol painted on the rock **(45 mins)**. 7

Go through the gate and continue straight on. You reach more open ground. Soon the path passes above the ruin of a stone hut. 8 (*Here you could cut right off the pass to a trough and a spring which you will see about 200m down the hill to replenish your water bottle, but be aware that the spring W slows to a trickle at the end of summer. Retrace your footsteps.*)

The path runs on between hawthorn and rocks. As you reach the top of a rise the path passes a sign for the *Salto del Cabrero* 9 and just before reaching a stone wall arcs right then left and passes through a gap in the wall by a marker post **(55 mins)**. 10

Go through the gap and follow the path roughly parallel to the wall, to your left. After some 150m the path angles right, cutting across a more open stretch of land towards the back of the *Salto* whose grey massif is now directly ahead of you. Shortly you reach a stand of three isolated oaks where the path divides at another marker post. 11 Here bear right, taking care as you pick your way through the sharp rocks: this is perfect ankle-twisting terrain. In spring watch out for the wild peonies that

grow between the rocks. Near the bottom of this rocky descent the path cuts sharply right, then left again – you'll need hands-on here – before reaching a vast flat area at the eastern base of the *Salto* **(1 hr 10 mins)**. 12

This could be a good spot for a picnic: there is shade beneath the oaks. (It's possible to scramble up to the top of the *Salto* from here. Some of the climb is hands-on, there's no clear path and you should allow an hour to get up and down. You should first angle right, then look for the most obvious path: climbing straight up looks tempting but is very difficult.)

From here walk directly away from the *Salto* across the vast open plain where goats and cows are often grazing. At the far side pick up a path that passes through a gap in the plain's perimeter wall then climbs gently across a tract of land where vegetation becomes much sparser.

The path levels and Benaocáz comes into sight. Look for a farm up ahead: you need to leave it well to your left. Soon you begin to gently descend and pass to the right of an old lime kiln. 13 A sign explains how lime was made. Just beyond the kiln the path zigzags down through the rocks to a gate made of an old bed base **(1 hr 35 mins)**. 14

Go through the gate then loop steeply downwards. Care is required on the loose scree, especially after rain. You reach a flatter area where the path runs beside a wall topped by a fence. Here you may spot griffon vultures perched on the cliff to your right: look for the streaks of white guano. The path passes through a green gate 15 then picks up a beautiful section of the old drover's path which is cobbled in parts.

The path crosses a stream by a small bridge, swings right, climbs, then passes through another gate. The path becomes a track which soon reaches the outskirts of the village. You pass a

new housing development to your left. Continue on past Hostal San Antón 16 and when you reach a garish villa to your left, branch left and continue to the village centre and its pretty main square **(2 hrs 10 mins)**. 17 You could drop into Bar Las Vegas for a drink or food: it has great views out to the south and if you are returning to Grazalema by taxi this is a good rendezvous point.

To reach the bus stop retrace your steps then turn left down Calle San Blas by the Caja de San Fernando bank. Take the next left and descend to the bus stop. The bus passes by every day at 15.40h. 20 minutes later you alight in the main square of Grazalema.

GRAZALEMA HIGH PEAKS CIRCUIT

Distance: 12 kms **Duration:** 6/6.5 hours **Rating:** Medium/Difficult

Map: IGN 1:50000 Ubrique (1050/14-44)

W Water: no springs along the way so take plenty

5 The Walk of the Twin Peaks

This full day excursion takes you to the top of two of the Grazalema Park's highest peaks, El Simancón (1561m) and El Reloj (1535m). After a steep climb from the village the forested lower slopes of the Sierra del Endrinal give way to a lunar-like landscape of deeply weathered limestone peaks. A final steep climb brings you to the top of the Simancón from where a huge swathe of the Subbética opens out before you: on clear days you can see all the way to Morocco and the Atlantic Coast. The path up and down the Reloj is more tricky to follow due to the lack of waymarking but if you feel confident clambering over rocks you'll have no problem finding a way up. Remember, too, that at times you'll be pushing through gorse and broom: this is a route best tackled in long trousers. In autumn, spring or winter have waterproof clothing in your pack because weather conditions change rapidly in the Grazalema massif.

If the amount of climbing appears daunting the walk can be shortened slightly by setting out from the car park beside the camp site at the top end of the village.

The Route

The walk begins in the main square of Grazalema in front of the town hall, the *Ayuntamiento*. 1 Leave the village square by passing between the Unicaja bank and the *Ayuntamiento* along Calle José María Jiménez. Bear left at the end of the street then climb to the top of Calle Doctor Mateos Gago. Here turn left into Calle Portal then take the next right and head up Calle Nueva, passing a spring, to the top of the village. Here bear left at a sign *Quesos Frescos de Grazalema*, pass the Fromandal cheese factory then turn right onto the Grazalema – El Bosque road. **(10 mins)**. 2

After a few yards you reach a car park to the left hand side of the road (you can leave a car here if doing the shortened version of the walk). Turn into the car park and walk along it eastern side, past the entrance to the camp site, to a wooden telegraph post. Just beyond it you pick up a path to the left of a green metal gate. The path loops left then climbs steeply up between two fences.You shortly pass through a green metal gate 3 and continue on up with the jagged ridge of Peñon Grande over to your right.

After a steep climb through the pines the path levels then descends for about 50m to a wooden sign. Take the right hand option marked *Llanos del Endrinal/Puerto del Boyar* **(35 mins)**. 4 You shortly pass a large cairn. The path descends, crosses a flat area betwen the pines then arcs round to the right. After 40m you come to a fork. 5 Here cut left on a less distinct path which runs through a gap in a stone wall and, beyond it, reaches a fence. Cut left and follow the fence along. At the end of the enclosure follow the fence as it cuts right then after 30m turn left 6 and cross the tumbledown wall. You reach a flat, more open area. Angling left you pick up a footpath, marked by a cairn and a blue dot on a rock, which climbs up through the rocks and pine trees. It is overgrown in parts with gorse and hawthorn but is easy to follow: a few blue dots help plot your course. Eventually the path cuts right to reach a much more rocky, swathe of ground **(1 hr 30 mins)** 7 before it runs up to reach a saddle. 8

The Simancón's denuded massif is now over to your left. At the top of the saddle angle left keeping an eye open for cairns which lead you along the right flank of the Simancón. After angling gently upwards the indistinct path angles hard left 9 then zigzags steeply up to the summit: small yellow arrows, some on a black background, guide you up to the top which is marked by a large cairn **(2 hrs 15 mins)**. 10 At just over 1560m this is

the highest point on the walk. The views are to be savoured: this is a great place to break for a picnic or a snack.

To the east, connected to the base of the Simancón by a high ridge, you'll clearly see the summit of the Reloj, the next point in the walk: Ronda is visible behind it in the far distance. Leaving the summit of the Simancón drop steeply down the mountain's eastern flank towards the saddle linking the two mountains: seen from above the saddle is slightly lighter in colour than the surrounding rocks. Look for cairns, follow the path which feels easiest, and soon you'll arrive at the beginning of the saddle. 11 Follow the saddle's ridge along, just to its right, still looking for cairns. At the eastern end, by a small swathe of open, more grassy ground, angle hard left. After a steep scramble over deeply weathered rocks you arrive at the summit of the Reloj **(2 hrs 45 mins)** 12 which is also marked by a cairn comprised of the remnants of a trig point.

From the top of the Reloj you'll see, in the valley floor to your right and to the south, a circular stone wall surrounding a well: this is your next destination. Leaving the summit follow the crest of the Reloj's ridge south for about 100m to a cairn 13 where you angle left (the stone circle is still clearly visible down below) then clamber down across the rocks following a line of cairns. Soon the path angles right, then left once more, before running along the left edge of a flattish area about the size of a tennis court 14 before it once more descends steeply. As you drop downwards be careful not to miss the point where the path cuts hard right: look for cairns. 15 The path then loops down to a flat area in the floor of the valley where it runs up to the circular stone wall

(3 hrs 10 mins) 16 which surrounds a well. Resist the temptation to fill up your water bottle: cattle graze here and the water is not suitable for drinking.

Bear left round the well following a path which climbs slightly for 30m then reaches a junction where an arrow painted on a rock points right. Ignore the arrow and rather cut left along a clear footpath where the going becomes much easier. Soon a black plastic pipe crosses the path then runs just to to its right: a little further on it leads to a small concrete drinking trough 17 for livestock. The Reloj is now up above you, to your left. The path runs on and passes just left of a sink (a collapsed limestone cave) 18 as it zigzags and rollercoasters slowly back towards Grazalema through low-growing oaks and pines. The path drops down, adopts a more level course and passes a rectangular corral 19 then runs up to a rickety wire-and-post gate **(3 hrs 45 mins)**. 20

After running across a more open tract of land the path climbs then again runs downhill and passes just to the right of a second limestone sink. Soon it arcs down between huge rocks 21 then divides. 22 Take the right hand option which climbs gradually up through the pines then merges with a better defined path. Follow the path to the top of the ridge 23 where, after passing a marker post, you drop down towards the campsite. The first houses of Grazalema come into site as you pass a wooden sign which tells you that Grazalema is just 15 minutes away. 24 After passing several marker posts topped by white arrows you pass a stone corral then reach the fence of the campsite where the path divides. Cutting left along the fence you soon arrive back at the path you followed earlier in the walk. Here turn right, go back through the green metal gate then head back down to the square in Grazalema **(4 hrs 25 mins)**. 1

ZAHARA DE LA SIERRA CIRCULAR WALK

Distance: 16 kms **Duration:** 6/6.5 hours **Rating:** Medium/Difficult

Map: IGN 1:50000 Ubrique (1050/14-44) & Olvera 1036 (1036/14-43)

W Water: no springs along the way so take at least 1.5 litres

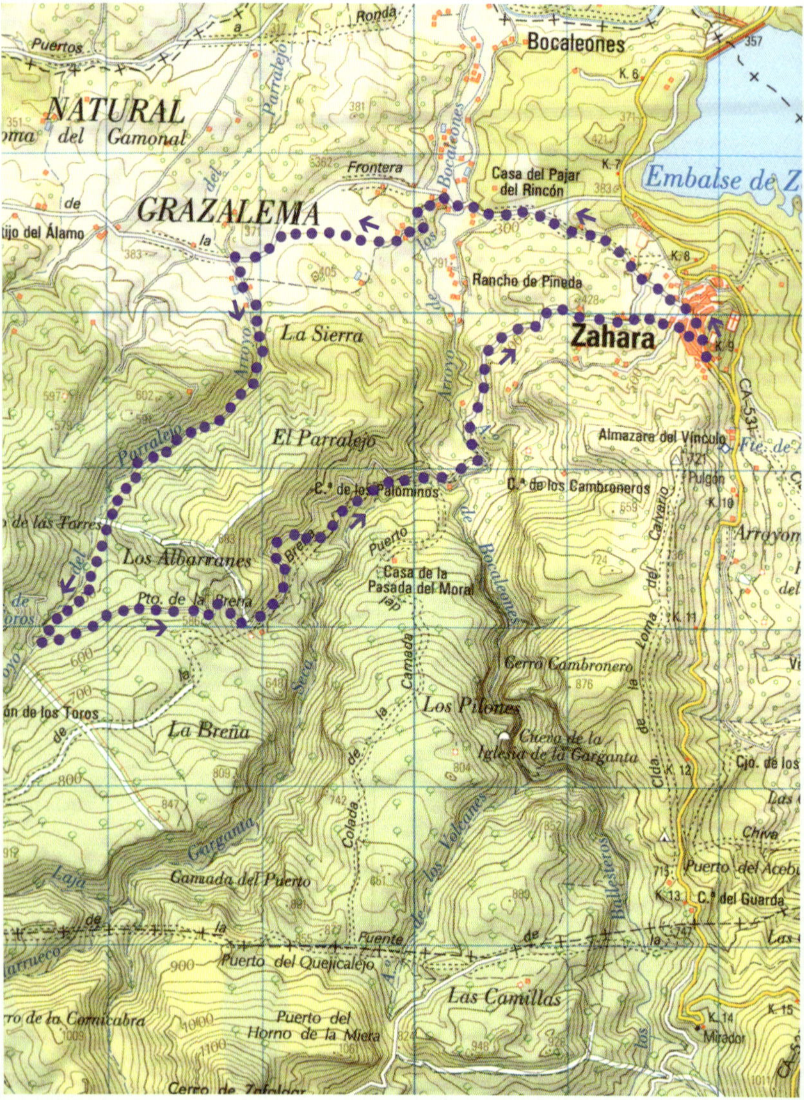

6 The Walk of the Griffon Vultures

This circular route begins and ends in one of the prettiest villages of the Grazalema Park, the quintessentail *pueblo blanco* of Zahara de la Sierra. The day begins with a steep descent to the Bocaleones stream. After crossing open farmland you follow a narrow path up the valley of the Parralejo stream then, after a long climb up to the Breña pass, drop down a broad forestry track. You then pick up a narrow path which leads on down the valley at which stage great views open out to the gorges of Garganta Seca and Garganta Verde, home to one of Europe's largest colonies of griffon vultures. The walk ends with a longish pull back up to Zahara: you'll be glad of a cold drink when you get back to the square. This itinerary is not recommended after heavy rain when crossing the Parralejo can become difficult. The amount of prickly gorse on the first part of the Parralejo ascent means this is a route best undertaken with a pair of long trousers in your day pack.

The Route

The walk begins in the main square of Zahara. 1 With your back to the church cross the square and drop down the road to the left of the town hall (*Ayuntamiento*) following a sign for *Salida*. You reach a fork by *Super La Cuesta*. Bear right then take the first left into Calle Peñas immediately passing *Autoservicio Jucemar*. At the end of this street, just past house no. 33, bear hard right and descend towards a sign *Principe Felipe*.

You reach a pedestrian crossing by a palm tree. 2 Cross the road, turn left and then cut immediately right and drop down a concrete track following a line of telegraph poles. The concrete ends as it swings left to a green gate. Don't go through the gate but rather continue straight on down a dirt path, still following the telegraph wires. The track swings right and meets with a concrete road. Here turn left and continue your descent. You pass a farm to the right of the track then reach a tarmac road **(20 mins)**. 3

Here turn left. After 500m the road bears right, then left, before descending and crossing the Bocaleones stream and, just beyond, a picnic area. Carry on along the road which bears right, climbs, passes a small cottage with a brown bench then reaches a house with ceramic pots on its gate posts. 4 Here branch left up a dirt track. Head for a black metal gate. Just before reaching it, bear left and climb. The track bears hard left then right and arrives at a small farm **(30 mins)**. 5 Here bear left and follow a dirt track across a field. Having crossed the field the track arcs right and cuts beneath a number of olive groves. Stick to the main track. Soon it descends, passes through a wire-and-post gate (often left open) then meets with the tarmac road. 6

Turn left and follow the road for 350m. Just before you reach a small bridge with metal crash barriers 7 turn left off the road along a dirt track. You pass two houses then reach a third building. Head straight on, passing just behind the farm. 8 The track narrows to become a path. 100m after the farm house it splits into two parallel branches. The upper one is easier to follow. Follow the path, indistinct at times, gently upwards on a course roughly parallel to the Parralejo. The path soon passes through a wire-and-post gate. **(50 mins)**. 9

A fence now runs to the right of the path. Soon you should see a path marked by blue dots cutting hard left, away from the stream. Don't take this turn but rather continue on your same course, ignoring an opening that you soon pass down to the right which leads through a wire-and-post gate to the stream.

Continue along the left bank. The path narrows, passes across a more open swathe of ground, then improves. You pass a huge carob tree then a gap in the fence leading to a metal drinking trough. Soon the path cuts right, then left, and passes through a gate just to the left of a sign for *Coto Privado de Caza* **(1 hr 15 mins)**. 10

Careful! Here you descend and cross the stream for the first time. Bearing left after just 15m you cross back to the left bank. The fence now runs to your left. Where it cuts sharply left you should again cross the stream and, shortly, cross back once again to the left bank. Shortly the path descends, crosses over a fifth time, then divides. Here take the right fork, continue straight on over a small rise then pass just to the left of an enormous oak tree with a red, metal sign **(1 hr 25 mins)**. 11

Continue straight on along a narrow path taking: care should

be taken because there are steep drops to your left. Soon you cross a final, sixth time back to the left bank of the stream. Here go through a wire-and-post gate 12 and after 30m pass through a second, smaller gate. Beyond it you reach a stone-walled enclosure. Continue climbing parallel to the stream: so long as you stick close to the wonderful old stone wall to your right, and keep an eye open for cairns and the most obvious path, you can't go wrong. At the far end of the enclosure the indistinct path bears left, climbs a steep bank, then meets with a broad track. 13 Here turn left and head gently upwards past stands of olive and oak. Eventually the track bears right, passes a helicopter landing circle, and reaches the top of the pass, El Puerto de la Breña **(2 hrs 5 mins)**. 14

Breaking out into the next valley you now see the rocky defiles of Garganta Seca and Garganta Verde across the valley. The track bears left, descends and passes through a green metal gate. 15 Ignore a first track which cuts down to the right marked with a sign for *Depósito de Agua*. After descending for some

20 minutes you reach two faded wooden signs to the right of the track. 16 Here angle hard right off the track and drop down another track to a black gate. Go through the narrow gate to its right 17 and immediately turn left on a narrow footpath. After 300m you go through a wire-and-post gate and continue on downwards. Eventually you go through a gate made of an old bed base. Your path now cuts slightly left and upwards then meets with the track you left higher up the valley. Bearing right and descending the track crosses the Bocaleones stream **(2 hrs 55 mins)**. 18 **If you are walking this route in the warmer months you could cut right just beyond the stream. When you reach a metal gate cut right along a narrow path which leads to a pretty and shaded bathing spot between the rocks.*

Beyond the stream the track bears left then climbs through the olive groves. Steel yourself for a steep climb. After levelling the track passes between two white buildings with solar panels then climbs again as Zahara comes into view. Descending again you reach a pretty farm to the left of the track with a palm tree. Just before reaching a green gate next to the farm where the track bears left, turn right away from the track **(3 hrs 40 mins)**. 19

Follow a narrow path steeply up through an olive grove. The path runs indistinctly up the left side of the grove then loops across a dry stream. Continuing along the top of the grove it improves then meets with a steep concrete track leading up towards a pylon. At the next junction 20 go left, pass *Molino La Ermita* and at the next junction turn right up a steep street with a *No Entry* sign. You pass a nursery *(guardería)* then the road bears left and you reach a wider street by a pedestrian crossing. Cross the road heading for a sign for *autoservicio*. Go straight up this street and you return to the square of Zahara **(4 hrs 10 mins)**. 1

El Parque Natural de Los Alcornocales & THE GAUCÍN AREA

Pujerra
Benalauria
Algatocín
Jubrique
Benarrabá
Genalguacíl
La Sauceda
Gaucín
Casares
Jimena de la Frontera
E-15
ESTEPONA
N-340
MANILVA
AREA MAP

El Parque Natural de Los Alcornocales & the Gaucín area

THE AREA

El Parque Natural de los Alcornocales (the Park of the Cork Oak Forests) covers no less than 165,000 hectares of western Andalusia. It offers some of the best bird life in Europe, a whole string of beautiful white villages, wonderful places to stay and some of the best walking in Southern Spain. Amazingly this guide was amongst the first in English to list walks in the area. Most of the Park lies within the province of Cádiz with just a tenth or so falling within Málaga. This is the most southerly of mainland Spain's protected areas, running all the way from El Bosque in the in the north to the Strait of Gibraltar in the south. The area encompassed within the boundaries of the Park corresponds roughly to that covered by the last reaches of the mighty Betica range whose mountains gradually decrease in height as they stretch south towards Africa.

Like the province of Cádiz itself the Park's character has been indelibly marked by its proximity to both the Atlantic and the Mediterranean: it literally falls *Entre Dos Aguas*. The whole of this region receives astonishingly high rainfall considering its southerly position. This is primarily due to the prevailing westerly winds which are forced upwards as they meet the Aljibe, Blanquilla and Cabras mountain ranges. These high levels of humidity are also maintained during the spring and summer thanks to the *Levante* wind which gathers moisture as it blows hard across the Strait from North Africa. This is then discharged in the form of thick, morning mists which wrap around the mountains and cloak the Mediterranean in a white mantle before being burned off by the harsh, summer sun. These morning mists can provide you with a surprisingly cool start to some of these walks, even in summer, when it would otherwise be too hot for comfortable walking.

The region's warm, humid climate has fostered abundant vegetation and the Park contains an exceptionally diverse flora as well as some of Andalusia's most extensive stretches of forest. Most notable of all is the vast tract of cork oak forest which has given the Park its name. Nearly all the walks described in this chapter take you through stands of *alcornoques* (cork oaks). Stripped of their bark their russet-coloured trunks have a beauty all of their own. These magnificent trees have long been a vital part of the local economy, not only for cork production but also as a source of food for the prized Iberian pigs. You're almost certain to come across them, grubbing for acorns, on any of these walks.

And these great swathes of wooded hill and mountainside are home to abundant wildlife. There are ginets, mongoose, martens, foxes, badgers, polecats, wild boar and deer. But what makes the area truly exceptional is its birdlife. This is one of the best areas in Europe for ornithology, not only because of the diversity of natural habitats but also because the seasonal migrations to and from Africa bring, literally, millions of birds straight over the Park. Be sure to pack a good field guide and your binoculars. You're bound to see eagles, kites, vultures, buzzards, egrets, storks, kingfishers, owls and many, many more birds. The list that you'll find in the back of this book contains all of the feathered things that you're most likely to see.

In order to make the walks as varied as possible I've added the area around Gaucín to that encompassed by this chapter. Although the village falls just outside the boundaries of the Park it is a natural neighbour of the Alcornocales, sharing a similar climate, geology and vegetation. And there are currently moves afoot to include Gaucín within the boundaries of the Park.

Both Gaucín and Jimena would make good bases for any of

the walks listed in this chapter. Both are fine examples of the classic Andalusian *pueblo blanco*, crowned by a castle and with a labyrinth of whitewashed houses spilling down the hillside. Gaucín has a large, mostly British ex-pat community, a fact that is reflected in the price of both food and accommodation. In Jimena there are fewer foreigners. Benarrabá, on the other hand, remains virtually undiscovered, as does Genalguacíl, and both have cheap-and-cheerful, friendly hotels (see accommodation listings).

Other Walks

There are endless possibilities for further walks within the Park. The 1:75000 park map could be a good starting point for deciding which areas to explore next. And you could link the walks described in this chapter with those of the Grazalema Park: the GR-7 footpath cuts through the heart of the Park via Jimena and Castellar although waymarking is often absent.

La Buitrera del Colmenar is a mighty, deep-sided gorge which is home to a large colony of vultures. You can reach it by walking north along the left bank of the Guadiaro from El Colmenar (also known as Estación de Cortes), crossing the river and heading for La Casa del Conde, then dropping down towards the river. Never be tempted to enter the gorge during the wetter months.

The Laja Alta walk which begins just to one side of road leading from Jimena to La Sauceda takes you up to a jagged limestone outcrop and a rock shelter with paleaolithic rock paintings. You can find details of the walks in either the Castellar or Jimena tourist offices.

Maps

The only map covering the whole of the Park as well as the Gaucín area is Parque Natural, Los Alcornocales (1998: Instituto Cartografía de Andalucía). But the 1:75000 scale is barely

detailed enough for these walks.

The best maps for walking are the standard 1:50000 maps of the Instituto Nacional Geográfico. The Gaucín and Benarrabá walks are covered by the map Cortes de la Frontera (1064/14-45). The two Jimena walks are both covered by the map Jimena de la Frontera (1071/14-46). The La Sauceda walk (The Queen's Bath) is covered by the map San José del Valle (1063/13-45).

BEST PLACES TO SLEEP & EAT

JIMENA DE LA FRONTERA

Casa Henrietta

Tel: 956 648 130 Email: info@casahenrietta.com

A delightful village inn with 8 beautiful bedrooms and great views out across the valley. Superb value for money, with a kind and friendly owner and a great restaurant right next door. (Taxis: Juan de Dios 956 640 191 or "Quini' 956 640 108). **Best Eats:** here or just a few metres down the hill in Bar/Bistro Oba

La Viña de Linan

Tel: 956 640 936 Email: valeriejubb@tiscali.co.uk

A top of the range B&B with a beautiful decked area and pool, hidden away in the forest beneath Jimena with exceptionally helpful owners. €90-€110 including breakfast. (Taxis: Juan de Díos 956 640 191 or "Quini" 956 640 108). **Best Eats:** here or decent food in any of the restaurants up by the square or Bar Cuenca.

Hostal El Anon

Tel: 956 640 113 Email: reservas@elanon.net

Five village houses have been fused together to create this intimate, multi-levelled hostal. Bar and restaurant serving Spanish and international food. €60 + 7% VAT. (Taxis: Eduardo 956 640 293 or Eugenio 956 640 192). **Best Eats:** here or in the bars and restaurants around the Plaza de la Constitución or Bar Cuenca.

GAUCÍN

La Fructuosa

Tel: 617 692 684 Email: lafructuosa@yahoo.es

An intimate, Spanish-owned B&B at the heart of the village with stylishly decorated rooms and great views. €85-€95 incl.

breakfast. (Taxis: José María 600 294 138 or Mundo 608 451 434). **Best Eats:** La Fructuosa's excellent restaurant is now only open on Friday and Saturday nights but plenty of workaday restaurants in village.

El Nobo

Tel: 952 151 303 Email: elnobo@telefonica.net

A delectable house on a spur beneath the village with amazing views out to Africa and *corden bleu* cusine. €125. (Taxis: José María 600 294 138 or Mundo). **Best Eats:** here or at La Fuente in village.

BENARRABÁ

Hotel Banu Rabbah

Tel: 952 150 288 Email: hotel@hbenarraba.es

A modern hotel with views across the Genal valley from the front-facing rooms. Friendly staff and reasonable food at the restaurant next door. A reliable budget option. €48-€60 + 7% VAT. (Taxis: Sebastian 952 150 164). **Best Eats:** here.

ALGOTACÍN

Hotel La Fuentecilla

Tel: 952 150 371 lafuentecilla@depcapc.com

Another great budget option which is within easy driving range of the starts of the Gaucín and Benarrabá walks and also within range of some of the Grazalema walks. Approx. €60 + 7% VAT. (Taxi: 952 150 017) **Best Eats:** here.

JIMENA DE LA FRONTERA SOUTHERN CIRCUIT

Distance: 9 kms **Duration:** 3.5/4 hours **Rating:** Medium

Map: IGN 1:50000 Jimena de la Frontera (1071/14-46)

Water: no springs along the way so take plenty

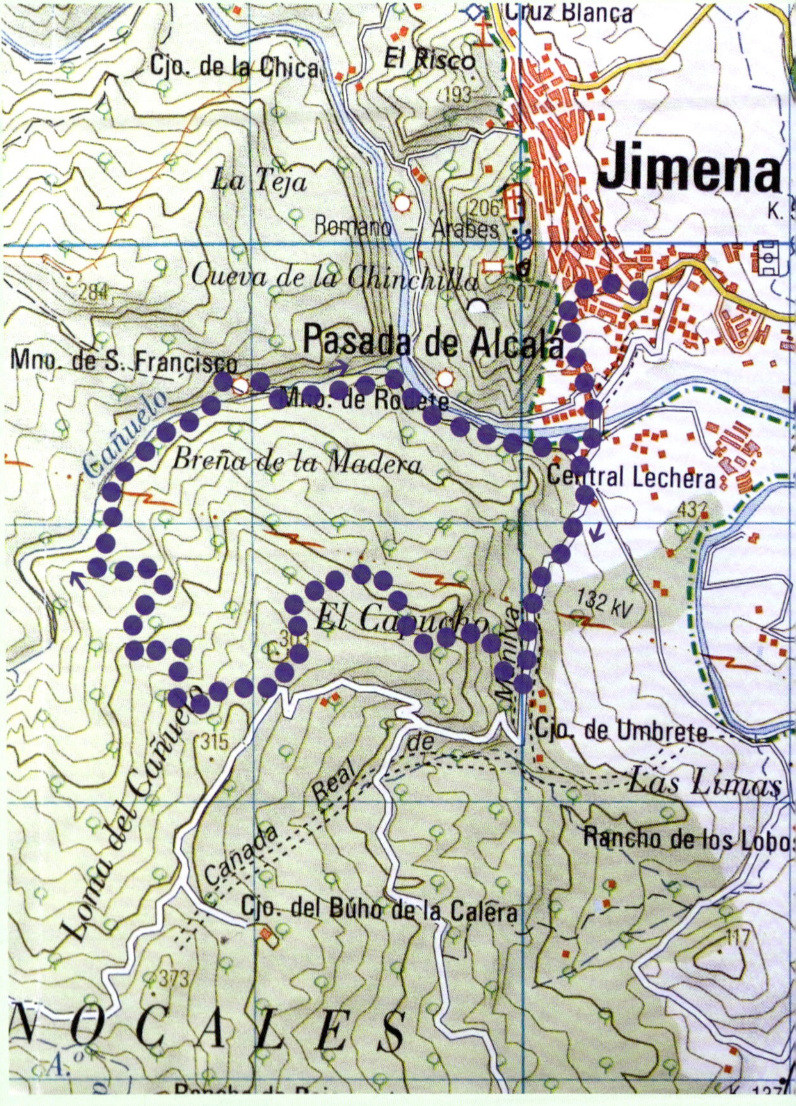

LOS ALCORNOCALES

1 The Walk of the Old Mill

This circuit makes for an easy half-day walk out from the pretty white village of Jimena de la Frontera. I've recommended allowing 3.5/4 hours for the walk but you could easily take far longer: the exceptionally pretty section of path leading down the Arroyo del Cañuelo should not to be rushed, there are beautiful rock pools for bathing and the old mill, *El Molino de San Francisco,* is a heavenly spot for a picnic. On the higher sections of the walk there are great views back to Jimena and its castle and out across the beautiful Hozgarganta valley. Apart from an initial steep section there isn't too much climbing involved. Remember to take plenty of water and your swimming gear if tackling the walk in the warmer months.

The Route

The walk begins next to the bell tower (1) in Jimena de la Frontera's Plaza de la Constitución which is to the left of the road as you arrive at the bottom of the village. You can normally find a parking space in the car park immediately beneath the square. Leave the square at its top, left-hand corner and head up Calle San Sebastian following signs for *Castillo/Fortaleza*. Take the first turning left and head along to the end of Calle Barrera. Here angle right across a small square, turn left down Calle La Vaca, then bear right into Chorro de la Calle. Pass a spring (2) and at the end of the road bear sharp left, then right, and drop down the hill past a row of houses. Continue straight on past a sign marking the beginning of the *Sendero: Río Hozgarganta*. Your road merges with another then crosses a bridge over the Hozgarganta river **(10 mins)**. (3)

After a few hundred metres the road bears right and begins to climb before levelling, now running parallel to a row of telegraph posts. There are lovely views back to Jimena. Careful! Just past an entrance to a farm tucked in to the left of the road, at a point where there are eucalyptus trees, turn right off the road at a cairn by a low wall and climb through a barbed wire fence **(25 mins)**. 4

Beyond the fence angle right and when you reach a stand of eucalyptus bear left and climb steeply up parallel to the trees and a (dry) stream bed. Crossing the (dry) stream bed 20m above the last of the eucalyptus trees you arrive at a ruined farm. Cut left in front of the farm and, just beyond its stone-walled corral 5 bear sharp right and pick up a rough track which loops steeply up above the farm. You'll be following this track nearly all the way to the top of the ridge: look for cairns but be aware that these get knocked over by the cattle and goats.

The track climbs steeply up the Loma del Cañuelo then loops right towards a fence. Looping once more to the left the track continues to ascend with the fence over to your right. Shortly before reaching the top of the ridge your path runs up to the fence which you should cross by way of a ladder. 6 Once over the fence angle left, parallel to the top of the ridge, along a track which soon runs between two fences, one with a stone wall at its base. The vegetation becomes sparser as the track drops slightly down and reaches a fence with a wire-and-post gate **(45 mins)**. 7

On the other side of the gate you'll see the tarmac road immediately ahead of you. Continue parallel to the road, just to its right. After 125m you reach an indistinct track cutting directly in from the road. 8 Here bear sharp right: you should see cairns. The track becomes better defined as it passes over the top of the ridge then bears left: there may be a chain across the track at this point. Follow this track all the way down through the cork oaks to the bottom of the valley. The track loops lazily downhill:

you can occasionally cut off a corner. There are good views of the *lajas* (glossary) on the other side of the valley.

Towards the bottom of the valley the track becomes stonier and looser underfoot as wild olives begin to take the place of the cork oaks. Just before reaching the valley floor the track loops hard left. Here look to the right of the track for a large cairn atop a boulder. 10m beyond the cairn 9 cut right away from the track on a narrow, indistinct path. **(1 hr 25 mins)**. (If you reach a concrete bridge across the Cañuelo, you have come too far and should retrace your footsteps to the sharp bend described earlier).

The oleander-filled bed of the Cañuelo is now to your left. The path is overgrown in parts but is easy enough to follow. Soon it crosses the stream then runs on down the left bank of the Cañuelo. Cross the stream once again, this time via stepping stones. The sandy path improves as it winds through the rocks. You cross the stream a third time. 10 You'll now be able to see the water channel just above your path which supplied the San Francisco mill. You now pick up a beautiful cobbled footpath that once would have been used by the millers when tending to the mill race. The path climbs slightly away from the river before swinging right and adopting its previous course. Soon you arrive at the derelict mill of San Francisco 11 which is a truly wonderful picnic spot. And just beneath the mill is a great place to swim.

75m past the mill the path descends and crosses the stream. Look for a cairn. The castle of Jimena is visible up ahead. You pass another good bathing spot and the path climbs slightly away from the stream into the cork oaks then passes between two huge rocks. Head on down the valley sticking to the most obvious path. The Hozgarganta river soon comes into sight. The path again becomes cobbled and leads you through a wire-and-post gate **(2 hrs)**. Beyond the gate the path swings right and

now follows a fence on a course roughly parallel to the River Hozgarganta. Where the fence cuts uphill 12 continue straight ahead and eventually you arrive back at the tarmac road you followed earlier in the day. Turn left, cross the river, then retrace your footsteps back to the Plaza de la Constitución **(2 hr 40 mins)**. 1

JIMENA NORTHERN CIRCUIT

Distance: 9.5 kms **Duration:** 3.5/4 hours **Rating:** Medium

Map: IGN 1:50000 Jimena de la Frontera (1071/14-46)

Ⓦ **Water:** no springs along the way so take plenty

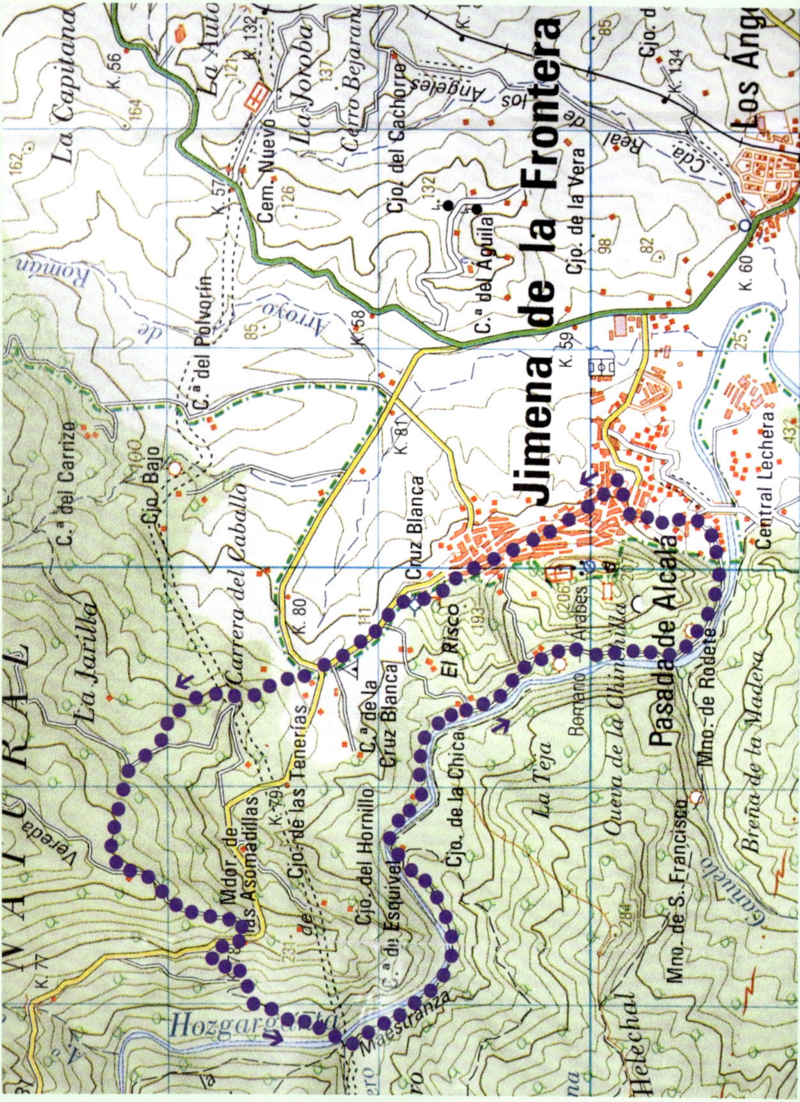

2 The Walk of the Eagle & the Kingfisher

Although this is rather shorter than some of the walks described in this section it makes for a memorable half-day excursion. Climbing up from Jimena there are glorious views back towards the village and its lofty castle and out to the eastern reaches of the Alcornocales Park. This is great territory for the observation of raptors and you're almost bound to see eagles (booted and short-toed) as well as griffon vultures. Later you loop down into the luxuriant vegetation of the Hozgarganta where, in warmer weather, you can take time out to swim in the crystal waters of any number of rock pools. The birdlife here is exceptional and you may be lucky enough to spot the irridescent flash of a kingfisher between the trees and enormous boulders which line the course of the river.

The Route

The walk begins at the bottom of Jimena de la Frontera in the Plaza de la Constitución, next to the bell tower in the centre of the square. ① From here head across towards the Unicaja bank then cut left past the taxi rank along Calle Sevilla and follow this street all the way through the village. 40m beyond the very last of the village houses cut left ② along a paved path which leads up past a white cross ③ then descends once more to merge with the road. After passing by a campsite you come to the road from Jimena to Algar (CA-3331) **(15 mins)**. ④

Go straight across the road passing a sign marking your route and climb up a wide cobbled path. The cobbling comes to an end and, climbing between two fences, you continue up along a rougher path. Views open out east towards La Crestellina and to Casares at its southern end. The path levels, descends for 150m, then reaches a green metal gate. ⑤ Go through the gate then turn right on a broad track which immediately comes to another green gate **(35 mins)**.

Don't go through the gate but rather cut left through another green gate by a G.R. marker post, and continue climbing steeply upwards over a rocky tract of land, more or less parallel to a fence to your right. Look for cairns and G.R. marking. After heading steeply up for just over 100m you reach a track. Here turn left following the direction marked by a sign *Sendero Vereda de Ubrique a Las Asomadillas*. Follow this sandy track on west. It soon merges with another as it runs on through stands of pines and cork oaks. Great views open out towards Jimena, over to your left. Your track runs up to meet another, broader track **(45 mins)**. 6

Here bear left (there's a marker post). Soon the track runs above a ruined farm: more green arrows mark your course. The track loops right then hard left, descending, then runs up towards a green and white gate. Approximately 30m before reaching the gate cut right 7 on a path which leads through an arch made of pine poles. Just beyond, to the right, is a *mirador* (glossary). It's worth climbing up for a great panoramic view of the Hozgarganta valley. Otherwise carry straight on down the track. Shortly you reach the CA-3331. 8

Turn right and follow the tarmac road for approximately 150m to another marker post, just to the left of the road. Here 9 cut left through the white road bollards and pick up a narrow footpath which loops down into the Hozgarganta valley passing through stands of oak, pine and lentiscus. It soon adopts a more level, westerly course before again looping steeply downhill: marker posts show the way. Eventually you reach a broad track where you should turn left. 10 Soon you reach a fork. Take the lower, right hand fork and continue on down towards the valley floor. The track soon narrows to become a path 11 and shortly before

Sendero
Ubrique

you reach the river runs up to a board explaining about the ecosystem of the Río Hozgarganta **(1 hr 20 mins)**. 12

Just beyond the sign go through a green metal gate, drop down, then bear left and follow an indistinct path along the left bank of the river. After 50m the path cuts right crosses the bed of the Hozgarganta via two runs of concrete stepping stones. You now pick up a sandy path which runs parallel to the river on its right bank which soon becomes cobbled in parts. There are great views up to the jagged *lajas* (glossary) of the upper reaches of the valley. Sticking to the most obvious path, and looking for white arrows and green painted stripes, you arrive at an open swathe of land in front of a farmhouse **(1 hr 50 mins)**. 13

Angle left across the open area between you and the farm to a wire-and-post gate. Beyond the gate, bear right, then drop down and cross back over the Hozgarganta via another run of stepping stones. 14 Having crossed the river you should angle right and, winding past thick stands of oleander, pick up a lovely narrow path which now runs close to the river's left bank. You pass through a wire and post gate 15 and soon a pretty house with a palm tree comes into view up ahead in the distance. When you reach a white marker post 16 pointing up hill ignore this sign: you should rather head straight on, closer to the river, along a narrower path.

Just before you reach the house with the palm tree a track runs up from the river to cross your path. Turn left, climb up the track for 30m, then cut right 17 along a narrow cobbled path. You pass beneath the house with the palm tree then pass a sign with a map and a second one explaining how a mill works. Continuing on your same course you pass above another mill where there's another board explaining how grain was milled, and another map. After climbing slightly away from the river via a path that has been worn out in the sandstone boulders over the

centuries you arrive at a more open area where the path, neatly cobbled, runs up to three way junction. 18

Here cut right and continue along a path which runs parallel to the Hozgarganta. After passing Huerta Mondeño the path merges with a track which runs on past another ruined mill then reaches the extraordinary water channel of El Cao. 19 It once supplied water to the factory where the cannon balls used during the seige of Gibraltar were manufactured. Head straight on past a row of houses: one of them was the original cannon ball factory. The track arcs left, then right, and runs up to meet with a road. Here cut left and climb up towards the village. After a steep ascent the road arcs right. Just past a house with a triple arch cut left and climb up a rough brick steps. At the top angle left, then right, to reach a small square. Here head straight on then take the first right to arrive back to your point of departure **(2 hrs 35 mins)**. 1

LA SAUCEDA CIRCUIT

Distance: 11 kms **Duration:** 4/4.5 hours **Rating:** Medium

Map: IGN 1:50000 San José del Valle (1063/13-45)

Water: no springs on walk so take plenty

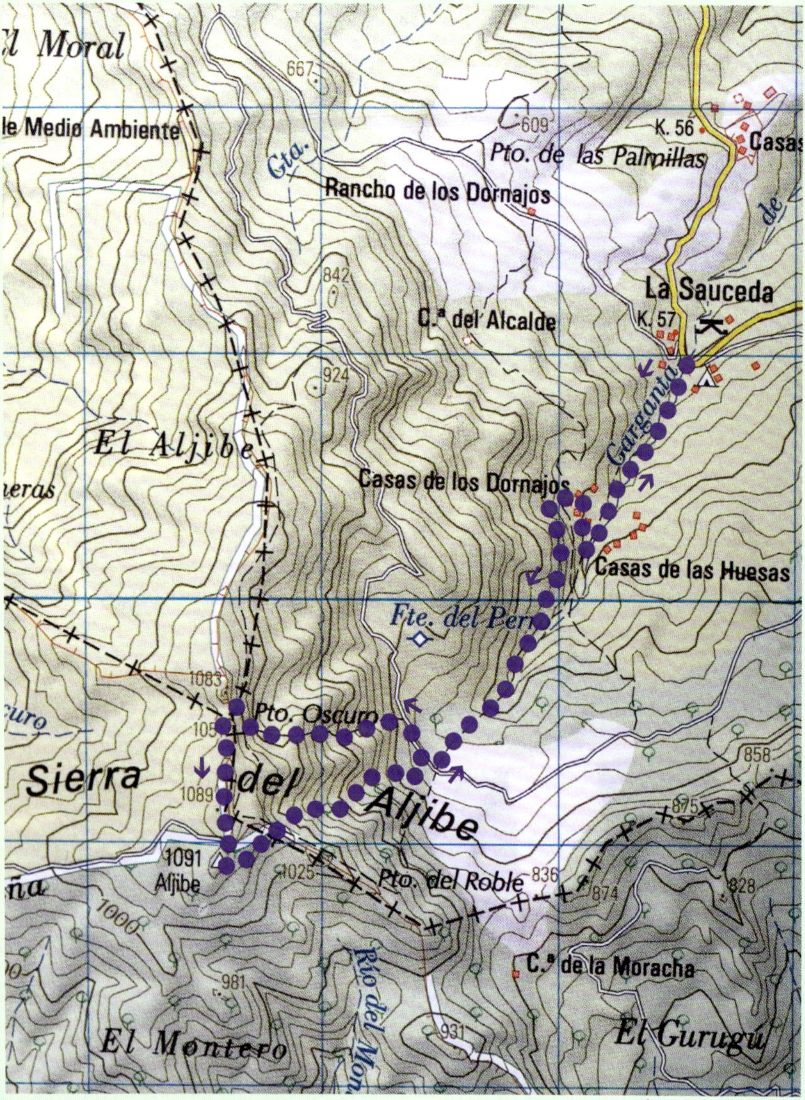

3 The Walk of the Queen's Bath

This averagely demanding walk takes you up to the rocky outcrop of El Aljibe (1092m), the highest point of the Alcornocales Park. You have a steep climb of nearly 500m up from La Sauceda but you're amply rewarded for your efforts. The path runs up past enormous moss and lichen covered boulders where the thick vegetation of the *canuto* (glossary) provides you with shade when you most need it. From El Aljibe you can see Gibraltar, Morocco, the mountains of Ronda, Grazalema and Gaucín as well as any number of white towns and villages. Legend tells that during the final phase of the Reconquest Queen Isabel bathed in the Pilita de la Reina, a recess hewn from a rocky outcrop just a few yards from El Aljibe. The settlement of La Sauceda (it has several small stone huts where you can stay but be aware that you may coincide with school groups) was one of the last redoubts of a whole community of smugglers who brought contraband from Gibraltar to the villages of Cádiz and Málaga provinces.

Getting to the start of the walk

Take the CA–3331 from Jimena de la Frontera towards Algar and Puerto de Galís. After 22km you'll see signs for *Nucleo Recreativo Ambiental La Sauceda* just to the left of the road. There's plenty of parking space on the opposite side of the road

The Route

The walk begins next to the arched entrance of the *Nucleo Recreativo Ambiental La Sauceda*. (1) Pass beneath the arch, climb up past a sundial, cross a small bridge then head straight ahead between a reception area (normally closed) and two ruins. You reach a gate and a sign *Cabañas 1200m*. (2)

Beyond the gate follow a pretty path marked with small white metal flags and painted white dots up through the oak trees, close to the left bank of the Garganta de Pasada Llana (marked on the 1:50000 military map Garganta de Rosada Llana and on other maps as Pasadellana) which you soon cross via a small wooden bridge.

You arrive at the hamlet of La Sauceda 3 where you should angle slightly right. Passing by a line of stone barbecues and a number of the converted *chozas* (glossary) cross the stream by a small wooden bridge 4 then, angling right, continue up past more *chozas* to the hamlet's ruined chapel. To its left you'll see an old bread oven. Head for a solar panel over to the left of the oven, climb for about 10m, then swing left onto a broad track that runs along through the cork oaks, hugging the right bank of the Garganta de Pasada Llana.

The path can be slightly difficult to follow because of its constant divisions: the secret for this first part of the walk is to keep the river close to your left and to look for marker posts and cairns. You pass by enormous moss and lichen-covered boulders, waterfalls and huge cork oaks. The exuberant vegetation is a result of the unusual microclimate of the Park's steep-sided river valleys or *canutos* (glossary). After 500m the track narrows to become a path which crosses two (dry) stream beds then bears round to the right, now climbing more steeply. After crossing a number of (dry) stream beds the path broadens and meets a track by a water tank **(45 mins)**. 5

Turn right onto this forestry track. Vast views now open out across the heart of the Alcornocales Park. The track continues to contour round the northern flank of the Sierra de Aljibe. After 500m you come to a wooden marker post just to the left of the track. 6 Here branch left on a path which climbs steeply up through the oaks. An oleander-filled stream, El Canuto de

los Sauces, is now to your left. Cairns and marker posts guide you upwards. Your path runs up to meet a clearer defined path where you bear left by a marker post 7 and continue climbing. Soon your path crosses El Canuto de los Sauces, bears right, and continues to climb.

After a very steep pull the path bears left then levels as the vegetation becomes sparser: reafforestation is taking place with autoctonous species. You come to a marker post 8 where you turn right then after 200m reach a second junction with two marker posts and a sign *Sendero Pico del Aljibe*. 9 Here swing left on a broad track that continues to climb. Soon a wall runs to either side of the track and you reach a huge rock and a fence. Go through this fence immediately to the left of the rock. 10

Be sure to head round to the far side of to climb of the rock and climb up to see *La Pilita de la Reina,* 'The Queen's Bath'. It was probably never a bath for a Queen but certainly was a pre-historic burial niche. Swinging right past the rock then left you arrive at a second, higher outcrop, El Aljibe (1092m) **(1 hr 45 mins)**. 11 On a clear day the views from here are sensational: the panorama takes in the Sierra de Grazalema, the Sierra de las Nieves, El Hacho above Gaucín, Gibraltar, the Strait and even the mountains of North Africa. This would be an obvious place for a long, lazy picnic in clement weather.

When you come to leave you have a choice. You could simply retrace your steps. If you prefer to take a different route down make your way back to the gap in the wall by the Pilita de la Reina. Here, instead of crossing the wall and fence, follow the wall down for 40m then pick up an indistinct path that angles away from the wall through the broom and heather. Crossing an area rather denuded of vegetation it descends towards another wall. Cairns mark the way. Follow the wall down to a sign for *Reserva Andaluza de Caza* then, just beyond the sign,

go through a wire-and-post gate. 12 Angling slightly left for 10m you reach a clear path where you should bear right and descend.

The path drops steeply down through the oaks. At first you follow a (dry) stream, crossing from one bank to the other before you bear left and cross a second (dry) stream. 13 Here you should cut right and follow the path steeply downwards with the stream over to your right: cairns mark the way. Cross another (dry) stream by a large cairn then angle down an indistinct path to meet with the forestry track which you followed earlier in the day **(2 hrs 30 mins)**. 14 Turn right along the track and when you reach the water tank once again branch left and retrace your footsteps back to your point of departure **(3 hrs 15 mins)**. 1

GAUCÍN SOUTHERN CIRCUIT

Distance: 7.5 kms **Duration:** 3/3.5 hours **Rating:** Easy/Medium

Map: IGN 1:50000 Cortes de la Frontera (1064/14-46)

Ⓦ **Water:** no springs along the way so take plenty

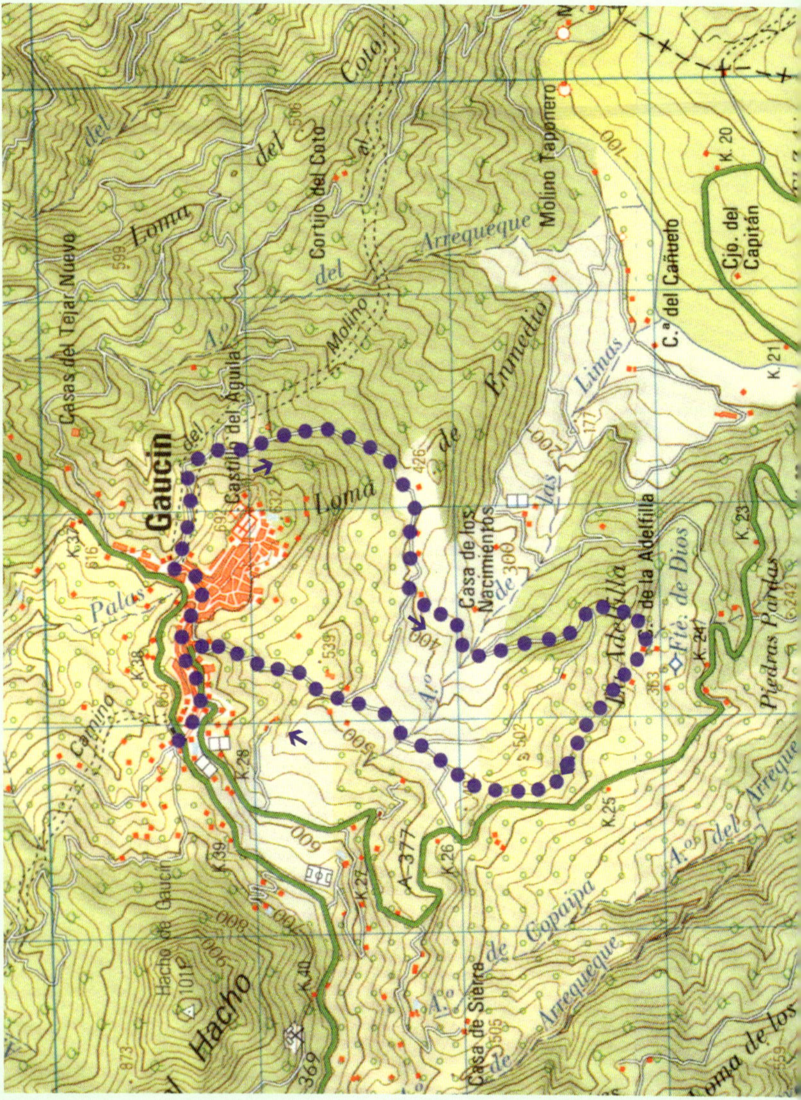

4 The Walk of Melanie & the Tiger

This easy half-day walk skirts round the mountain beneath the beautiful village of Gaucín then cuts down into the Genal valley to the *Ermita de Juan de Dios*, a mountain chapel where a colourful annual pilgrimage is held. There are lovely sections of ancient path, a fair amount of track and even a short section of what is reputedly Roman road. Throughout the walk you're treated to soaring views out across the Genal valley and back to the hilltop chapel and the castle above Gaucín. This is a great walk for the variety of wildflowers, you have a good chance of spotting eagles hunting down in the valley and will certainly see bee-eaters during the summer months. Be prepared for a stiff final pull back up to the village and be sure to take plenty of water. I owe special thanks to my friends Melanie and Tiger for sharing one of their favourite walks with me.

The Route

The walk begins at the petrol station *(la gasolinera)* on the outskirts of Gaucín, to one side of the main road which leads through the village from Ronda to Algeciras. 1 There's plenty of parking space immediately opposite the garage. Cross the road and head for the village centre, immediately passing a small supermarket and Bodeguita Chaparra. Just past a zebra crossing swing left along Calle Barrio Alto. Pass the Molino del Carmen and continue on through the village passing between the Unicaja bank and the *Mercado de Abastos*.

Turn left just past the Cajamar bank and head along Calle Queipo de Llano. At the end of the street, just past Bar Portisuelo, turn right 2 and climb for 30m then swing left on a track that immediately begins to descend. The track drops down through groves of almonds and carobs, skirting round beneath the village. At the next fork by a white building, just to the left of the track, bear right **(25 mins)**. 3

The track continues to descend and passes beneath a white building where you'll be greeted by barking dogs. When you reach a grove of carob and olive trees, ignore a left turn leading to a gate 4 but rather continue straight on. You reach a more open area of meadow. A fence now runs to either side of the track. The track runs towards a ruined farm then angles right then passes to the right of a gate where it narrows to become a path. This pretty path soon drops down to meet with another track. 5 Here, continuing on the same course, you meet with another track by a green transformer mast **(50 mins)**. 6

Bear right here, following a line of cypresses uphill for 300m. When you reach a junction where there's a carob tree to your left and pine trees straight ahead turn left. You immediately reach a large red gate. 7 Squeeze by to the right of the gate. Big views open out across the Genal valley to the mountain of La Crestelina and you'll now spot green and white waymarking. The track soon passes by a sandy area where bee-eaters nest. Shortly after passing beneath electricity lines you reach a fork. 8 Here bear sharply right on a track (marked by a cairn) which heads up towards the mountain of El Hacho before looping back round to the left. Soon you meet with a better-surfaced track. 9

Continue up on your same course, climbing gently up between oak and pine trees towards a pylon. After crossing over a rocky scree slope the track passes just to the left of the pylon. When you reach a second pylon 10 swing left and drop steeply downhill: soon you'll spot the barrel-vaulted *ermita* (glossary) beneath you. The track drops down to the picnic area in front of the Chapel of Juan de Dios **(1 hour 15 mins)**. 11 The chapel is the destination of a summer *romería* (glossary) when the villagers bring the *Santo Niño* (the Christ Child) down from Gaucín. It's a

nice place to break for a picnic.

When you come to leave, with your back to the main entrance of the chapel, up ahead you'll see tracks to both left and right. Take the left hand option and head up a wonderful old section of track which climbs up between ancient groves of almonds. Soon you pass by an odd group of modern buildings to the left of the track. (12) Continue on up the track which is now cobbled in parts. As it levels the Gaucín to Casares road comes into sight down beneath you.

Shortly before the track drops down to meet with this road you reach a three way junction. (13) Here take the middle option (being sure not to take the track which angles hard right: the owner of the farm doesn't appreciate visitors). Climbing up and over a ridge (14) Gaucín comes into sight once again. You're now following a section of ancient road which locals referred to as the *La Calzada Romana*: it has recently been resurfaced all the way up to the village. Continue straight on up towards Gaucín following a line of pylons.

Prepare yourself for a steep climb. Soon you pass by Finca El Alborrán then a little further up go past the track cutting in to El Nobo. (15) Continue straight up to the first houses of the village where the track becomes paved. Angling right you pass by the oddly numbered houses 5, 3, 7 then 35 where you should cut left (16) and head up a narrow, paved street. When you reach the top turn left along a one way street past the *Cuartel* of the Guardia Civil to return to your point of departure **(2 hours 20 mins)**. (1)

GAUCÍN WESTERN CIRCUIT

Distance: 11 kms **Duration:** 4/4.5 hours **Rating:** Medium

Map: 1:50000 Cortes de la Frontera (1064/14-46)

W Water: no springs so take plenty

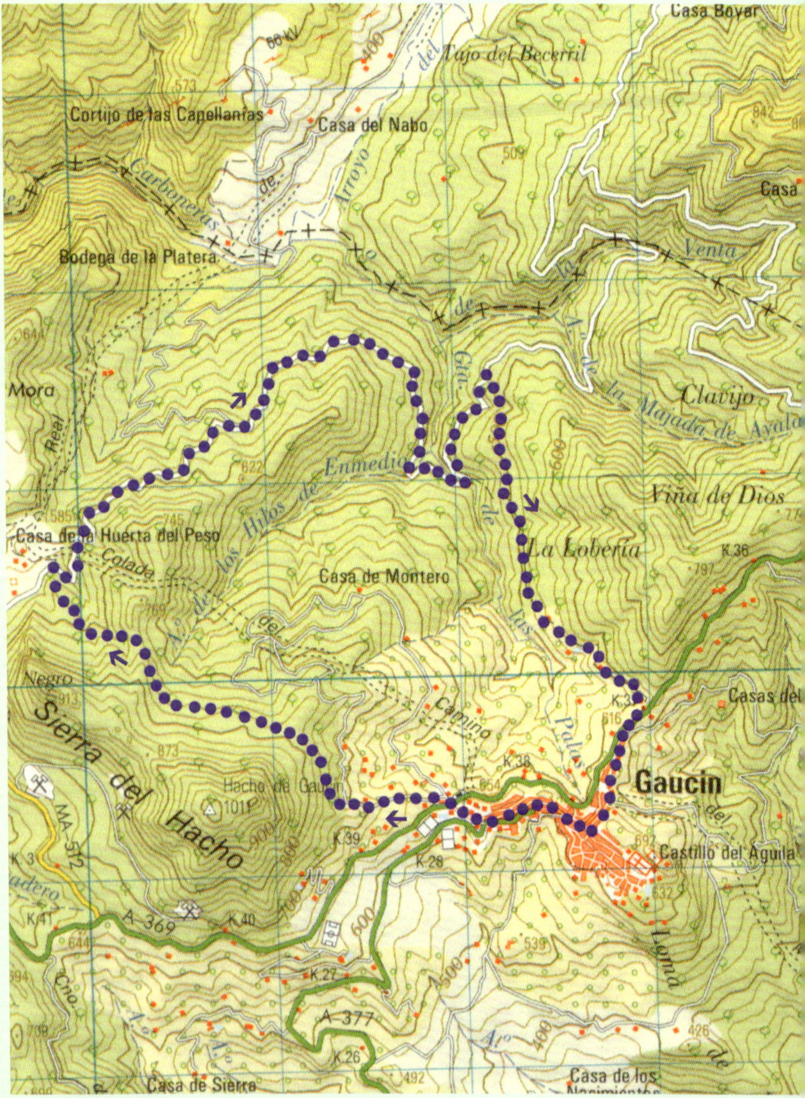

LOS ALCORNOCALES

5 The Walk of the Cork Cutters

This route makes for a lovely half-day walk out from Gaucín. It's easy to follow, the views change with every turn in the path and the ancient stands of cork oaks through which you pass have a unique beauty and are home to abundant bird life. There's a steepish haul first thing as you head up the north-eastern flank of El Hacho and another at the end of the walk when you head back up to Gaucín. After following a narrow, slightly overgrown path early in the day (you may feel more comfortable in long trousers at this stage) there's a longish section of forestry track mid-walk where you can abandon yourself to the wonderful views out towards the Sierra del Pino and the Sierra del Líbar: your feet can take care of themselves at this point. You may meet with teams of cork cutters if undertaking the walk during the winter months when the sap is down: the oaks are particularly memorable when seen after their nine-yearly cork cut.

The Route

The walk begins at the *Campsa* petrol station *(la gasolinera)* 1 on the outskirts of Gaucín. There's plenty of parking space directly across the road. By the entrance of the petrol station (at the Gaucín end) head along calle Camino del Montorio. Directly opposite house no. 16, just before reaching a green gate to your left, cut hard left 2 and pick up a path which runs just to the left of a line of eucalyptus trees. The path climbs steeply up between two fences past groves of olives and almonds. Ignore a track that branches off to the right.

Ahead you'll be able to spot the path you'll soon be following, cutting across the northern flank of El Hacho. When you reach a fork 3 keep left and continue to climb. Shortly the path swings hard to the right and runs on, now parallel to a track which is just above you. It becomes rather more overgrown as it passes just beneath a large, statuesque rock where it divides. 4 Take the left fork and continue climbing: the path soon becomes better defined as it passes a post 5 with white and yellow P.R. waymarking then runs on up to a pylon at the top of the ridge **(20 mins)**. 6

Here go through a wire-and-post gate then, bearing slightly to the left, follow a narrow path which winds its way down through the thick undergrowth beneath the oaks and conifers. It soon becomes clearer and leads you to a fence and another wire-and-post gate. 7 Beyond the gate the path continues to wind on through thick undergrowth before angling right and descending towards a pylon. Just a few metres before you reach the pylon 8 cut left and continue along the narrow path that snakes through the cistus, gorse and oaks then, descending, runs past a *calera* (glossary). 9 Passing beneath overhead cables it soon descends to another gate with a sign for *Coto Privado de Caza*. 10

Go through the gate and bear left along a more clearly defined path. You shortly come to a rocky defile to the left of the path. 11 Bear left here, following the path through the breach in the hillside. On the other side the path runs on, just beneath a green–posted fence then descends, crosses a (dry) stream, 12 then loops round to the right. You now lose the fence and shortly come to an indistinct fork. 13 Here bear left. The path winds steeply down then crosses another (dry) stream. Just beyond the stream the path divides. Take the lower, right hand fork and drop down the hill parallel to the stream that you have just crossed.

After crossing the second of two small (dry) streams the path angles away from the fence then runs uphill and meets with a

track leading towards a newly-built house. 14 Here turn right and drop down the track towards a pylon. Just before reaching the pylon **(1 hr)** 15 you come to a junction with a broader track. Here arc hard right and head along a broad forestry track: you'll be following the track for the next forty minutes so you could forget these notes at this stage. The track gradually descends as views open out to the west. Passing a quarry, then a farm 16 where pigs and goats are raised, you reach a junction. 17 Carry straight on, ignoring a left fork down towards Finca La Capellania.

Continue along the main track ignoring a smaller track which you'll soon see leading up to the right. 18 The track contours lazily round the valley and eventually Gaucín comes into sight. Soon the track loops sharply left, crosses a tributary of Garganta de las Palas 19 then a few hundred metres further crosses the Garganta de las Palas itself. 20 The track now bears hard left, crosses a cattle grid, then runs on for about 600m and crosses a third stream bed.

Careful! 225m past this stream look for a small white sign *Camino de Gaucín a Cortes* in a tree to the right of the track **(1 hr 45 mins)**. 21 It's easily missed but you should also see cairns to the left and right of the track. Here bear sharply right away from the track and follow a path up through the heather, gorse and lavender. The path winds up through the cork oaks and eventually passes through a gate made from an old bed base 22 where it broadens and soon runs up to meet with a better-defined track by a green metal gate. 23

Bearing right you eventually pass by a group of modern buildings and a furniture warehouse, *Las Palas*, then come to the Ronda-Gaucín road. 24 Turn right then just past the bandstand cut left along Calle Queipo de Llano following a sign for *Centro Urbano*. 25 After passing a small roundabout head straight along Calle Los Bancos then arc right into Calle del Corral. Continue on past the Unicaja bank then cross the street and, passing just right of *Modas Teresa*, head to the very end of the Calle Barrio Alto. Here bear right and, having passed the Guardia Civil headquarters, you reach the Ronda-Gaucín road and your point of departure. **(2 hrs 30 mins)**. 1

BENARRABÁ CIRCUIT

Distance: 12.5 kms **Duration:** 5.5/6 hours **Rating:** Medium

Map: IGN 1:50000 Cortes de la Frontera (1064/14-46)

Ⓦ **Water:** spring in Genalguacil @ 2 hrs

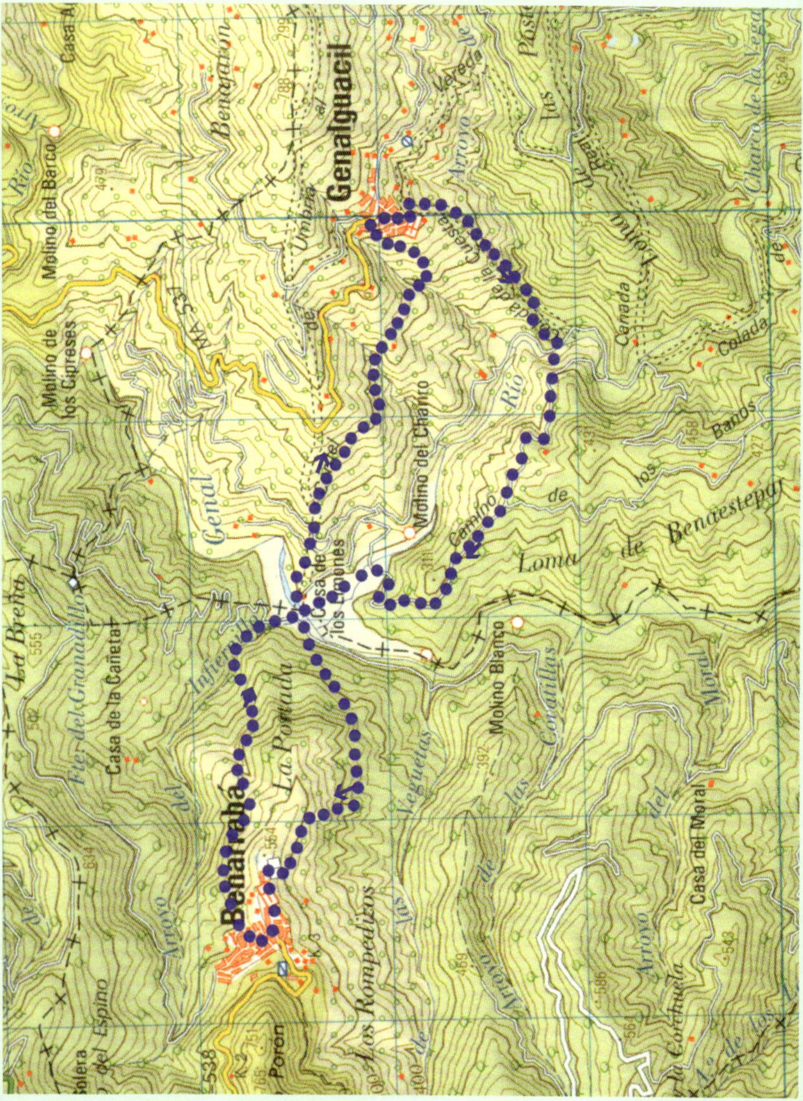

6 The Walk of the Vizir's Garden

This lovely figure-of-eight makes for a longish day walk and links two beautiful, little-known villages. A good deal of the walk takes you along narrow paths and there are wonderful views out across the Genal valley and south towards the Med'. If you do the whole route you have three fairly stiff climbs but the path is easy to follow and there are shady sections beneath the oak and chestnut trees. It's possible to shorten the walk considerably by swinging right just before you cross the Genal for the first time. But this would mean missing Genalguacil, an exceptionally pretty village and a highlight of the walk: the abundance of sculpture is fruit of the good offices of a dynamic young mayor who for years has offered food and lodging to aspiring young artists in return for their donating a work to the village. Be sure to visit the beautiful square and one of the bars close by or have a leisurely picnic on one of the benches in front of the church: the views are simply stunning.

The Route

The walk begins at Hotel Banu Rabbah at the far side of the village of Benarrabá. (1) From the hotel walk back towards the village passing the football pitch and then the school. Just past the school, opposite a line of tiled benches, turn right down Avenida Miguel Pérez Delgado following a sign for *Iglesia* then take the next right into Calle Sol. (2) The street bears sharply left then right. When you reach house no.16 cut right on a dirt track which drops down hill away from the village. (3)

As you loop downwards you'll begin to see yellow and white P.R. marking and white arrows and bands on the oaks. Stick to the main track, ignoring side tracks which cut right and left. You reach a solitary portal with white posts and a rickety cross beam 4 which seems to serve no obvious purpose. Here the track loops left then right and resumes it course. A green metal posted fence soon runs to your left and, descending still, the track loops past a citrus grove before cutting through an area of ancient cork oaks. The track contours gradually round the mountainside and crosses a cattle grid. 5 After the grid the track runs up hill, levels then descends for approximately 200m to a marker post. 6 Here you should cut left and drop down on a steep and eroded path: P.R. marker posts show the way. The path eventually meets with a track where you cross the Arroyo del Infiernillo 7 then bears right along the valley floor. It soon crosses back to the other side of the stream then runs up to a bridge over the Genal **(30 mins)**. 8

Cross the river (there's a nice spot for swimming here) and swing hard left at a sign for *Genalguacíl* and *Cordel de la Umbria a Río Genal* along a track which immediately cuts left and runs along the pebbly right bank of the Genal. After just 40m, swinging right away from the river, go through a small wooden gate 9 and follow a path which climbs up behind the farm of Casa Los Limones **(55 mins)**. Climbing steeply after about ten minutes you pass through another small wooden gate. 10 Here cross directly over a track and continue up through the cork oaks. Soon you cross the track once again. The countryside opens out and there are big views out across the Genal valley. The path runs up to meet the track for a third time **(1 hr 25 mins)**. 11

Here angle right and cross the track a final time. After 25m, just before reaching a gate, bearing right you again pick up the footpath. It descends slightly, levels, then passes a pylon as it arcs round a gully before running up to a small farm. Just past the farmhouse turn left by a pylon 12 and follow the path steeply upwards. Passing above a (dry) spring the path merges with a track which loops up past a small football pitch before reaching a junction at the outskirts of the village. Turn right and follow the

tarmac road into the village centre, passing a tiled plaque and a map showing the footpaths in the area south of Ronda. 13

At the next fork keep right, pass a spring *La Fuente de la Alberquilla*, W then head all the way along Calle Real, passing the Unicaja bank and the Casa Consistorial, to the church **(2 hrs)**. Turning right you arrive at the village's beautiful square, La Plaza de la Constitución. 14 On the far side you'll see an arched doorway leading to restaurant El Refugio and Los Jardines del Vizir: both are good spots to break for refreshments or you might prefer to picnic in the square.

After your break leave the square via the street running to the left of the church, the same one by which you entered. At the far end, just to the left of a *mirador* (glossary) 15 with two contemporary sculptures, drop down a concrete road. After just 15m swing sharp right along another concreted section of road. Passing a line of wafer-bricked posts with wooden rails the road divides. Here fork left and drop steeply downhill, always sticking to the main path. You eventually come to a farm just to the right of the path where there's a (dry) watering hole immediately in front of you. 16 Here bear left and after just a few metres the path merges with a track which you follow on down hill.

The track soon reaches a junction with another track. 17 Here turn right and continue on down to the river. 18 Turn left on a track which cuts along the river's pebbly bank then runs up to a farm. In front of the farm cut right and cross the river Almarchal: in the wetter months you may need to remove your boots. Once you're over the river **(2 hrs 30 mins)** bear left then, some 30m before reaching the ruined arch of an old bridge, swing right through the thick riverine vegetation on a narrow path 19 which zigzags steeply up and away from the river. After passing beneath a salmon coloured building the path climbs up to a track where you bear left. 20 The track loops left then right and continues climbing gradually upwards, then levels as it runs back towards the Genal.

You arrive at an abandoned farmhouse where the track divides. 21 Fork right here. Soon you pass another ruin, then a monolithic modern house with a wooden cabin, before the track loops steeply back down to the river Almarchal. Just before it reaches the river you meet with another track. Turn left here and cross over the river bed **(3 hrs 10 mins)**. 22

The track now runs indistinctly up to the bridge you crossed earlier in the walk. Cross back over the Genal and turn left along a broad track. At first it hugs the river's right bank but soon begins to angle away from it as it climbs steeply upwards. Cross a cattle grid and after just 50m pass by a spring 23 which can be dry at the end of the summer months. Carry on up the main track and, after about a quarter of an hour of climbing, watch out for the point where a line of pylons runs up to meet with your track **(3 hrs 35 mins)**.

Ten metres past the second pylon 24 turn right off the track: there's a rickety wooden sign for *Benarrabá/Hotel*. Pass between two drain covers, bear slightly left and climb steeply up, and up, to the village. The path eventually meets with the road by the college you passed earlier in the walk. Turn right here to arrive back at Hotel Banu Rabbah **(4 hrs)**. 1

La Axarquía

Ventas de Zafaraya
Periana
Alcaucin
Canillas de Aceituno
Sedella
Arenas
del Bey
Jayena
Canillas de Albaida
Competa
Árchez
Benamargosa
Corumbela
Benamocarra
Sayalonga
Frigliana
Iznate
VÉLEZ
MÁLAGA
Algarrobo
Torrox
Maro
Nerja
E-15
Torre del Mar
La Herradura
N-340
Torrox Costa

AREA MAP

LA AXARQUÍA

The Area

The Axarquía was the name given by the Moors to the swathe of land just back from the Mediterranean which stretches east from Málaga towards the Sierra Nevada. Axarquía literally means 'the land to the East' – as opposed to the Algarve, 'the land to the West'.

The landscape is rugged, often spectacularly so. A series of valleys have cut deep courses through the chain of the Tejeda mountains in their rapid descent to the sea. There are marked differences in climate and vegetation between the higher passes and the coastal fringe and the region offers exceptionally varied walking. A belt of white villages, nearly all of them with views down to the Mediterranean, pepper the southern flank of the mountains. Rising up behind this string of settlements to over 2000 metres, the Sierra de Tejeda provides a stunning backdrop, especially during the winter months when there is often snow on its higher reaches.

The tortuous nature of much of this area meant that it attracted its fair share of *bandoleros* who worked the passes that lead through the mountains from the coast to Granada. And as late as the early fifties there were still bands of Republicans at large who had fought on after the Civil War. They, too, were able to make the mountain chain a formidable redoubt.

The most attractive part of La Axarquía is its eastern end and the walks that I have chosen are all in the beautiful area of mountains and lush river valleys surrounding Cómpeta, Frigiliana and Canillas de Albaida. All of these villages have exceptionally pretty village centres with whitewashed walls, terracotta tiled roofs and narrow backstreets with balconies brimming with geraniums. My personal favourite is Canillas, with its diminuitive *plaza* and pretty Santa Ana chapel dominating the village. It also now has a reliable little inn right on the square.

The contrast between the land to the north and south of these settlements could not be greater. Beyond the very first ridge above the villages the landscape changes dramatically. Before you is a vast arena of limestone peaks where there's virtually no sign of human habitation. This is in marked contrast to the swathe of land between the villages and the sea that is extensively cultivated and sprinkled with numerous small farmsteads.

Cultivation is aided by an exceptionally benign climate and careful irrigation. Many of the water channels date back to the Moorish period. The hillsides, especially round Cómpeta and Canillas, are covered with olive groves and vineyards where the sweet Moscatel grape is grown. Nearly all the farms here have one or more of the characteristic platforms or *secaderos* (glossary) that are used to sun-dry and fortify the grapes which are used to make the famous *vino de moscatel*. A tasting should be an obligatory part of any visit but, unless you are a lover of really sweet wines, be sure to ask for *seco* in the bars and restaurants.

Many of the walks described here take in sections of the lush, sub-tropical river valleys so characteristic of the lower Axarquía. Everything, it would seem, will grow here. There are groves of citrus, avocado, mangos, pomegranate, and even custard fruit, lichees and sugar cane. These fertile valleys provide a welcome respite if you are walking during the hotter months. The section of the river valley north of Canillas is particularly attractive.

In spite of a growing numbers of expatriates who have made the area their home (you'll spot more and more villas being built amongst the farms, many without any type of building licence),

these villages have still managed to retain their Spanishness. Frigiliana has become a popular destination for coach trips up from the coastal resorts. The village is best avoided during the middle part of the day but regains much of its dignity by the evening. And it is, it must be said, a very pretty village.

The variety of scenery you will encounter on your walks is truly remarkable and you will meet with few other walkers on your rambles. The benign climate means that this is an area well suited to winter sorties. Málaga can be reached in little more than an hour.

Other Walks

Elma Thompson has written a series of leaflets called *Exploring La Axarquía* which you can find it in shops in Frigiliana and Nerja. Most of her routes leave from Frigiliana: they tend to be easy half-day rambles.

La Maroma. At 2065 metres La Maroma is the highest peak of the Sierra Tejada and is nearly always visible wherever you are in the Axarquía. The ascent of the mountain is not technically challenging but it does take a full day. The classic route leaves from Canillas de Aceituno and follows the old *Camino Arriero de la Nieve*, the route once followed by muleteers who in pre-refrigerator days brought ice down from covered pits in the high sierra.

Maps

The best maps of the area are the standard 1:50000 map of the Servicio Geográfico del Ejército, Series L. As this guide goes to press the area has not yet been mapped by the IGN for their 1:50000 series.

The walks described in this section are covered by sheet (*hoja*) Zafarraya 18-43 and sheet (*hoja*) Vélez-Málaga 18-44. The Marco Polo bookstore just off the Plaza de Almijara in the centre of Cómpeta (952 516 423) generally has both maps in stock. You can also find maps in the English bookshop in Nerja. The area is also covered by the 1:25000 CNIG series but you'll need several maps if you wish to use this scale.

BEST PLACES TO SLEEP & EAT

CÓMPETA

Hotel Balcón de Cómpeta

Tel: 952 553 535 Email: balconcompeta@hotmail.com

The most reliable hotel in town with friendy staff and ample experience of walkers and their ways: a number of UK walking holiday operators use this as their base. Good rooms with baths rather than showers and views down towards the Mediterranean: the best rooms have balconies. €60-€75 + VAT. (Taxis: hotel can organise). **Best Eats:** Las Gemelas for a meal with a view or La Casona's quirky upstairs dining room.

Casa La Piedra

Tel: 952 516 329 or 657 056 166 Email: casa@2sandra.com

A self-catering set up in an old house on a pretty square looking down to the sea. Sandra, the owner, knows many of the walks in the area. Las Piedras makes a great base if you plan to spend a number of days in the area. €50-€60. (Taxis: Paco 952 516 056 or Cesario 952 516 205). **Best Eats:** Las Gemelas for a meal with a view or La Casona's quirky upstairs dining room.

CANILLAS DE ALBAIDA

Finca El Cerrillo

Tel: 952 030 444 Email: info@hotelfinca.com

A beautiful converted farmhouse with pool, great views and beautiful bedrooms. Friendly owners who have plenty of information on local walks. Picnics prepared for walkers: my favourite place to stay by far in the area but often fully booked. €100-€110 + VAT. (Taxi: José 608 952 880). **Best Eats:** here or at La Almijara in Canillas.

Posada La Plaza

Tel: 952 554 807 Email: reception@posada-laplaza.com

A comfortable small inn right on the pretty main square of the village. Both rooms and food are excellent value. Popularity with walking groups means that the inn is often full in Spring and Autumn. €55-€70 + 7% VAT. (Taxi: José 608 952 880). **Best Eats:** here or at La Almijara restaurant.

FRIGILIANA

La Posada Morisca

Tel: 952 534 151 Email: info@laposadamorisca.com

An attractive small hotel just outside of Frigiliana with views down to the sea with reasonable food. €50-€90 + VAT. (Taxi rank: 625 288 811 or 696 969 469). **Best Eats:** The Garden Restaurant at top of town or Bodega Pepe.

Hotel Villa Frigiliana

Tel: 952 533 393 Email via: www.ihmhotels.com

A large hotel with very comfortable rooms overlooking the Plaza del Ingenio in Frigiliana. Great position but expect to hear passing traffic which can go on until late at weekends. €75-€105 + VAT. (Taxi rank: 625 288 811 or 696 969 469) **Best Eats:** The Garden Restaurant at top of town or Bodega Pepe.

NERJA

Hotel Paraiso del Mar

Tel: 952 521 621 Email: info@hispanica-colint.com

A good choice if you want some serious comfort before or after tackling the Liman trail. The best rooms have sea views and the owner Enrique is constantly charming and helpful. €85-€125 + VAT. (Taxi rank: 952 524 519). **Best Eats:** Casa Luque, Bar Redondo, La Biznaga.

MARO TO FRIGILIANA VIA THE CAMINO LIMÁN

Distance: 13.5 kms **Duration:** 5.5/6 hours **Rating:** Medium/Difficult

Map: 1:50000 Vélez-Málaga (1054) & Motril (1055)

Ⓦ **Water:** El Pinarillo @ approx. 1 hour into walk

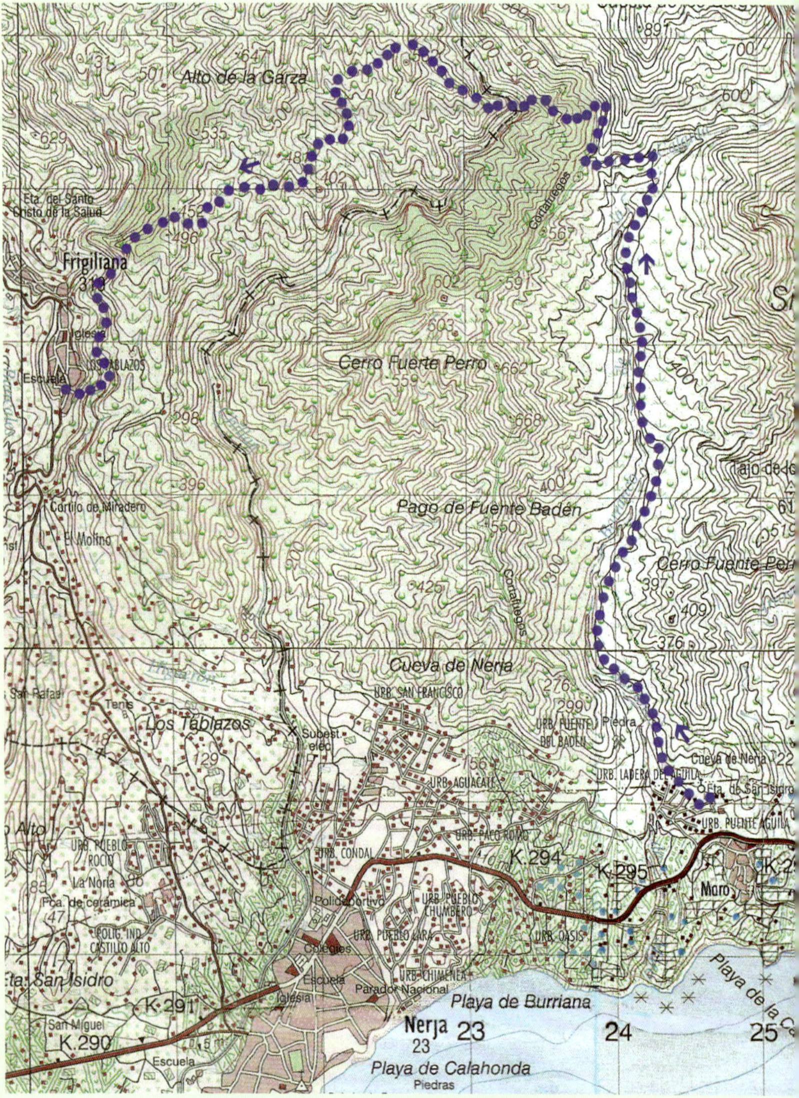

1 The Walk of the Chillar Canyon

This mountain trail, known to locals as El Camino Limán, is without question one of Andalucía's most spectacular walks. The itinerary begins in gentle mode as it heads along a broad forestry track which leads north from the Cueva de Nerja: it is well worth a visit before you set out. Once you've passed the picnic area of El Pinarillo things take on a different tempo as the trail roller-coasters its way west to Frigiliana via four deep gorges. It scarcely seems possible, when you behold such wild mountain scenery, that you're just a few kilometers from the urban sprawl of the coast. This is a walk to be savoured so get going early with a picnic and plenty of water: this also means you'll get shade from the pines on the approach to El Pinarillo. There are regular buses between Frigiliana and Nerja but you'll then need to take a taxi up to the Nerja cave. Or you could leave a car close to the square in Frigiliana then taxi to the beginning of the walk.

The Route

The walk begins just outside the car park of the Nerja Cave, next to its green entrance gates. (1) With your back to the gates turn right. You immediately pass signs for *Fuente del Esparto* and *Area Recreativa El Pinarillo*. After a few yards you pass a green barrier. Ignore a track branching left but rather head straight along a broad forestry track which climbs gradually upwards. You'll see wooden marker posts with white arrows marking your way. You reach a fork where one sign points left for *Area Recreativa El Pinarillo,* another right for *Sendero* **(35 mins)**. (2)

Here branch left. The track continues to climb and eventually arrives at El Pinarillo. Here the track divides again. (3) Bearing left you pass a map of the park then head straight on through the picnic/camping area. You can replenish your water bottle about 50m past the map at taps next to a bar-b-q. W At the far end, after passing a threshing circle, you come to a green barrier. 4 Beyond it drop down a broad track and cross the (dry) river bed.

Just 20m beyond the river the track divides. Take the narrower left hand path which climbs steeply and shortly crosses the track that you have just left. Head on up a deeply eroded path. You reach a broader track where you'll see a marker post. 5 Don't turn right here (this would lead you up to the Fuente del Esparto) but rather turn left along a broad track. It leads you to the top of a pass and passes by a *No Entry* sign. 6 Magnificent views open out to the north and west. Continue along the track which arcs hard right and runs up to a chain across the track. **(1 hr 20 mins)**.

Continue on past the chain remembering that you'll be cutting left onto a narrow path after approximately 950m. You pass two marker posts just to the left of the track then, at a point where the track cuts right, reach a third post and a large cairn. 7 Here cut left on a narrow path which zigzags steeply down into the Chillar gorge. You'll see the occasional marker post as you descend. The path drops down past a small ruin, crosses a water channel, then continues on down. Eventually you arrive at the river bed **(1 hr 50 mins)**. 8

Here bear right at a blue arrow on a rock along the river's east bank for approximately 30m then cross to the opposite bank by way of stepping stones. Look for blue arrows. After running close to the river's west bank for about 50m (where there are two great rock pools for cooling off in the warmer months: the highest one is the deepest) the path angles left and begins to climb. You reach a point where the path divides by a marker post. 9 Here turn left and continue to climb steeply upwards. The path is marked with green and blue painted dots. Eventually

you reach the top of the second steep pass of the walk **(2 hrs 20 mins)**. 10

Beyond the pass the path, deeply eroded in parts, descends into the next valley, soon crossing a (dry) stream bed. 11 It then climbs for a short distance before descending once more and crossing another stream where there's a cairn and a marker post. 12 After crossing two more (dry) stream beds it climbs to the top of a third pass where views open out into the next valley. 13 Here the vegetation becomes much sparser, the result of a forest fire in the not-so-distant past. The path again descends and crosses another (dry) stream bed 14 before climbing once again to the top of the fourth and final pass from where the Higuerón valley is now visible to the west. 15 The path runs along the spine of the ridge and, after passing a marker post where there are views both east and west, runs gently downhill just east of the ridge for a short distance then reaches a divide by a marker post **(3 hrs 10 mins)**. 16

Here cut right by a rock with a large blue dot and drop steeply downhill on a beautiful narrow path which leads down through a stand of pines to the valley floor and a sign for *Frigiliana-Fuente del Esparto* 17 where, swinging left and descending, you pass a white hut then a large water tank. The track leads on down the valley then loops across to the river's west bank towards a large green water pipe where it becomes concreted. 18 Follow the track steeply upwards. After a final steep haul up past groves of avocados you reach the Unicaja bank and, just beyond, the Plaza del Ingenio and the Frigiliana taxi rank. **(3 hrs 45 mins)**. 19

FRIGILIANA CIRCUIT VIA LA CRUZ DE PINTO

Distance: 12 kms **Duration:** 4.5 hours **Rating:** Medium

Map:1:50000 Vélez-Málaga (1054)

Water: No springs on the walk

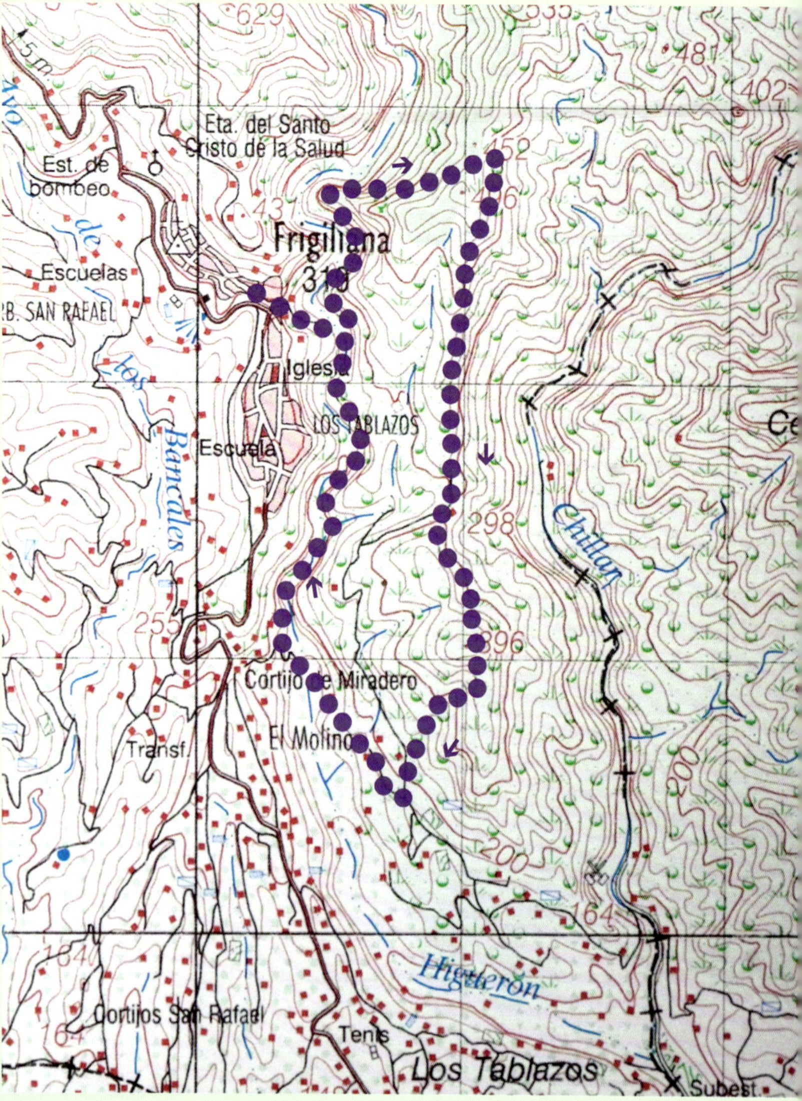

2 The Walk of the Moor & his Parrot

This half day ramble has an astonishing variety of scenery considering that you're never more than 5 kilometers from Frigiliana. From the village you drop down into the spectacular gorge of the Río Higuerón. After cutting north along the river a dramatic path (the final section of the Limán Trail which is also described in this book) leads up the gorge's eastern side before cutting south along the top of a ridge to La Cruz de Pinto, a hilltop shrine dedicated to La Virgen del Carmen. You then loop back down to the gorge where you follow a path through one of its narrowest sections before the final steep pull back up to Frigiliana. You could pack long trousers for the rather overgrown middle section of the walk. Remember that the path through the gorge on the walk's final section can be dangerous after heavy rain: you'll need to take a view. If in doubt head straight across the river at waypoint 13 then climb the track which arcs up the western side of the gorge. You can then return to the Plaza del Ingenio along the Frigiliana-Nerja road.

The Route

This walk begins in Frigiliana in the square at the entrance to the village, La Plaza del Ingenio. ① With your back to a series of tiled pictures head down the hill then cut left along the road that runs to the right of the Unicaja bank signposted *Río Higuerón*. This concreted road loops steeply down to the river. ② Cross to its eastern bank then swing left on a broad, pebbly track. You soon pass a large water deposit, just to the left of the track, and then a small white hut. Just beyond the hut you reach a sign for *Sendero de la Fuente del Esparto, 5.5 kms*. ③ Here cut right on a narrow path with climbs steeply up the side of the gorge to the top of the pass **(35 mins)**. ④

Continue for just a couple of metres beyond the pass then cut right off the footpath at a small cairn: ignore the marker post pointing left in the direction of the Fuente del Esparto. You pick up a narrow path which leads up to the highest point of the ridge. 5 Here bear left and continue along the apex of the ridge. Ahead in the distance you should be able to spot a pylon and, just behind it, the narrow footpath that will later lead you up to the Cruz de Pinto. Faint red, blue and yellow waymarking, as well as cairns, help you to plot the correct course.

You reach a dip in the ridge where the path angles right 6 then runs on just to the right of the ridge's highest point. Soon you pass a massive circular cairn. Continuing along the ridge you come to a second large cairn 7 where the path divides. Take the left fork and continue along the top of the ridge. Shortly you descend and pass immediately left of a pylon. The path angles right then reaches a fork where a path angles left, a track right. 8 Cut left on the path which climbs up the left side of the ridge. After a steep ascent you arrive at La Cruz de Pinto **(1 hr 5 mins)**. 9

From this high vantage point there is an amazing 360 degree panorama of the sea, the coastal villages, Frigiliana and, to the north, the crumpled massif of the Sierra de Almijara. Facing the north side of the shrine, and the small black door protecting its votive offerings, cut east along the ridge for about 40m then swing right and pick up a path which leads down the hill's southern side. After descending for about 100m it passes left of a rocky outcrop then cuts right through a small col (10) then descends steeply through the valley back down into the Higuerón valley where, after approximately 10 minutes, it reaches a track by a sign for *Parque Natural*. (11) Here bear left and descend for approximately 200m to a point where the track that you've been following converges with three more. (12) Here loop sharply right onto the most westerly (lower) of the tracks which climbs slightly before levelling. A line of telegraph posts runs beside the track. Soon you pass Cortijo Floreana. The track begins to descend, passing by a number of small houses/farms and groves of olives and avocado, then finally a small horse stable before it reaches the fertile valley floor **(1 hr 35 mins)**. (13)

Cut right just before you reach the Higuerón and head along its right bank. You soon pass just left of a red-tiled building. The indistinct path loops back and forth across the river and then, as the gorge narrows down, climbs along the stream's east bank via a steep stone staircase beyond which it descends steeply for a short distance. The path, cobbled in parts, passes a spring (often dry) then continues to loop back and forth across the river. You eventually reach the point where you first crossed the Higuerón at the beginning of the walk. 2 Here cut left across the river and retrace your footsteps back up to your point of departure **(2 hrs 20 mins)**.

1 It would be a shame not to stick a euro in the box of a rather bizarre kiosk in the square and listen to a Moor, and his parrot, discussing the finer points of Andalusian history.

CÓMPETA CIRCUIT VIA THE CASA DE LA MINA

Distance: 12 kms **Duration:** 5/5.5 hours **Rating:** Medium

Map: 1:50000 Zafarraya (1040) & Vélez-Málaga (1054)

Ⓦ **Water:** no springs on walk so take plenty

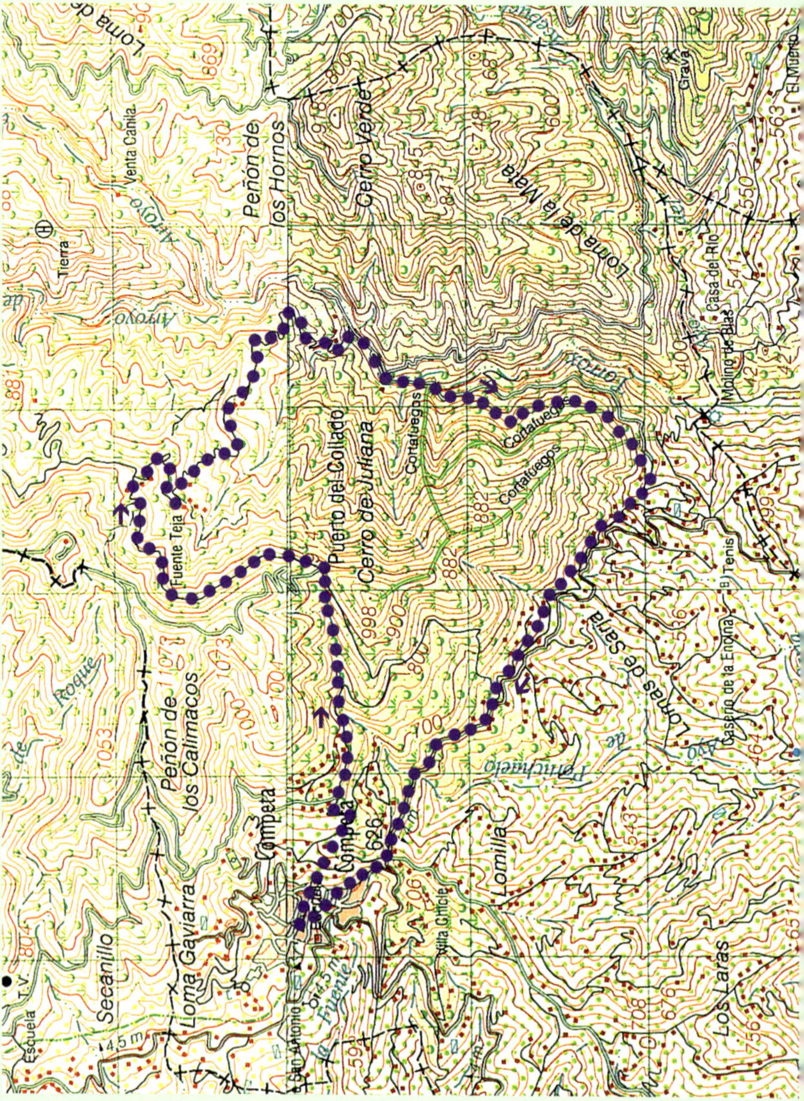

3 The Walk of the Cool River

Though most of this itinerary follows forestry tracks rather than paths, it makes for a memorable walk. Be prepared for a steep climb out from the village all the way up to the Puerto Collado. Once you you reach the pass a stunning panorama opens out of virtually uninhabited Sierra which stretches away to the north and to the east. It's amazing to consider that the crowded beaches of Nerja are little more than 10 kms distant. After a looping slowly round the mountain to the Casa de la Mina you descend to the Fábrica de la Luz where you are rewarded with some shade: this leafy retreat makes a perfect spot for a picnic. When you come to leave you may need to take boots and socks off to cross the river during the wetter months of the year. If undertaking this walk in the warmer months you could stop for a dip in the river pools just beyond the Fábrica. You have about 1km of asphalt road to negotiate towards the end of the walk as you climb up past the Venta de Palma before dropping back down to the village square.

The Route

The walk begins in the main square of Competa, the Plaza de la Almijara. (1) Leave the square at its top, right-hand corner along Calle Carretería then take the first right into Calle Toledo. This narrow street loops left then right and runs up to a small square with a fountain. Here turn left at a sign for *Plazoleta*. The street climbs then loops right and arrives at La Plaza de la Vendimía. (2)

Go straight across the square and cut right up Avenida (Avda) de Nerja, passing just left of Bar La Vendimía. The street loops steeply up hill. At the second of two green railings to your right, opposite Edificio Las Adelfas, cut right up Calle Lugar Tejarejo (and not Calle Tejarejo which is the previous street). The street swings round to the left then climbs up to meet with the road that runs round the top of the village. 3

Go straight across following the sign for *Sendero: Casa de la Mina/Pradillos*. The road climbs steeply up through the area known as Cruz del Monte, passing a number of modern villas. Shortly you reach a picnic area and a second sign *Sendero: Casa de la Mina/Pradillos* where you should turn left. The road soon loops round to the right and reverts to a dirt track before reaching a ceramic sign for *Cruz del Monte*. 4 Ignore a third sign for *Sendero: Casa de la Mina/Pradillos* but rather head straight on along the track. Soon you leave last of the villas behind and the track runs gently down through pine trees. At a point where the track arcs round to the right look out for a red mark painted on a rock, just to the left of the track, in an area which has been quarried. **(25 mins)** 5

Here cut left away from the track and climb steeply up beside a (dry) stream. The path at first follows its right hand bank. You pass an old *calera* (glossary) on your right. Follow the stream bed up this gulley until you meet with a scree slope which you follow along to its left. Where the scree ends you reach a square concrete drain cover with a faint red arrow indicating that your path now swings right, still climbing. After passing a fenced water deposit you emerge on a broad track opposite a sign for *El Puerto del Collado*, the highest point on this walk. 6

Here turn left onto the track (not hard left on a track which cuts back towards Competa) following another sign for *Sendero: Casa de la Mina/Pradillos*. Beautiful views open out to the rumpled mountains of the Almijara Sierra and down to the Mediterranean.

Follow this track all the way to La Casa de la Mina, a white building which is clearly visible up ahead with a second building to its left, the Hotel Casa de la Mina (currently closed). The track

eventually runs past the metal entrance gates of the hotel then passes above Albergue Casa de la Mina **(1 hr 25 mins).** 7 Where the Casa's wooden posted fence ends cut right off the track and, passing just right of a tennis court, drop down a narrower dirt track towards La Fábrica de la Luz.

Looping downwards the track runs past a line of eucalyptus trees then reaches Fuente La Teja 8 (sometimes dry) where the track divides. Don't bear right towards a house girthed by cypress trees but rather bear left and, after a short climb, continue your descent. Soon you pass a farm with low buildings to both sides of the track. You then pass another farm, Ulla Finca, and then another small farm to the right of the track. Pines give way to groves of olives as the track drops past a ranch with finely groomed horses.

Continuing your descent you pass a house number 158, with its ugly breeze block wall, then shortly you reach the shade of the river bed and arrive at the Fábrica de la Luz **(2 hrs 20 mins)**. 9 It's a great spot for a picnic with plenty of shade provided by the palm and eucalyptus trees, the soothing sound of running water and the majestic cliff faces to contemplate.

When you're ready to leave head on down the river bed which may entail removing your boots and socks in the wetter months. You soon reach a fork 10 where you'll see a sign nailed to a tree pointing towards *El Acebuchal*. Ignore the sign and take the right fork. After about 100m you cross the river once again, this time via a small wooden bridge.

25m beyond the river the track divides. Here branch right, remembering that in approx. 800m you'll be cutting away from the track which now begins to climb gently uphill. About quarter of an hour after crossing the river look for a cairn and a stone arrow to the right of the track 11 marking the point where you cut right on to a narrow path. The first few metres are steep

and loose and may require the use of hands as well as feet: care should be taken for the first 50 metres where there are drops to the left. The path soon improves as it contours round the hillside across an area of loose scree. Eventually it climbs a steep dirt bank, crosses a black plastic water pipe, and runs up to a concrete track. Here turn left and descend for just 50m to a pylon with a white base. 12 Here turn right, and climb up a steep path passing to the right of Casa El Pájaro.

The path soon meets with the track once again. Head straight across, climb, and when you meet the track a third time bear right and follow it round the hillside between houses and villas. When you reach a fork take the right-hand option and climb towards a white water tank.

Soon your track merges with a better-surfaced one which runs more or less parallel with the road to Competa, passing by several modern villas. Eventually the track drops down past a small shrine to meet with the road from Torrox to Competa. 13 Bear right here and climb for about ten minutes along the tarmac to Venta La Palma **(3 hrs 35 mins)**. 14

Continue on past Venta La Palma on the right hand side of the road and when you reach a sign indicating that the road swings hard to the left, cut right and drop down a narrow path. It meets with a tarmac road, the Avenida de Torrox. Here turn right and follow this road into the village and back to the Plaza de la Vendimía 2 from where you retrace your footsteps back to your starting point, the village's main square **(3 hrs 50 mins)**. 1

EL ACEBUCHAL

CÓMPETA CIRCUIT VIA EL PUERTO BLANQUILLO

Distance: 16 kms **Duration:** 7/7.5 hours **Rating:** Medium/Difficult

Map: 1:50000 Zafarraya (1040)

Ⓦ **Water:** Fuente El Chorillo @ 4 hrs 20 mins

4 The Walk of the High Axarquía

This long loop out from Cómpeta is a wonderful day walk and takes in a stunning slice of the Almijara Sierra. Be sure to get going early if planning to walk this route in the warmer months and be prepared for a rigorous start to the day: from the main square in Cómpeta to Puerto Blanquillo there's a height gain of 575m. Your efforts will be amply rewarded: the approach to Blanquillo climbs through wildly beautiful terrain and once you're over the pass the landscape changes dramatically as you drop down the lush, subtropical Cueva del Melero valley. You may encounter lorries on the section of road that leads from the quarry down to Canillas de Albaida so plan your walk so you negotiate this section between 2pm and 4pm when work stops for lunch. And remember that you can shorten the walk by returning to Cómpeta from Canillas by taxi or knock 200m off the initial ascent by taking a taxi up to the football ground.

The Route

The walk begins in the Plaza de la Almijara in Cómpeta. (1) Leave the square at its top, right-hand corner and head up Calle Carretería. The street climbs steeply then bears round to the right. Soon you pass a fountain and, opposite house no. 60, turn left and climb steeply up a narrow street of concreted steps. Take the higher option at any junction. When you reach a tarmac road, turn left. Passing by Bar David you reach the Plaza del Carmen (just ask for 'La Plaza' if you miss the path).

Here bear right along Camino de Jata following signs for *Campo de Fútbol*. At the top of the street bear left at a fork to reach the road that runs around the top of the village. (2) Cross the road and continue up past a group of modern houses. The concrete road zigzags up to the entrance of the village football ground.

Just before you reach the entrance to the ground go right, then left, and where the road ends drop down to a sandy path which cuts along the right side of a white wall, topped by a fence. The path begins to climb steeply upwards, crosses a water pipe, then passes a water deposit before its angles right and meets with a track **(30 mins)**. 3

Turn left along the track. It climbs gently upwards and soon passes through a swathe of pines then reaches a junction by two metal posts. Here swing right and continue climbing. Soon, looking ahead of you, you'll see that the track later makes a huge loop left: you should be able to spot a sandy path close to the beginning of the loop that cuts steeply up and away from the track. Be ready to cut right here at a cairn **(55 mins)** 4 on this path which follows a line of pylons steeply upwards.

The path merges with a track 5 and continues up towards a stand of pine trees. You begin to reap the reward for your efforts: the track levels and the views get even better. Up ahead you'll now see a fire observation post with antennae on the roof atop a steep, convex hill.

Huge views open out to the east as you continue on round the base of the hill, leaving the hut above you to the right. Shortly you pass by the concreted road which leads up to the hut. The track descends for a short distance, climbs again, then once more runs downhill. Careful! At a point where the track arcs hard left you should cut right on a narrow path 6 which immediately passes by a rock with a red circle **(1 hr 45 mins)**.

The path passes an abandoned farm then descends. Faint red arrows and dots mark the path. You pass by a *calera* (glossary) 7 hewn from soild rock. Eventually the path bears left, descends through pines, then runs up to a second ruined farmstead. An arrow 8 directs you past the left hand side of the farm and its threshing circle.

The path runs parallel to a low wall for a short distance, climbs, and passing by a second *calera* arrives at a third ruined farm whose wall has been daubed with the words *La Casa de Donados*. Beyond the farm the path swings left and begins climbing up the left bank of the Arroyo de Pradillos.

Keep your eyes on the left of the path. Careful! At a point just 10m before the path crosses the bed of the stream 9 bear left at cairn: it is easily missed. Follow cairns and red dots up to the top of the pass of Puerto Blanquillo **(2 hrs 30 mins)**. 10 This is the highest point of your walk: you are now 1202m above sea level. A few metres further on the path meets with a broad track.

Turn left onto the track and after 250m, at a cairn and a marker post, 11 swing right off the track and follow a loose, sandy path which zigzags steeply downwards. It soon improves and runs just left of a (dry) stream. The path shortly crosses the stream, climbs steeply, then drops down to the stream of Arroyo de la Cueva del Melero. Ahead of you is a farm.

Careful! Don't cross the stream but rather bear sharply to the left 12 and head down the left bank of the stream for approximately 60m then cross to the other bank and the terraces beneath the farm. The path runs parallel to an old fence then descends, more or less parallel to the right bank of the stream. Soon you pass through a rickety wooden gate 13 which is often left open. You pass through a second gate made of an old bed base: you begin to see more wooden posts with white arrows marking your way. Beyond the gate a metal fence runs just to the right of the path. Where the fence angles right the path crosses a (dry) stream then angles left, then right, and crosses a second (dry) stream. The path, which is now cobbled in parts, loops down to the Cueva del Melero stream which it crosses then runs up to another gate made from a bed base. 14 Beyond the gate the path crosses once more to the far bank before crossing back

to the left bank. The path widens to become a track **(3 hrs 35 mins)**. 15

After climbing for a short distance the path descends: a metal fence soon runs just to your right. Following the fence along past a water tank you come to a fork. Here angle down to the right, still following the fence. After 150m you reach a gap in the fence marked by a post and a red arrow. 16 Cut right through the gap then bear sharp left (red dot) along a narrow path which loops back and forth across the stream through thick stands of oleander. Eventually you arrive at the Fábrica de Luz de Canillas **(4 hrs 5 mins)**. Here you cross the stream a final time. 17 Passing directly beneath the Fábrica, with the stream just metres to your right, you come to the Fabrica's car park. Head straight on down the tarmac road which hugs the left bank of the Río Llanada de la Turvilla.

You soon pass a quarry. Be aware that lorries fill up with gravel here so ideally this part of the walk should be done between 2pm and 4pm when work stops for lunch. You pass the spring of Fuente El Chorillo 18 W where you can replenish your water bottle and, continuing down the valley, you arrive at a paved road which leads up to the Chapel of San Antón **(4 hrs 50 mins)**. 19

Climb up to the chapel for great views and a rest then retrace your footsteps back down to the tarmac road. Cross straight over, following a sign for *Competa* with a walker icon. Head up a section of steep, concreted track. You soon pass a large water deposit just to the left of the track. Continue up the track for another 60m and just before you reach a second water deposit cut right at a second sign for *Competa.* 20 The sandy track bears sharply left after just 75m then passes above a house with a swimming pool.

The track narrows to become a path which runs along beside an irrigation channel. You reach a three way fork where you take the lower path which shortly runs up to a tarmac road. Turn right onto the road and after 300m cut left onto the second of two concrete drives. Just before the gate, at a small cairn, 21 cut right along a narrow footpath which runs on through a beautiful swathe of irrigated terraces. The path arcs hard to the left and then once more right and reaches a fork. Take the higher path. Soon the path passes a builder's yard then meets with a tarmac road at the outskirts of Competa, Avenida de Canillas. 22 Go right here, then left, and head all the way along Calle de San Antonio to return to the main square **(5 hrs 45 mins)**. 1

CANILLAS DE ALBAIDA CIRCUIT

Distance: 11 kms **Duration:** 4/4.5 hours **Rating:** Medium

Map: 1:50000 Zafarraya

Ⓦ **Water:** At the head of Cajula Gorge @ 1hr 45mins

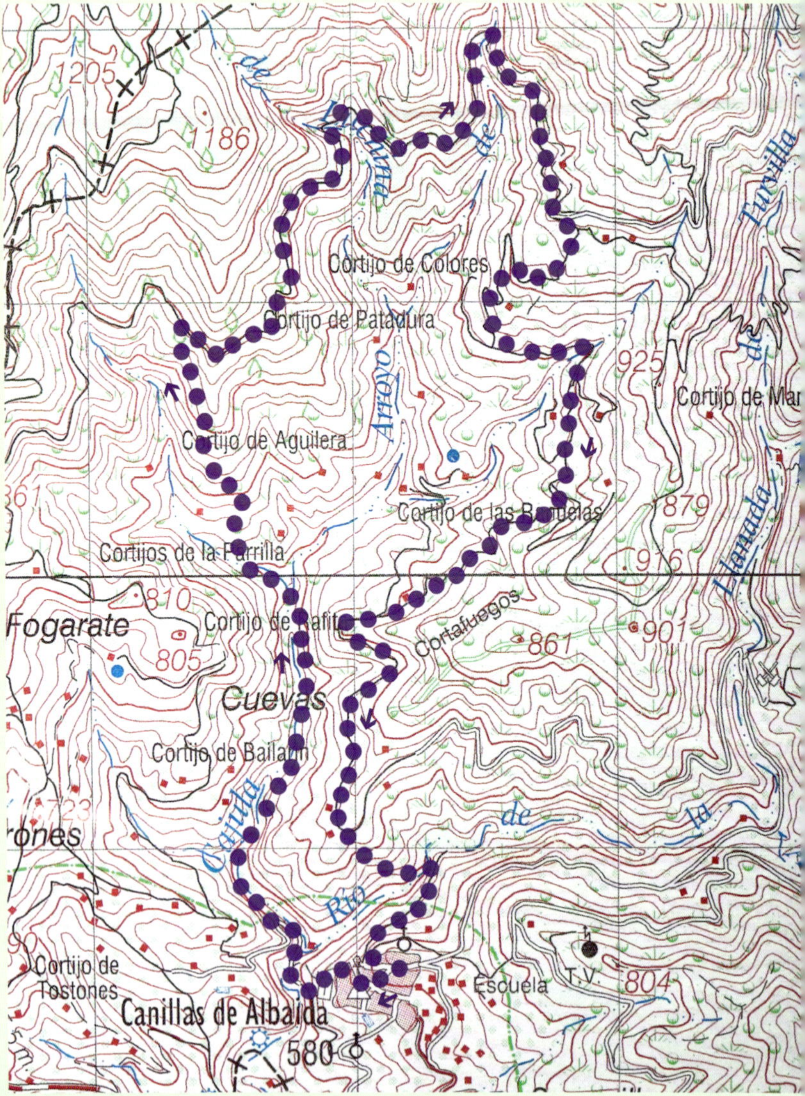

5 The Walk of Stepping Stones & Mountain Chapels

This is one of my favourite rambles in La Axarquía. It takes you out from Canillas de Albaida by way of an enchanting riverside path that meanders through thick stands of oleander, crossing back and forth across the Cájula river which is easily passable unless there has been heavy rainfall. After a steep climb, the middle section of the walk runs along dirt tracks and is quite different in feel. But it's easy to follow and there are fine views of the Sierra de Tejeda. The final section of the walk – there's a steep climb last thing – is along an ancient cobbled path from where there are beautiful views of Canillas and the Chapel of Santa Ana. Try to do this when the oleander which line the river banks are in flower: it is a real spectacle. There are some prickly plants on the middle section before you reach the forestry track so it's a good idea to take long trousers along.

The Route

The walk begins from the car park at the entrance of the village as you come from Cómpeta next to the shrine to the Virgin and Christ 1, between the school's college and its doctor's surgery, the Consultorio. With your back to the Virgin (no disrespect) turn left along the college's northern wall, pass a phone box and leave the square down Calle Llano de la Fuente, past a spring. At the bottom of this street turn sharp right into Calle Poeta Migiñas. It leads you to the pretty *plaza* of the village.

Head straight across the square into Calle Málaga which after a few yards becomes Calle Plazoleta. At the end of the street bear left and drop down Calle Axarquía. At the bottom of the street continue straight ahead to a green railing 2 where you pick up a narrow cobbled path path which passes a pylon then zigzags down into the Cájula valley to meet with a road. Here swing right, cross the river and immediately bear sharp right at a sign for *Río Turvilla* 3 on a concrete track running towards an old mill. It soon narrows to a path which follows the course of the Cájula river, crossing to and fro several times and sticking close to the water's course. The path eventually crosses the river one more time **(25 mins)** and zigzags higher above the river before it passes beneath a steep cliff, then a second overhanging rock face, before its descends and crosses the river once more. 4 Careful! 200m (it's worth counting them out) after crossing the river you reach a fork in the path. 5 Here cut left through a gap in the oleander, cross the stream's course once more via stepping stones, then climb steeply up the other side with a fence now running to your right. After about 75m the path broadens to become a track.

You'll now see a small farm building up ahead of you but - careful! – before reaching it branch right off the track at a sign for *Camino Río*. 6 Follow a narrow path that cuts through a grove of young avocados. It winds, passes the stumps of a line of poplars and then continues on its rather serpentine course, occasionally marked by cairns. About 300m beyond the line of poplar stumps your path crosses over another which has a black plastic water pipe following its course. Cross the path and pipe then bear hard left and wind down to the river which you again cross on stepping stones 7 then duck beneath a branch barrier marking the boundaries of a farm: the path you are on is a public right of way.

The path climbs the far bank, loops round to the left and follows along the stream's east bank, sticking close to the water. A ruined farm comes into sight on the other side of the river. When you're almost opposite the ruin cross the river a final time and follow a path up to the house. You pass just beneath the house 8 then, bearing left, climb steeply up a valley parallel to a tributary of the Cájula. As you climb you'll see a solitary modern

building on the crown of a hill. Remember this landmark – you'll pass by it later in the walk.

The path swings right, descends, and crosses the (dry) stream 9 then bears right again and winds uphill. You come to an area of terracing where you continue to climb. Up above to your right you'll now spot a small farm. Choose the easiest path up across the terraces to the right wall of the farm where, passing a metal post, you meet with a dirt track. Here you should turn right **(1 hr 15 mins)**. 10 You now begin descending towards the solitary building you saw earlier.

When you reach the house the track bears sharply left and runs on towards the head of the Cájula gorge and a small cluster of houses. The track winds, descends and crosses el Arroyo de Luchina via a concrete bridge with rusting railings. 11 It then climbs again, runs past a pretty farm and, just beyond it, a line of cypress trees before dropping down to a point where several tracks converge. Ignore two tracks cutting right, and one cutting up hill to the left: you should continue of the main track which passes just right of a water deposit where there's a tap W where you can fill your water bottle **(1 hr 45 mins)**.

Bearing right the track climbs gently upwards on a course roughly parallel to the Cájula, back towards Canillas. It eventually runs past two pylons, then a water tank, and then a house with a line of cypresses marking its boundary **(2 hrs)**. Just beyond this house the track swings to hard left and a track branches down to the right with a chain across it. Ignore this turning and continue for just 50m and then – careful! – turn right off the track 12 on a narrow path (cobbled in parts) which zigzags down to the river Llanada de Turvilla. Somewhere just off to one side of this path would make a memorable picnic spot.

Cross a bridge 13 over the river, bear right and wind up the other side of the valley towards the Santa Ana Chapel. Pass beneath

the chapel – the gorge is now down to your right – and after a steep climb the path merges with a track that leads you just beneath the cemetery.

Just beyond the cemetery and a pylon bear sharp left, then right and immediately left again, and retrace the route that you followed earlier in the walk back to your point of departure **(2 hrs 45 mins)**. 1

SAYALONGA CIRCUIT

Distance: 10 kms **Duration:** 3.5/4 hours **Rating:** Easy/Medium

Map: 1:50000 Vélez-Málaga (1054)

Ⓦ **Water:** Las Tres Fuentes @ 1 hour

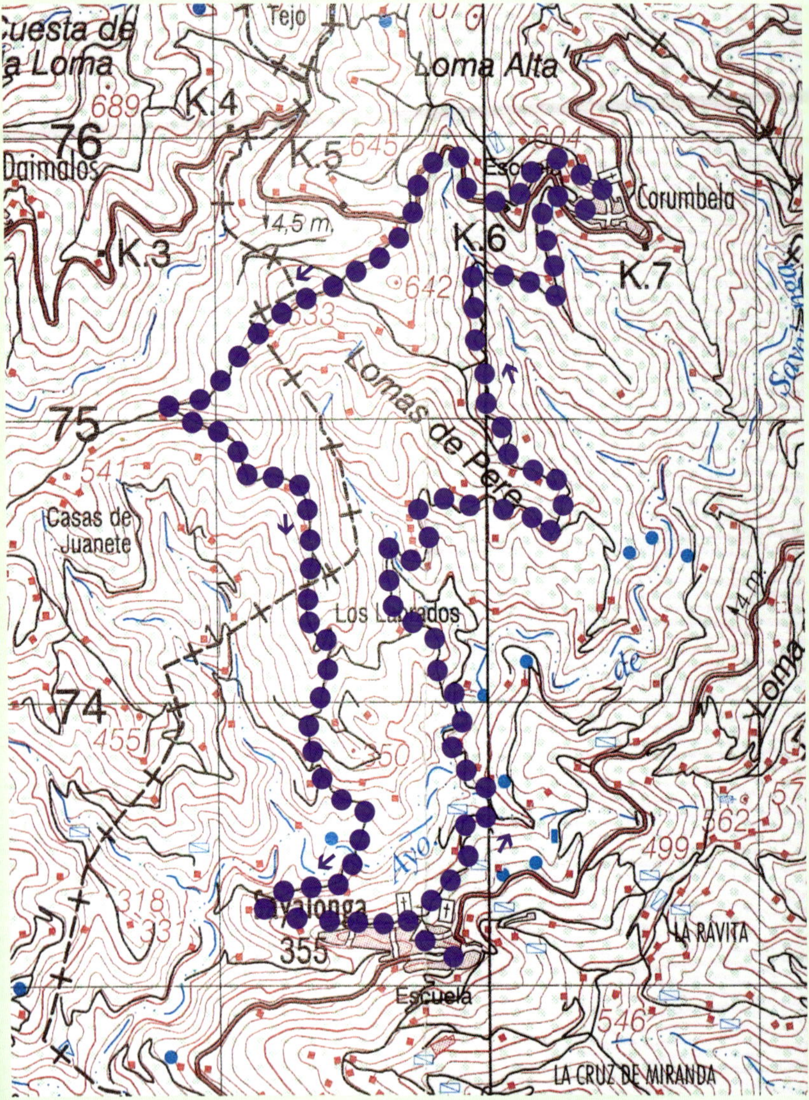

6 The Walk of the Bountiful Valley

This easy half-day excursion links two attractive villages, Sayalonga and sleepy Corombela. The walk takes you down through the subtropical orchards of Sayalonga's terraced river valley where there is an astonishing variety of fruit trees: avocado, citrus, medlar, walnut, olive, almond and pomegranate are all cultivated on the valley's terraced slopes as well as the sweet moscatel grape. A steep climb brings you to Corombela passing by several small farmsteads and on the return leg there are sweeping views of the Sierra de Tejeda and the Mediterrranean. Most of the walk is along tracks and this is an easy circuit to follow. There's a short section of tarmac road when you leave Corombela but you'll see little passing traffic.

The Route

The walk begins in Sayalonga's pretty main square, Plaza Rafael Alcoba. 1 From here take the street that leads in front of the *Ayuntamiento* into Calle Cristo and follow signs for *Cementerio Redondo*. Branch right into Calle Rodríguez de la Fuente then at the end of this narrow street turn left (unless you wish to visit the 'round cemetery', the only one of its kind in Spain. If so, go right here then later retrace your footsteps). Pass beneath the Santa Catalina church then take the next right and descend to a sign marking the beginning of the walk: *Corombela, 5kms*. 2

You shortly reach a fork where you bear right, passing beneath the cemetery, along a concreted section of track which descends through fertile groves of fruit trees. Your route is occasionally waymarked with white and yellow stripes. The track meets the river runs along beside it for a short distance and then crosses over an arched bridge **(20 mins)**. 3

Continuing along the river bank you shortly pass Casa El Molino.

The track climbs through more lush, well irrigated terraces. There are good views here back to Sayalonga. Soon the track heads directly away from the river up a side valley then bears left, climbing steeply. A fence runs to the right of the track. You pass over a (dry) stream where there is storm drainage and continue climbing with the stream to your right. After a steep ascent the track loops hard right, crosses the stream bed, then angles left and passes beneath a line of houses that straddle a ridge before angling right and descending for about 50m. The Med' now comes into view, to the south. You reach a fork in the track **(45 mins)**. 4

Here bear hard left and continue climbing. Cómpeta is visible over to the right and soon Corombela comes into sight. Having passed a number of small farms the track descends, passes over a gulley then comes to the paved picnic area of *Las Tres Fuentes* (The Three Springs) W on your left **(1 hr)**. 5

The track winds up towards Corombela, passes above a five-a-side football pitch then meets a tarmac road **(1 hr 20 mins)**. 6 Cross the road and head up Calle Las Pitas into Corombela. Bearing left past the bakery and you arrive at Bar Cantero, an excellent place for a cool drink after the long climb from Sayalonga. Here swing left past the Covirán supermarket 7 into calle Las Pitas.

At the end of this street bear slightly left and follow a track that runs just above the Corombela/ Daimalos road, passing through groves of almonds, olives and medlars. The track climbs, passes Villa Almenara, then drops down past a ruin to meet the

tarmac road. Bear slightly right and follow the road to the top of the pass. After ten minutes, at a point where the road swings sharply right, turn left onto a track **(1 hr 45 mins)**. 8

The track immediately passes by a farm with *secaderos* (glossary) for grapes. You soon reach a fork 9 from where there are views down to the sea: on a clear day there are sweeping views of the Sierra de Tejeda and its highest point, La Maroma (2069m). Here, bearing right, the track leads past several small farms before it runs down hill past two houses with wafer-bricked gate columns. Another house with a row of arches comes into view up ahead. Just before reaching this house swing left 10 on a track that cuts steeply downhill. With Sayalonga clearly visble on the other side of the valley the track passes two small farms, then a crumbling ruin.

Keep to the main track which continues to descend, looping left then right. The track passes just to the left of a ruined farm 11 then arcs right. You pass an odd-looking kit house with twin balconies and after a steep descent reach another track by a

farm with with twin palm trees next to its entrance, Cortijo Pepe y Angelina. 12 Here turn left and continue your descent, passing a water tank then an ice cream kiosk (which now serves as a shed) to reach the river **(2 hrs 15 mins)**. 13

Cross the river (you may need to remove boots and socks in the wetter months) then bear right and follow a concreted road steeply upwards. After passing a pylon you come to a white building to the left of the track, the home of an extended family of pigs. Immediately before this building 14 branch left and climb steeply on a stoney path which runs between two fences. It soon widens and meets with a concreted section of track. At the end of this track bear left then immediately right at a black metal railing to reach the first village houses and Calle La Loma. At the end of this street bear left then immediately right into Calle Morales. When you reach a sign for the *Cementerio Redondo* turn right along a narrow street to Plaza de la Constitución then bear left along Calle Cristo to arrive back in Plaza Rafael Alcoba **(2 hrs 40 mins)**. 1

The Alpujarras

Trevélez
Capileira
Pampaneira
Busquistar
Mecina Fodales
Cáñar
Lanjarón
Órgiva
Berchules
Mecina
Válor
Ugíjar
Darrical
Murtas
Torvizcón
Turón
Berja
N-323
Vélez de Benaudalla
Albondón
Rubite
Sorvilán
Albuñol
Lújar
Polopos
MOTRIL
Adra
La Rábita
E-15
Castillo de Baños

THE ALPUJARRAS

THE AREA

The Alpujarras are a series of high villages that cling to the southern flank of the Sierra Nevada and face out across the Mediterranean to the Atlas mountains of Morocco. The area surrounding these villages is encompassed within the Parque Natural de La Sierra Nevada that was created in 1989 and covers an area of 171,0000 hectares. As well as the Alpujarras the huge Park includes mainland Spain's most lofty peaks, the highest of them being the mighty Mulhacén, rising to 3481 metres. The area's great natural beauty and its huge biological and geomorphological diversity has meant that since the mid-eighties the Sierra Nevada has been one of UNESCO's Biosphere Reserves. And the higher area of the Park has just recently been upgraded to *Parque Nacional* status.

The life-giver of the mountain range is the melt-water that runs down off the high Sierra for nearly the whole of the year. Over the course of the centuries it has cut a series of deep river valleys or *barrancos* (glossary) that radiate out from the central Sierra. Since the arrival of the Moors in the Middle Ages, a number of meticulously crafted *acequias* or irrigation channels have brought this same water to the carefully tended terraces that have been cut out of the hillsides surrounding the villages. To see these swathes of richly cultivated land in this otherwise harsh, often barren landscape, is like coming across an oasis in the desert. It's no wonder that the Moors were loathe to leave these villages and lingered on for almost a century after the fall of Granada. They were abandoning a truly monumental feat of engineering. It wasn't until 1568 and the last desperate Morisco uprisings that they finally gave up the land for lost, accepted their defeat and limped across the Strait back to Africa.

The villages they left behind still have an unmistakably North African feel with their flat-roofed, whitewashed houses huddling tightly together on the steep hillsides. One of their most striking features are the covered passageways or *tinaos* that often span the narrow streets forming both a porch and a platform for a room above. The *tinaos* seem to bind the villages together and occasionally form narrow tunnels between the houses, conveying a distinctly soukh-like feel.

Times have changed since a young Gerard Brennan found in the Alpujarras a remote, undiscovered corner of Europe. For the past twenty years, Bubión, Trevélez and the villages at the western end of the Sierra have become a popular weekend resort with the Spaniards. Thanks to the arrival of more and more visitors there are numerous hotels and hostals, and good restaurants too. The downside of this sudden increase in tourism is that the character of some of the villages is beginning to change. There are more souvenir shops, pub-style bars and Spanish rather than Alpujarran cuisine in the restaurants. And the legendary *tapas* (so big that they can be a meal in themselves) are beginning to disappear.

In the past decade the area has begun to attract growing number of New Age travellers from the North of Europe. As well as the impromptu camps of VW and Bedford vans you come across in and around Orgiva there's a more established, alternative community. Yoga, Zen-Buddhism, aromatherapy, permaculture and creative workshops are all now a part of life in the Sierra along with goat herding, ham curing and cheese making. Get hold of a copy of Chris Stewart's *Driving Over Lemons* for a tender and entertaining account of moving into this area in search of the Good Life.

And walkers have arrived, too. Many come to climb the higher peaks or to undertake higher traverses of the Sierra. There's a

good system of mountain refuges and more are on the way. And the last few years have seen a huge increase in the number of waymarked routes, both G.R. and P.R. Thanks to the isolation of the Alpujarra, and the comparatively recent arrival of paved roads, the footpaths linking the villages are mostly intact and they make for wonderful walking. Most routes described have at least one steep climb – there's no such thing as a gentle *barranco* (glossary) – but the walking is varied and often spectacular.

Because of the height of the villages – most of these walks start from a height of about 1000 metres – you can still walk comfortably in the Alpujarras in June and September, although during these months you should start out early. During the winter months the snow rarely settles for long below 1200m and this can be a wonderful time to visit, especially when the almond trees are in blossom. Spring is a double treat when the flowers are at their best and the temperatures mild enough for lazy picnics along the way.

Other Walks

The G.R.7. This long-distance route, running all the way from Andorra to Algeciras, cuts across the middle of the Alpujarras. You could easily follow the G.R.7 from village to village for five or six days, but you'll need maps because the way marking is sometimes confusing. There is good documentation available now for the walk: the Nevadensis in Pampaneira is the best place to pick up guides/pamphlets.

The G.R.240 or **La Ruta Sulayr** is a new long distance footpath which loops all the way round te Sierra Nevada on a generally higher course to that followed by the G.R.7. Good documentation on the route is available: the Walk of the Sun Mountain in this guide follows a part of this stunning footpath.

Eastern Alpujarra. There's also good walking at the eastern end of the Alpujarras though for me it doesn't quite match up to the area described in this book. A good base here is Casa de Las Chimeneas in Mairena (958 760 352). A little closer to Trevélez in Bérchules is Hotel Los Bérchules (958 852 530) and El Paraje (I highly recommend) (958 064 029) which is just outside of the village. Both offer good value accommodation and have information on local walks.

Southern Alpujarra. There are a number of lower walks out from the Alquería de Morayma (958 343 221), a beautiful small inn close to Cádiar. Spanish owner Mariano has his own route descriptions and has been pioneering in his defence of the region's patrimony.

Shorter Routes. Elma Thompson's leaflets *Exploring the Alpujarras* describe a series of more gentle walks, most of them radiating out from Bubión and Poqueira.

Longer Routes. The Lonely Planet guide *Trekking in Spain* describes the high traverse of the Sierra Nevada (you need to camp) as well as the route up to the Mulhacén.

Maps

If you choose to go for the individual IGN 1:50000 series you'll need Güéjar Sierra (1027), Lanjarón (1042) and Berja (1043). Trevélez falls right on the border of two maps, 1027 and 1042. Alpina's 1:40000 map Sierra Nevada/La Alpujarra is good and benefits from a larger scale though I've found that some tracks are missing from the map.

By far the best place to pick up maps and guide books to the area is the excellent Nevadensis Centre in Pampaneira. The amount of assembled literature and maps are really impressive and some of it is in English, too. Any serious walker should pass by here at the beginning of any visit and it is, conveniently, located in one of the first villages you pass through coming from the west.

BEST PLACES TO SLEEP & EAT

FERREIROLA

Sierra y Mar

Tel: 958 766 171 Email: reservas@sierraymar.com

A delightful guesthouse in an unspoiled village and always my first choice as a base for walking. Owners José and Inge have unrivalled knowledge of walks in the Alpujarras. €62 incl. breakfast VAT. (Taxi: José Luis y Paco 958 766 005). **Best Eats:** Restaurante La Parra or El Aljibe in the next village.

TREVÉLEZ

Hotel La Fragua & Hotel La Fragua 2

Tel: 958 858 626 Email: reservas@hotellafragua.com

La Fragua is a basic, small hotel at the top of the village with simple yet comfortable rooms. The sister hotel, La Fragua 2, has larger bedrooms with great views. The cosy restaurant of the same name is just yards from both hotels. Miguel and Antonio, the genial owners, could not be more welcoming. €40-€55 + 7% VAT. (Taxi: José Luis 958 858 727 or 609 911 657). **Best Eats:** in sister restaurant Mesón La Fragua.

BUBIÓN

Casa Rural La Sevillana

Tel: 958 763 153 Email: casasevillana@hotmail.com

Simple accommodation just to one side of the main drag through the village, with friendly owners and staff. Good value. €55-€65 incl. VAT. (Taxi José 958 763 025). **Best Eats:** Restaurante Teide & several good tapas bars nearby.

CAPILEIRA

Finca Los Llanos

Tel: 958 763 071 Email: reservas@hotelfincalosllanos.com

A quiet place with pool, at the top of the village. Well set up for hikers with masses of info on all local walks. €65-€75 including a good buffet breakfast. (Taxi: hotel can arrange transfers).
Best Eats: Restaurante Corral de Castaños, The Pizzería or El Asador for meat eaters.

MECINA FONDALES

Hotel Mecina Fondales

Tel: 958 766 254 Email: victor@hoteldemecina.com

Good value rooms, many with views, in the tiny village of Mecina Fondales close to the start of most of the walks listed here. €88 excl. breakfast. **Best Eats:** L'Atelier.

L'Atelier

Tel: 958 857 501 Email: mecinilla@yahoo.com

An exceptionally friendly vegetarian restaurant which also has simple guest accommodation for up to 7. €50 + 7% VAT. Very close to the start of the Arab Baths walk out from Ferreirola.
Best Eats: here.

FERREIROLA CIRCUIT

Distance: 8.5 kms **Duration:** 3.5/4 hours **Rating:** Medium

Map: IGN 1:5000 Lanjarón (1042/20-43)

Ⓦ **Water:** spring in Busquistar @ 1 hr 40 mins and mineral water @ 5mins

1 The Walk of the Ruined Mills & the Arab Baths

This walk begins and ends in the tiny village of Ferreirola. For most of the way it follows old muleteer tracks that twice cross the steep-sided *barranco* of the Río Trevélez. Although there are two steep uphill sections this is an easy half-day walk which you can easily stretch out by picnicking along the way or by stopping for a drink or meal in Busquístar. This itinerary has a kilometre or so of tarmac but there's virtually no traffic and the views across the gorge are fabulous. José and Inger, owners of the delightful Sierra y Mar guest house in Ferreirola, kindly shared this route with me: their charming B&B is one of the best walking bases in the area. Ferreirola and Busquístar are not in the least touristy and this could be a great first walk in the Alpujarras.

The Route

The walk begins in the main square of Ferreirola, La Plaza de Santa Cruz, in front of the church. (1) Pass in front of the four fountains and the village wash house then continue past Villa Kiko along Calle Rosario. At the end of the street bear right past the doctor's surgery, *el Consultorio*, then take the first left and pass beneath a *tinao* (glossary). You soon pass a signpost for *Mirador* and a map of the long distance footpath, the GR142.

The path soon passes by a spring with ceramic tiles, *La Fuente Gaseosa*, (W) then crosses a small bridge. After passing above a beautiful *era* (glossary) and a information board the path runs past a second spring (W) to the left of the path, *La Fuente Paula*. After crossing another bridge the path climbs up over a more rocky area then reaches a fork. (2) Here keep right. After just 50m you reach a second fork (3) where you should once more bear right. The path gradually drops down towards the bottom of the gorge where, describing a final loop, it arrives at a ruined mill beside the river **(20 mins)**. 4

Cross the river then follow a narrow path which climbs steeply up the southern side of the gorge. After climbing for some 15 minutes you reach a wooden marker post. Here the path narrows, angles hard right and then, reaching a flatter area, loops back to the left and passes a green gate in a whitewashed wall. 5 Shortly you pass an overgrown ruin, a mill dating back to the Moorish period. The path broadens, angles right, levels and then passes between two white buildings, house numbers 4 and 5 **(50 mins)**. Continuing straight ahead you passing to the left of another house then come to a *Stop* sign and a tarmac road. 6

Bear left along the road. Views open out to the south towards the Contraviesa mountain range. The road runs past Cortijo Venta Relleno then, just before reaching an abandoned mining complex (iron ore was mined here until the 1970s), arrives at the junction of the Juvíles-Cástaras road. 7 Here fork left away from the road and pick up a footpath which zigzags steeply back down into the *barranco*: there's a sign for *Busquístar* and red and white G.R. waymarking.

Reaching the bottom of the gorge the path crosses a bridge over the river Trevélez where it passes another ruined mill **(1 hr 25 mins)** then climbs steeply up the north side of the gorge. After passing a number of terraced fields you reach the road running round the bottom of Busquístar, Calle Laurel **(1 hr 40 mins)** and an information board with a map of the area. 8

Here turn left and head along this street to its the junction with Calle San Francisco. 9 Here you have a choice. If planning to visit Busquístar, or refill your water bottle, turn right and climb up into the village centre where there are bars and a spring. If not, you should cut left and begin to descend, passing a sign for *Ferreirola, 2.7 kms* and another which lets you know that you're following the ancient *Camino Real*. The path descends steeply,

crosses a bridge and passes by some ramshackle byres. Your path comes in to meet with a track **(1 hr 50 mins)**. 10

Here head straight on, climbing slightly. At the point where the track loops hard round to the right you should carry straight on, again picking up the old footpath by a G.R. marker post. This is a beautiful section of the walk as the path cuts between stands of evergreen oaks and clumps of gorse and cistus before cutting past a dramatic, rocky outcrop.

Soon you reach a fork in the path. 11 Here maintain your same course, ignoring the turning left that would take you steeply down into the gorge. Ferreirola shortly comes into view as the path loops downwards. As the path runs on towards the village up head you'll now be able to see Mecina and Mecina Fondales. Eventually the path drops down and meets with the path that you followed out of Ferreirola earlier in the day **(2 hrs 15 mins)**. Here turn right and retrace your footsteps back to the village **(2 hrs 30 mins)**. 1

PAMPANEIRA CIRCUIT

Distance: 8.5 kms **Duration:** 4/4.5 hours **Rating:** Medium

Map: IGN 1:5000 Lanjarón (1042/20-43)

Ⓦ **Water:** springs in Capileira @ 2 hrs, Bubión @ 2hrs 45mins

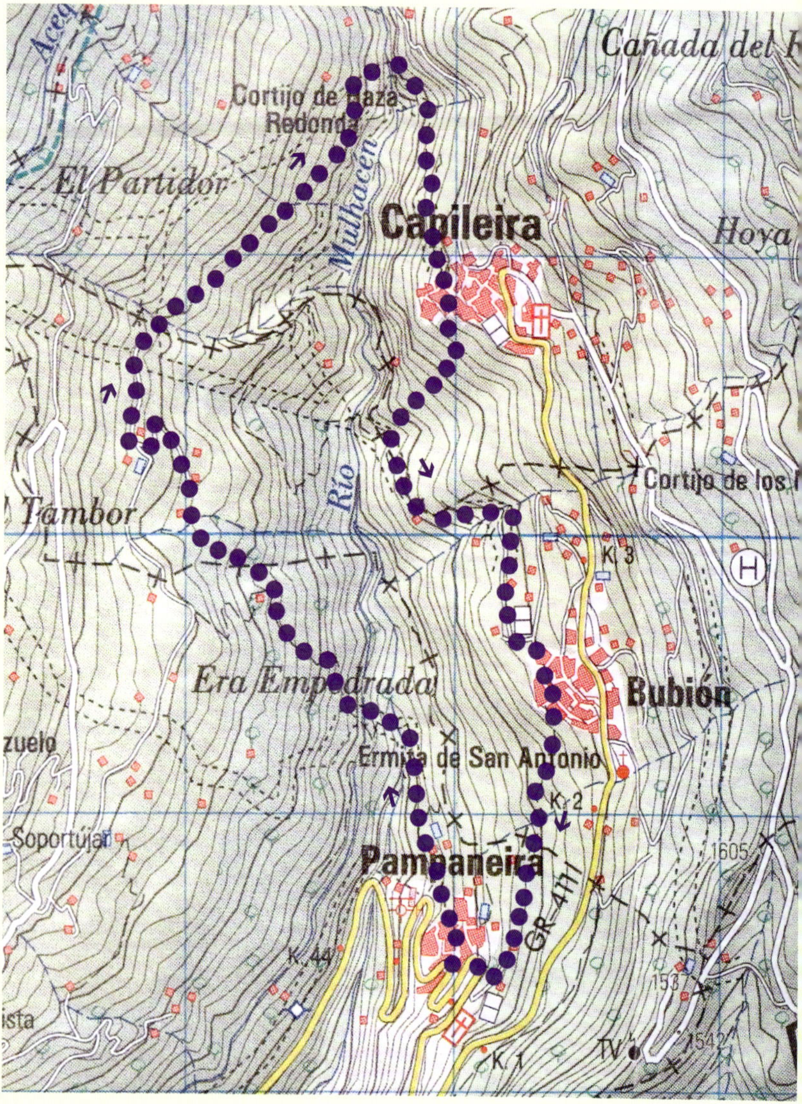

2 The Walk of San Antonio's Spring

This challenging gorge walk makes for a great first taste of the abrupt Alpujarran topography. The circuit takes in three of the region's most attractive villages and a fabulous slice of the plunging Poqueira *barranco* (glossary). Be prepared for a fair amount of climbing: first thing once you cross the river, then again as you tackle another steep ascent in the middle section of the walk from the river up to Capileira before the final steep climb up to Bubión. Your efforts will be amply rewarded by magnificent views south and north. You could break for lunch/ snacks in Capileira or Bubión.

The Route

The walk begins at the entrance to the village of Pampaneira in front of *Hostal Ruta Mulhacén*. (1) From here head for the village centre, passing the church and the Fuente de San Antonio. A plaque tells how, partaking of its waters, lonely hearts can find a partner. And instantaneously to boot. Keep to the top side of the square, pass beneath a *tinao* (glossary). At the end of Calle Antonio Álvarez drop down a flight of steps then turn left. Bearing right you pass a sign *Camino del Río*. The street bears right, then right again, and the cobbling ends. (2) Head straight ahead along a footpath. When you reach a fork by a pylon cut right (the left turn leads down to the village *lavadero* (glossary)). The path loops down to a track **(10 mins)**. (3)

Bearing right, and continuing your descent, you soon pass a farm, El Cercado before a final descent leads you down to the pretty bridge spanning the Poqueira gorge. (4) Beyond the bridge continue for 5m then, just before reaching a sign explaining what a *Molino Harinero* (flour mill) was, cut right on a track and after just 30m angle left up a narrow footpath. The path zigzags upwards and the loose surface improves. You soon reach a fork. 5 Here cut right and pass above another ruined mill: water still runs for most of the year in its *acequia* (glossary). The path continues to climb as views open out to Bubión across the gorge. Soon you pass twin marker posts 6 and the path passes just to the right of a long, low ruined farm. Continue straight on past the farm. The path angles slightly right, becomes less distinct, but soon improves as it continues to loop steeply upwards. After passing a waymarking post you reach a fork. 7 Here cut right and continue climbing: the footpath is slightly overgrown at this point. Soon you climb up past another ruin. 8

After climbing steeply for about 250m the path angles right then left before resuming its steep ascent, now with a (dry) stream to its left. It soon angles slightly right and passes across a rather swampy area to reach yet another ruined farm which it passes by at its lower, right hand corner 9 before angling left towards two newly built stone houses, both with solar pannels. Continue along the path that runs just left and above the first farm 10 and soon the path merges with the access track to the farms. Follow the track uphill. It soon loops hard left, then right, and climbs steeply to a point where there are two metal gate posts, sometimes linked with a chain. 11 Here cut right on a broad level track which passes behind another ruin. Soon you reach a point where this track angles sharply left. 12 Here continue straight on along a footpath which soon crosses a (dry) stream. After 50m it divides. Here cut right and descend steeply across and open tract of hillside: the path is loose, and occasionally divides, as you head down towards a small, overgrown ruin.

Just 30m before reaching the ruin 13 the path becomes much clearer as it angles left and cuts across a more flat, open area of meadow. Beyond it the path again descends steeply, parallel to a stream bed which runs to your left. Soon the path angles

hard left, 14 crosses the stream via a stone bridge, descends, then just before reaching another stream bed, divides. Continue straight ahead and cross the (dry) stream. After 5m the path divides. Bear left and climb. Soon the path crosses two more (dry) stream beds and shortly a stone wall runs to its left. An *acequia* (glossary) runs just left of the path which soon passes above a small, flat-roofed building. The path runs gently downhill to a junction where a sign points the way to Capileira. 15 Here, bearing right, you drop down a cobbled path then cross a pretty bridge which spans the Poqueira gorge. **(1 hr 30 mins)**. 16

The path loops right and climbs up the eastern side of the gorge. Having crossed a smaller bridge a final steep pull brings you up to the outskirts of Capileira and a small sign, *Puente Chiscar* and a larger one with a map of the Sendero Sulayr, a newly created G.R. footpath. **(1 hr 55 mins)**. 17

Here bear right (if you wish to visit the village head straight on up, then later retrace your steps to this point) and follow a line of black lamp posts as you skirt round beneath the village. When you reach a small spring W bear right again and, descending, you pass a sign for *Camino de las Higuerillas/ Molino de Bubión*. The broad track that you have been following narrows to become a path which zigzags down into the valley. Soon it passes above a small stone hut 18 then continues its descent, more or less parallel to a stream which is now to your left: the path doubles as a water course at times when the stream is in spate. Passing by a stone house with a terraced garden full of plants and flowers it continues steeply downhill, passes one more ruin, then after a final steep descent reaches a slate sign for *Puente Molino/Bubión* and a wooden marker post. Here turn left. 19 Soon you cross the stream via a small stone bridge. A broad path now leads you upwards, passing by a ruined farm and some enormous old chestnut trees before crossing a second small bridge **(2 hrs 35 mins)**. 20

The path runs angles up to the outskirts of Bubión where you reach a map and a P.R. waymark post. 21 Just past the village football pitch it cuts left then contours round the village before running on past the Museo Casa Alpujarreña to reach the village square and the church. 22 At the end of the square turn right at a sign *Ruta Barrio Bajo*. Descend past the main entrance to the church then, bearing left, you arrive at a G.R.7 sign for *Pampaneira, 1.5km* **(2 hrs 45 mins)**. After descending for 50m you pass a spring, W La Fuente del Barrio Bajo. 23

Continue along the path. It eventually merges with a track which runs on past a couple of ruined huts then passes to the right of the village water deposit **(3 hrs)** then reaches the village cemetery where it loops round to the right. Head straight on to the first houses of the village following a line of black lamp posts. At the end of this street cut left just before you reach a *tinao* (glossary) then at the next fork bear left and zigzag down to the village square and the church. From here retrace your footsteps to the beginning of the walk **(3 hrs 10 mins)**. 1

CAPILEIRA CIRCUIT

Distance: 9 kms **Duration:** 4.5/5 hours **Rating:** Medium

Map: IGN 1:5000 Lanjarón (1042/20-43)

Ⓦ **Water:** spring on your return leg @ 1 hr 55 mins

3 The Walk of the Poqueira Gorge

The shorter version of this walk begins and ends in the pretty village of Capileira and takes you up to the generating station of La Cebadilla. Although your destination is at a height of over 1600m you point of departure is in one of the highest villages in the Alpujarras (1432m) so there's not too much climbing involved. The views down the Poqueira river valley are exceptional and, although there's a half-hour stretch of track on the return leg, the final part of the walk takes you along the loveliest of paths which drops steeply down to Capileira. You could turn this into a longer circuit by continuing on up the Poqueira gorge, above La Cebadilla then picking up the route notes for *The Walk of the High Acequias*. This would turn a half day ramble into a challenging full day of walking: you'll need 8 to 9 hours to tackle the combined walks in comfort.

The Route

The walk begins at the *Ayuntamiento* (Town Hall) of Capileira. You see it on your right as you come from Bubión. (1) Cross the road and cut along the street leading into the village centre, immediately passing by Hostal Mesón Poqueira. At the end of the street turn left at restaurant El Tilo. Turning right you pass a spring *Fuente Plaza del Calvario*. Head past Bar El Tilo into Calle del Cubo then bear right in front of Apartamentos Vista Veleta.

Continue on this paved road following a line of black street lamps. Continue on past two *eras* (glossary) to a sign which points your way to *Camino de Abuchite*. (2) The road becomes a track which begins to descend. Soon you pass a water tank to the left of the path, then a spring, and after descending for some 300m reach a path which angles hard left away from the one you've been following. (3) Here cut left and drop steeply down a narrow path. Keeping to the main path you soon pass beneath a stone hut then, reaching the river, cross *El Puente Abuchite* by a sign for *Aguas de Alta Montaña* **(20 mins)**. 4

Beyond the river the path arcs left for just 15m then swings right and climbs: P.R. waymarking indicates your course. After 50m a wooden barrier runs to the right of the path. Continue following the same course as the barrier, ignoring a path which swings left up to a threshing circle. The path runs roughly parallel to the river, climbing gradually upwards. Soon you pass a ruined farmstead with a threshing circle. The path still runs more or less parallel to the river, occasionally looping up to a higher level. You pass just to the right of a ruined farm building **(40 mins)**. 5

After looping upwards the path crosses a small *barranco* (glossary) then passes through a ramshackle gate then runs past an isolated farm which it passes just to its left. Beyond the farm the path descends and crosses a stone bridge. 6 Soon you pass by another tumbledown farm. You come to a line of poplars where the path swings left, following the line of the trees upwards. After passing a threshing circle it climbs more steeply and soon passes three stone buildings before arriving at a transmitter mast. 7 Just to its right is a building with a bridge leading to its front door. A few metres past this bridge, turn right and drop down to a wide track which leads down to the river and the H.E.P. buildings. You come to the bridge crossing the River Poqueira, Puente Hondero **(1 hr 25 mins)**. 8

Cross the bridge and swing right past the chapel and buildings where the workers of the station once lived. The track climbs gradually upwards, heading back towards Capileira. Ignore a track that branches off right to Cortijo Roble Blanco but be ready to branch right 80m after passing beneath the electricity lines at a sign for *Camino Capileira* and a marker post **(1 hr 45 mins)**. 9

Heading along a broad track you'll soon see an *acequia* to your right. The track narrows to become a path. Shortly you pass just beneath a white building then, after crossing a water channel, arc left and continue on in the same course, just beneath the water channel. You pass a small byre and then a small spring 10 just to the left of the path. Reaching the entrance gates of a farm bear left. The path now runs just beneath a plantation of pine trees and soon reaches a fork and a marker post. Here contine straight ahead. Your path soon crosses the *acequia* then runs past a large water tank before it runs up to meet with a broader track. Here bear right **(2 hr 05 mins)**. 11

Views open out across the *barranco*. You reach another branch in the track and a marker post where you should cut right along a narrower path. You pass a small white hut then, shortly afterwards, a second hut. The path loops down towards Capileira and arrives at the outskirts of the village by a sign which shows the route that you have followed. 12 Head on past the sign then follow a steep cobbled track downwards. At the next junction head straight across, past a spring, into Calle Carril. At the bottom of this street bear left and retrace the route that you followed earlier back to your point of departure **(2 hrs 25 mins)**. 1

Note: This walk can be turned into a long 8 to 9 hour circuit. If this idea appeals when you reach Puente Hondero pick up the route notes for *The Walk of the High Acequias*.

LA CEBADILLA CIRCUIT

Distance: 10.5 kms **Duration:** 5/5.5 hours **Rating:** Medium

Map: IGN 1:5000 Lanjarón (1042/20-43) & Güéjar Sierra (1027/20-42)

Water: no springs on walk so take plenty

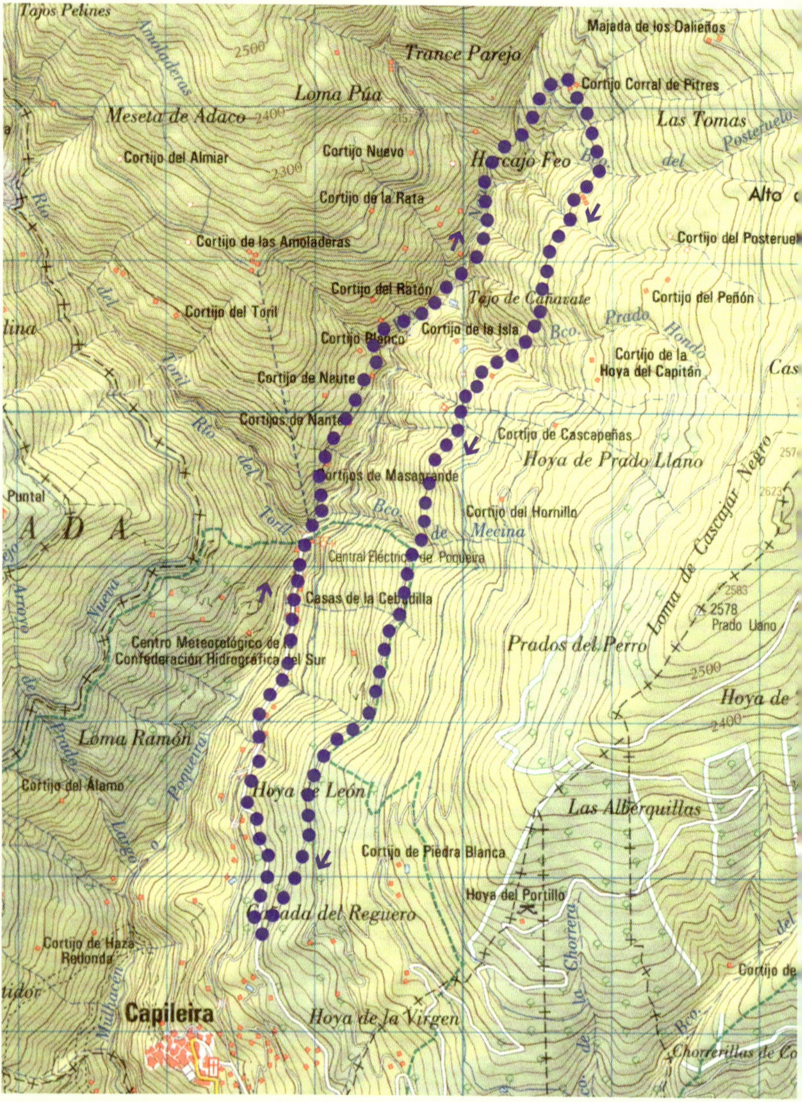

4 The Walk of the High Acequias

The high water channels of the Alpujarras or *acequias* stand testimony to the endeavour and resourcefulness displayed by the inhabitants of these mountain villages in channeling water huge distances through the harshest of terrain. Many of the channels that are in use today were built more than five centuries ago during the time of the Moors. This walk takes you up to some of the highest of these remarkable constructions, beginning at the Cebadilla power station to the north of Capileira. It's easy to drive here or you could take a taxi up from Capileira. After a short section of track which leads past the Cebadilla H.E.P. plant you cut north on a narrow path which follows the course of the Naute river past a number of abandoned farms. Eventually you reach the highest point of the walk, the isolated farm of Cortijo de las Tomas. This is a wonderful spot for a picnic with several 3000m peaks rising all around you including the mighty Mulhacén. From here you contour back round the valley before dropping down to the broad track which leads back to your point of departure.

Driving to the begining of the walk: Head up to the top of Capileira then take the *Pista Forestal 3* that loops up towards the *Hoya del Portillo*. At km 2.7 branch left onto a dirt track . Follow the track parallel to the Poqueira gorge for 4 kms. Shortly before the road arrives at the river you reach the buildings to the right and left of the track which once housed the workers of the La Cebadilla power station. Park as close to the Puente Hondero bridge as possible.

The Route

The walk begins on the eastern side of the Puente Hondero bridge by a sign *Aguas de Alta Montaña.* 1 Cross the bridge and bear right along the road. Arriving at the power station of La Cebadilla cross the river via a concrete bridge then bear left. Continuing on up you cross a second bridge and reach a sign marking the beginning of your path and a map of the higher circuits of the Poqueira valley **(10 mins)**. 2

Here cut away from the track on a narrow path which heads up the left bank of the river. You'll see occasional yellow and white P.R. waymarking. The path zigzags up then adopts a more level course before passing beneath a stone hut. 3 Here the path angles gently upwards, more or less parallel to the river, then passes beneath a second stone building *Cortijo Masa Grande*. Just beyond it you reach a wooden signpost for *Sendero Acequias del Poqueira*. 4 The path now descends slightly and passes behind a whitewashed farm building.

Soon you pass beneath another stone building 5 and a threshing platform then, descending steeply, cross a (dry) stream. The path runs along the stony left bank of the River Naute towards a ruined farm. Approximately 80m before the farm cross the Naute via a small stone bridge. 6 You shortly cross a second bridge, then a third, before arriving at the ruined farm, Cortijo de la Isla. Bearing right the path now runs past the farm's *era* (glossary) then threads its way through the rocks, running up the middle of the valley. Soon it loops right, passes over a small knoll, then crosses a small footbridge **(1 hr 10 mins)**. 7

Beyond the knoll the path descends, crosses a small bridge, then a second one, before resuming its ascent of the Naute valley. After passing another ruined farm 8 the rocky path loops higher and you come to a fork. 9 Cut right along the lower path: this section of the route can get boggy during the wetter months. The path soon drops down and crosses the river via another small bridge **(1 hr 25 mins)**.

Beyond the river you loop up past another P.R. marker post. The path, cobbled in parts, follows the river's left bank for a short distance then, descending, crosses a small footbridge. 10 Beyond the stream it runs straight before cutting left and climbing steeply, more or less parallel to the stream which it soon crosses once again via another footbridge. 11 The path, marked by cairns, climbs on up past a ruined corral 12 then crosses the water channel of *Aceqia Baja*. You come to the abandoned farm of *Cortijo de las Tomas* (**1 hr 50 mins)**. 13

This makes a perfect picnic spot with a glorious panoramic view of the *barranco* to the south, westwards to the peak of Terreras Azules and northwards to the towering massif of the Mulhacén. When you leave the Cortijo, with your back to the gorge and the path you have followed earlier, angle right past a P.R. waymarking post and follow the path upwards, parallel to the fenced corral of Las Tomas, to a sign for *Sendero Acequias del Poqueira*. 14 Here cut right. The path soon crosses a stream then, contouring on round the valley, crosses a second stream. 15 Still climbing it soon loops across a third stream. 16 Looking back towards Las Tomas the Poqueira refuge is now visible on the bare flank of the Mulhacén. Soon the path begins to descend and passes by a ruined farm 17 before climbing once again and passing another sign for *Sendero Acequias del Poqueira*.

After crossing another stream you pass beneath the ruins of Cortijo Peñon **(2 hrs 30 mins)** 18 then continue on parallel to right bank of *Acequia Alta* before angling right away from the water channel and descending. Soon you pass an information board which identifies the higher peaks that are visible from this point 19 then, passing by another ruined farm, descend past a sign for *Refugio de Poqueira*. Looping steeply downhill you cross another water channel 20 then continue your steep descent. After running across a flatter area the path angles left, crosses a (dry) stream then cuts across the hillside beneath a rocky outcrop towards a stand of pines where you pass yet another sign for *Sendero Acequias del Poqueira* **(3 hrs 20 mins)**. 21

Soon the path merges with a broad track. 22 Cutting left along the track you immediately pass by a white hut. After descending past a second white hut you reach a marker post to the right of the track. 23

Here cut right and descend for 225m. You again meet with the track. 24 Here angle hard round to the right and head down the Cebadilla access track back to your point of departure, the bridge over the Río Naute **(4 hrs 5 mins)**. 1

BUBION TO TREVÉLEZ LINEAR WALK

Distance: 18.3 kms **Duration:** 7.5 hours **Rating:** Medium/Difficult

Map: IGN 1:5000 Lanjarón (1042/20-43)

Ⓦ **Water:** spring @ 3hrs 30 mins

5 The Walk of the Sun Mountain

This long day walk follows a part of the newly created long distance walking path *Sendero Sulayr* which takes its name from the Arab for *Mountain of the Sun*. This extraordinarily varied walk takes in a magnificent swathe of the Sierra Nevada between Bubión and Trevélez and passes through pine forest, mixed woodland and high rocky terrain from where you're treated to soaring views of the southern flank of the Sierra Nevada as well as the Mediterranean and North African coasts. The walk begins with a long ascent of 900m from Bubión to the highest point on the walk, Las Aberquillas (2240m). From here the path cuts down across open hillside then through a swathe of oak forest to a broad forestry track which contours round the Río Trevélez gorge. You then follow a pretty section of the G.R.7 footpath down to Trevélez from where buses depart at 16h and 17.30h back to Bubión, every day of the year: provided that you get going soon after breakfast you'll have ample time to make either of these departures. Or you could take a taxi from Trevélez to Bubión then follow the route back across the mountain.

The Route

The walk begins next to the road that leads through Bubión up to Capileira at the top end of the village, just above the spring of Fuente Fuenfría next to an information board with a map of the *Sendero Sulayr*. ① Cut uphill, away from the road on a steep cobbled path. After 200m you reach a junction where you branch right and continue climbing up past a white hut. The path crosses a small *acequia* (glossary) and leaves the last of the village buildings behind. Views open out across the Poqueira *barranco* (glossary). The path winds up through a stand of oaks to meet with a track. ② Go straight across and continue climbing. Soon you cross the track a second time and, after another steep ascent, cross over a third time by a barrier 3 following the direction shown by a marker post *Trevélez, G.R.240/Hoya del Portillo*. Continuing its ascent the track runs up to meet with a tarmac road **(30 mins)**. 4 Cross the road and continue up the path marked by a sign *Camino de la Sierra*. Soon you meet once more with the road. 5

Here cut right and head south along the road. After 750m you pass a viewing platform to the right of the road. 6 Continue along the road as it loops hard left then after approximately 75m cut right at a marker post 7 onto a narrow footpath **(1 hr)** which climbs steeply up into the pine forest, still clearly marked with red and white G.R. posts. The path levels as it runs along a sandy stream bed then cutting slightly right runs along beside a dug out channel with the pine forest over to its right. The path is a little more indistinct at this stage but you'll soon spot another G.R. post. 8 Here the path angles left and climbs parallel to the pines: beyond the trees you'll hear a mountain stream that feeds a large reservoir which, at this stage, is out of sight. Soon you pass another marker post then descend to cross the stream via a small wooden bridge. 9

Heading straight ahead you reach a sign marking *Trevélez, 14.1km.* The path broadens as it runs up between the pines then loops left. After climbing for another 150m it cuts right at a marker post 10 and narrows down. It soon traverses another wooden bridge before once again entering the pine forest. Vast

vistas open out to the south as the path runs on and crosses another wooden bridge before looping up past a rocky outcrop **(1 hr 40 mins)**. After continuing its ascent through the pines the path runs downhill, crosses a (dry) stream then climbs once more before running into a stand of older fir trees. You arrive at a junction where there are three marker posts. 11

Here cut left along a broad forestry track. After about 350m the track loops right and shortly before it describes another loop left be ready to cut right 12 onto a narrow footpath which climbs up the right bank of a stream which it soon crosses via a wooden bridge. It then cuts left, still climbing, before angling once more right into a stand of pines. G.R. posts mark your way up to the parking area of *Hoyo del Portillo* where you will see a map, a wooden marker post and a barrier **(2 hrs 5 mins)**. 13 Here cut right along a broad track following a sign *Trevélez 11.8km*.

Views once more open out to the south as the pines thin out. After some 15 minutes the track runs past an information board describing mountain flora 14 where there's a spring wrapped round by a stone wall: in the warmer months this slows to little more than a trickle so don't rely on it as a source of water. At 2240m this is the highest point of the walk. Some 50m past the walled spring cut right, away from the track, at another sign *Trevélez 10.5km* 15 picking up a narrow path which cuts across a swathe of more open terrain before entering another stand of pines. You soon break out of the trees then loop down and cross a wooden bridge. 16 The path runs well to the left of a rocky outcrop: this is a great spot to break for your picnic now that you've conquered nearly all of the 900m ascent from Bubión. 17 The path widens then runs downhill towards another stand of pine forest. Here you pass a sign for *Parque Natural*. 20m beyond the sign at a marker post 18 cut left and head downhill, away from the pines.

The path becomes looser as you descend and soon arcs across another wooden bridge 19 before resuming its course down across the open mountainside. After descending for some 10 minutes the path angles sharply right 20 then after just 150m cuts back left then enters a stand of low-growing oaks. After running past a rocky outcrop it reaches a small reservoir where you can refill your water bottle from a black plastic pipe **(3 hrs 30 mins)**. 21 W You might be tempted to take a dip here if following this walk in the summer months.

Beyond the reservoir cross a wooden bridge then continue your descent through a lovely stand of deciduous oak forest. The path winds more steeply downwards to reach a broad track 22 where you come to another sign marking *Trevélez 4.8km.* Bearing left along the track you shortly pass by G.R.7 marker posts indicating a path which leaves the track to its right side. Ignore these and continue along the track which contours round the valley. Eventually, where the track loops hard left, 23 cut right

along a path which loops up into the pine forest. It soon levels, runs on between two parallel rows of trees, then again meets with the track. 24

Continue along the track until you reach a sign for *Parque Natural*. Here cut right off the track at a G.R. waypost 25 on a narrow path which cuts down then crosses an eroded gulley before it meets again meets with the track. Bearing left head on down the track, ignoring more G.R. markers to the right. Trevélez comes into view and you pass another sign *Trevélez, 2.4kms*. Just 20m past this sign cut right at a G.R.7 marker post 26 and drop down a steep, loose and narrow path which soon crosses directly over a track 27 and, continuing its descent, arcs left then right and crosses a *barranco* via a concrete bridge. 28

Soon you pass an information board for *Sendero Sulayr* and reach the first houses of the village **(4 hrs 20 mins)** and Calle

Charquillo. 29 At the end of this street cut left, pass the village wash house, then angle right to meet with a tarmac road which you should follow down into the village. After looping left then right it leads to a small square where you can quench your thirst at a spring or in Bar Cerezo or Bar Los Nogales.

Leave the square by cutting right past Ferretería Monica then before you reach Hostal Fernando cut left and head on down to a *Stop* sign. Here turn right and after 30m, just past house number 7, cut left and drop down a flight of steps then bear left to reach the square at the bottom of Trevélez **(4 hrs 35 mins)**. 30

The bus stop is at the top of the square next to a small kiosk which sells cold drinks, books and sweets.

Buses leave for Bubión at 16h and 17.30h on weekdays, weekends and public holidays. It's about a 35 minute ride back to your point of departure.

TREVÉLEZ LINEAR WALK

Distance: 14.5 kms **Duration:** 7.5/8 hours **Rating:** Medium/Difficult

Map: IGN 1:5000 Lanjarón (1042/20-43) & Güéjar Sierra (1027/20-42)

Ⓦ **Water:** no springs on the route so take plenty

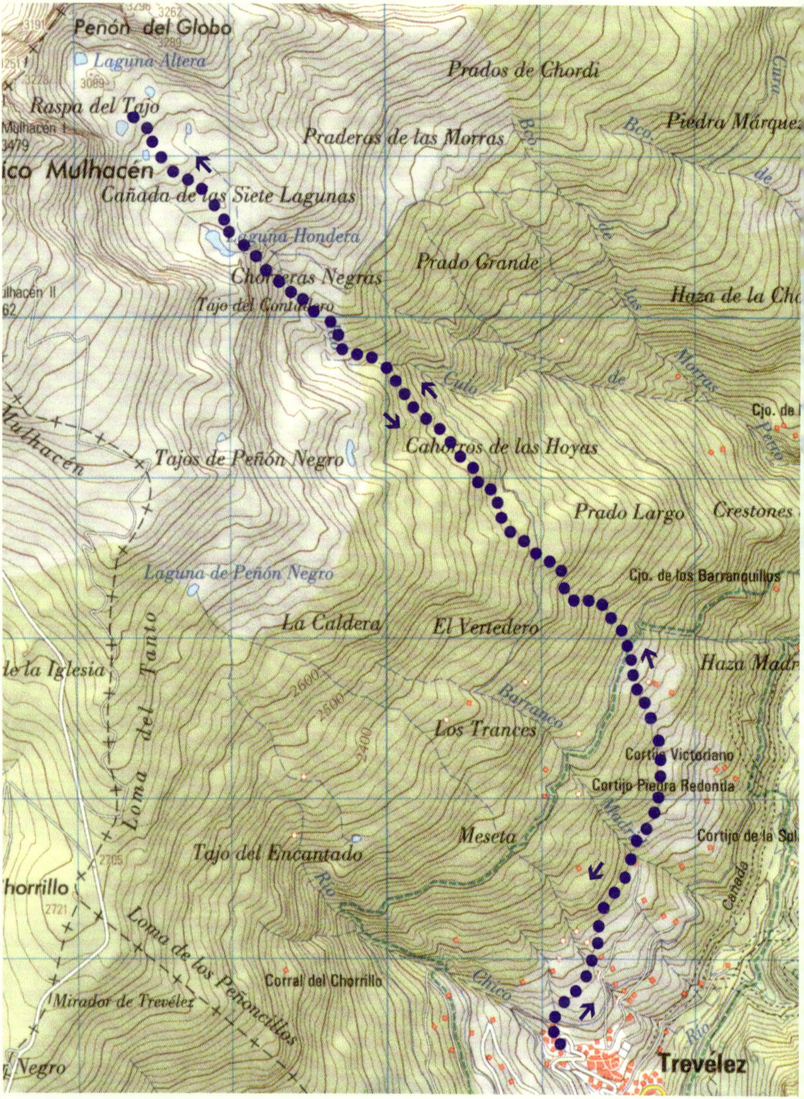

6 The Walk of the Seven Lagoons

This linear day walk takes you up to the high cirque (2900m) beneath mainland Spain's highest peak, the Mulhacén (3479m). This is one of the most exquisite corners of the Sierra Nevada and a wonderful place for a long, relaxed picnic: you could even have a bracing dip in one of the lagoons if you walk this route in summer. From Trevélez you have a climb of nearly 1500m so to enjoy this circuit you need to be reasonably fit and set out early in the day. You can shorten the walk by almost 3 hours by ending the climb at the ruins of Cortijo La Campiñuela from where you're treated to a stunning panorama of peaks and gorges. In the colder months there's often snow on the higher sections of the walk and conditions at this altitude can change rapidly: always check the weather forecast before leaving Trevélez. The walk decribed here ends at the Seven Lagoons but you could extend it by scaling the Mulhacén. The approach up its southern ridge from Laguna Hondera is marked by cairns. If you plan to do so add two and a half hours to the timings below.

The Route

The walk begins at the square in the *Barrio Medio* of Trevélez in front of Bar Rosales. (1) Go up the hill passing the Panadería Federico following signs for *Mesón La Fragua*. Just before reaching the restaurant bear sharp left, pass the *ayuntamiento* and Hotel La Fragua then turn right and pass beneath an archway. Turn right into Calle Horno. You pass by an old wash house and after 60m turn left at a metal sign *Camino a Siete Lagunas*. (2)

A narrow cobbled path leads up through the terraces. Soon the path narrows and crosses an *acequia* (glossary). You'll see yellow and white P.R. waymarking (it will mark your route as far as La Campiñuela). Cross a (dry) stream and continue to climb. You pass a whitewashed building 3 then cross a second small bridge. The path divides **(20 mins)**. Here carry straight on. You soon pass by a farm with solar panels then cross another small stone bridge. Shortly after passing between another group of farm buildings the path divides. 4 Here bear left and climb steeply up across the open mountainside. The path soon leads through a wire-and post-gate. Cairns and P.R. marker posts guide you up across rather looser terrain, more or less parallel to a flimsy fence which runs to your left. Trevélez is visible way down beneath you.

After a steep climb the path arcs right and runs parallel to a water channel *(Acequia Gorda)* and a fence. The path soon reaches another fence where it passes through a wire-and-post gate 5 then, crossing the water channel, climbs steeply through an area of young pines passing by another sign for *La Campiñuela/Siete Lagunas*. The pines thin out as the path zigzags steeply up through the shale to another fence where you go through another wire-and-post gate 6 then follow the fence along.

The path continues its steep ascent and you leave the last of the pines behind. It eventually swings right, crosses a water channel *(Acequia del Mundo)* 7 then comes to the flat swathe of land surrounding the ruined farm of Cortijo la Campiñuela **(2 hrs 15 mins)**. 8 The path runs between the farm and its threshing circle then swings to the right and begins to climb up towards the Río Culo de Perro. Beneath you, to your right, the dry water channel of *Acequia del Mundo* looks like a broad footpath. The path eventually winds down and crosses the Río Culo de Perro 150m upstream from a point where the banks of the stream have been shored up with concrete. 9

The path angles steeply upwards, less distinct at this point, but cairns guide you safely on up. After climbing for some 15 minutes the path divides. Bear left, still following cairns, and climb up the river Culo de Perro's rocky right bank (marked on some maps as *Chorreras Negras* – literally 'the small, dark waterfalls': you'll see why). Crossing back over the rocky river bed 10 a final steep climb takes you to the threshhold of the glacial cirque of Siete Lagunas **(3 hrs 45 mins)** 11 and the first of the lagoons, *Laguna Hondera*. In front of you a rocky divide links the Alcazaba (3360m) and the Mulhacén (3478m), both of which can be climbed from here.

You could end your ascent at this point. My preferred option is to climb to the third of the seven lagoons, the beautiful *Laguna Altera*. If you plan to do this follow along the left side of *Laguna Hondera* to its northwestern end. From here follow the course of the its principle stream up to another flat swathe of ground where, to the left, you'll see the second lagoon. Head across to the far left of this flat expanse then follow the stream up to a third level to reach the beautiful *Laguna Altera*. It is a fittingly beautiful recompense for the long climb up from Trevélez **(4 hrs)**. 12

After allowing yourself ample time to drink in your surroundings retrace your footsteps back to Trevélez **(6 hrs 30 mins)**.

Cazorla

Génave
Torres de Albanchez
Puente de Génave
La Puera de Segura
Arroyo del Ojanco
N-322
Segura de la Sierra
Beas de Segura
Hornos
Villanueva del Arzobispo
Emb. de Tranco
Torre del Vinagre
La Iruela
CAZORLA

CAZORLA

THE AREA

The Cazorla Natural Park, or the *Parque Natural de las Sierras de Cazorla, Segura and Las Villas* to give it its full title, lies at the eastern edge of the province of Jaén and is about a two hour drive north-east from Granada. The most common way to approach the Park is from the west by way of the endless groves of olives that stretch away as far as the eye can see. After this unremitting monoculture it comes as welcome relief to see, up ahead in the distance, the jagged outline of the Peña de los Halcones which towers above the town of Cazorla (886m) and which stands sentinel to the Natural Park to which it gives its name.

The Park is Spain's largest protected area and covers no less than 214,000 hectares of incredibly diverse terrain. There are vast extensions of pine forests, broad river valleys, deep canyons, spectacular waterfalls and jagged peaks of karst that rise to 2000 metres and more. You couldn't hope to find more beautiful walking country.

The abundance of game on the thickly forested hillsides meant that the region was long popular as a place to hunt. But by the fifties the pickings were becoming so scarce that the area was declared a National Hunting Reserve. The original idea was simple: to increase the number of moving targets. Red deer and wild boar were reintroduced, mouflon brought from France and fallow deer from the mountains of Segovia. Numbers were carefully monitored, hunting controlled and it soon began to pay big dividends. The population of the *Cabra Hispánica* (Spanish mountain goat) alone rose tenfold in less than two decades and Cazorla was back on the map as a place to pot game.

The subsequent declaration of the reserve as a Natural Park (1986) with much tighter controls on hunting has helped make the region one of the best in Iberia for the observation of wild mammals. Add to this an impressive roll call of birds of prey (several types of eagle, griffon and Egyptian vultures, goshawks, hobbies and many more besides), the region's exceptional flora – there are over 2000 species with no less than two dozen endemic to the Park – and you begin to get a measure of the uniqueness of the Park.

Most walkers base themselves in Cazorla at the south-eastern tip of the Park: the area immediately to the east contains some of the area's most dramatic scenery. Although the town attracts many visitors it makes an ideal base for tackling most of the walks described in this section. The town has accommodation for all budgets as well as some great restaurants: be sure to eat at least once in the delightful Plaza de Santa María at the south end of the town.

In recent years the number of agencies offering 4-Wheel drive excursions have multiplied as have the number of tourist developments lining the Guadalquivir valley. Segura, the starting point for the walk at the northern end of the park, is well away from the more touristy bits and is well worth an overnight stay.

The best time to walk in Cazorla is from late March to early June and from September to early November. Temperatures plummet in the winter months and roads are often closed with snowfalls. To really enjoy the walks in the Park you need to be in reasonably good shape: nearly all the routes described have at least one long, steep climb. Try to avoid the weekends and public holidays in Cazorla.

Other Walks

Don't waste time with the Park Authorities Office in Cazorla. They have no written or even verbal advice to offer. And the tourist offices in Cazorla are really just private travel agencies that try to sell you one of their own guided walks or jeep excursions. The Penthalon guide *Andar por El Parque Natural de las Sierra de Cazorla, Segura y Las Villas* by Gonzalo Crespo lists some routes in the Park in Spanish (nearly all up and down walks) but most require a lengthy drive first thing. At the northern end of the Park a number of routes have recently been waymarked out from the village of Siles. It's an attractive area although less dramatic than that around Cazorla. The Alpina 1.40000 map includes a booklet describing (in Spanish) some walking routes. These are highlighted on the individual maps but the route descriptions are very scant in detail.

Maps

The Pentathlon 1:50000 Plano Topográfico de las Sierras de Cazorla, Segura y Las Villas, based on the IGN series 'L', covers the whole of the area in just one map but is rather unwieldy. A good map that you can easily find in Cazorla is the Alpina 1.40000 series.

If planning to do all of the walks detailed in this chapter, you'll need four of the IGN 1:50000 maps: Orcera (887/22-35), Cazorla (928/21-37), Canal de San Clemente (929/22-37) and Santiago de la Espada (908/22-36). The Río Borosa walk spans all four maps.

BEST PLACES TO SLEEP & EAT

CAZORLA

Molino la Farraga

Tel: 953 721 249 Email: farraga@teleline.es

A beautiful converted mill in a leafy valley close to the Santa Ana church. €67 + 7% VAT. (Taxis: Urbano 608 854 701 or Antonio 953 720 837). **Best Eats:** here or at Restaurante La Cueva de Juan Pedro just 2 minutes away.

Hotel Guadalquivir

Tel: 953 720 268 Email: info@hguadalquivir.com

A friendly, family-run hotel close to Cazorla's main square and popular with walking groups from the UK. Rooms are basic, clean and comfortable. €48 + 7% VAT. (Taxis: Fran 659 670 592). **Best Eats:** La Cueva de Juan Pedro.

LA IRUELA

La Finca Mercedes

Tel: 953 721 087 Email: info@lafincamercedes.com

Just outside Cazorla, on the road to La Iruela. Comfortable rooms, great food, excellent value: a perfect base for your walks. Pool and garden. €39-€42 + 7% VAT. (Taxis: Urbano 608 854 701 or Antonio 953 720 837). **Best Eats:** here or at Bar La Cueva de Juan Pedro in town.

SEGURA DE LA SIERRA

La Mesa Segureña

Tel: 953 482 101 Email: lamesaseg@hosteleria.net

Beautifully decorated apartments at the heart of a pretty village with an attractive restaurant offering regional specialities. €60-€75 incl. breakfast and daily cleaning. (Taxis: in Orcera @ 7km, Sr Herrero 953 482 112). **Best Eats:** here.

WITHIN THE PARK

Hotel de Montaña Los Parrales

Tel: 953 126 170 Email: manoloparralaes@yahoo.es

A small hotel, between Cazorla and Hornos/Segura, in a peaceful location over-looking the El Tranco reservoir. Pleasant rooms, simple home cooking, rather chaotic service. Approx. €50 + 7% VAT including breakfast. (Taxis: see Cazorla listings). **Best Eats:** here.

Parador El Adelantado

Tel: 953 727 075 Email: cazorla@parador.es

The best thing about the parador is its beautiful, isolated position just beyond El Puerto del Tejo on the other side of the high ridge above Cazorla. But it's a long drive from the town (40+ minutes). €90-€120 + 7% VAT. (Taxis: see Cazorla listings). **Best Eats:** here.

CAZORLA SOUTHEASTERN CIRCUIT

Distance: 5.5 kms **Duration:** 2 hours **Rating:** Easy

Map: Alpina 1:40000 Sierra de Cazorla or IGN 1:50000 Cazorla (928/21-37)

Water: fill up at beginning of walk at the springs in the main square

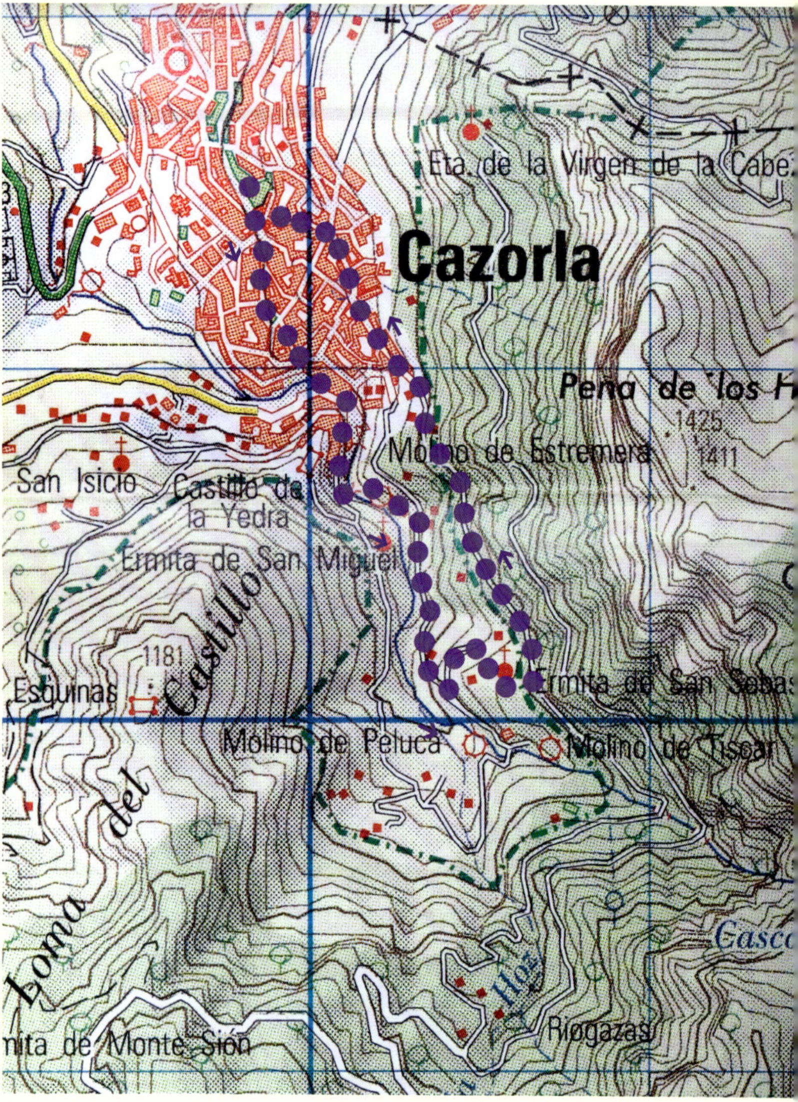

1 The Walk of Glenn's Mill

This is a short, easy walk out from Cazorla that covers little distance but gives you a feel for the valley and the kind of terrain that awaits you should you choose to do some of the longer circuits in the Park: it would be a perfect short walk on the day of your arrival. It leaves the village from the beautiful Plaza de Santa María then follows a dirt track gently up Cazorla's river valley to the small mountain chapel of San Sebastián before looping back to the village along a higher path. I can never walk this valley without fondly remembering Glenn Minard, an amiable American who lived for many years in one of the old mills that you pass by on this walk. He chose a heavenly spot to spend the later years of his life.

The Route

The walk begins in front of the hotel Cuidad de Cazorla in the main square of Cazorla, the Plaza de la Corredera. 1 Cross the square and go down the street just to the left of the Banesto bank, Calle de la Nubla. At the end of this street bear left following signs for *Casco Histórico*. Passing by a small square and then a drinking fountain head down a narrow street past a traffic light to the square of Santa María. Cross the square, pass in front of the La Cueva don Pedro restaurant 2 and follow the street upwards passing by the ruined church of Santa María to your left (under restoration when this guide went to press).

At the first fork bear left into Camino del Angel. After approx. 250m you come to a sign *Molino La Farraga*. Here bearing left cross the bridge over the Cazorla river in the direction indicated by a sign *Ermita de San Sebastián.* 3 Pass by Molino de la Farraga just to one side of the track where the eponymous Glenn once lived: it is now a B&B and a lovely one to boot.

Continuing upwards the dirt track soon meets with a concreted section of track. Here go right 4 and head up along a narrow track which hugs the left bank of the river and soon turns to dirt. Continue along the track until you reach a green sign post marking *Cazorla 2.15 km* **(30 mins)**.

Here swing hard round to the left 5 and climb up a dirt road passing a small shed built into the rocks. The track runs up to a house with a triple-arched terrace. Here bear right 6 following waymarking. After 80m the track divides. Don't branch left to a metal gate but rather continue straight on. Shortly you arrive at the Ermita de San Sebastián. 7 This is a fabulous place for a break: there are panoramic views across the Cazorla valley, up to the high sierra and westwards to the sea of olive groves that stretches away towards Úbeda and Baeza.

The path passes the chapel, bears left, then climbs up towards a stand of pines. Some 200m after the chapel, climbing parallel to a metal fence, you reach a dirt track. Turn left 8 onto the track and, passing by an enormous cairn 9 head back towards Cazorla. Heading along the path you soon pass a water deposit then, descending, pass a second deposit. Just before reaching the first of the town's buildings bear sharp left and drop down to meet Calle Paseo del Solar.

Continue steeply down Calle Paseo del Solar and 20m past a phone box cut left into Calle del Solar Bajo. 10 Continue down some steep steps then turn right into Calle de la Torre. At the end of this street bear left then right, and right again, into Calle de Mariano Extremera. Turn left at the very end of this street and then bear sharp right and follow the street along past the *Agencia de la Seguridad Social*. Turn left at the end, descend, then bear right into Calle Gómez Calderón. You arrive back at the Plaza de la Corredera **(1 hr 30 mins)**. 1

CAZORLA SOUTHWESTERN CIRCUIT

Distance: 14 kms **Duration:** 5 hours **Rating:** Medium

Map: Alpina 1:40000 Sierra de Cazorla or IGN 1:50000 Cazorla (928/21-37)

W Water: at spring by Gilillo path junction @ 2 hrs 45 mins and waypoint 22

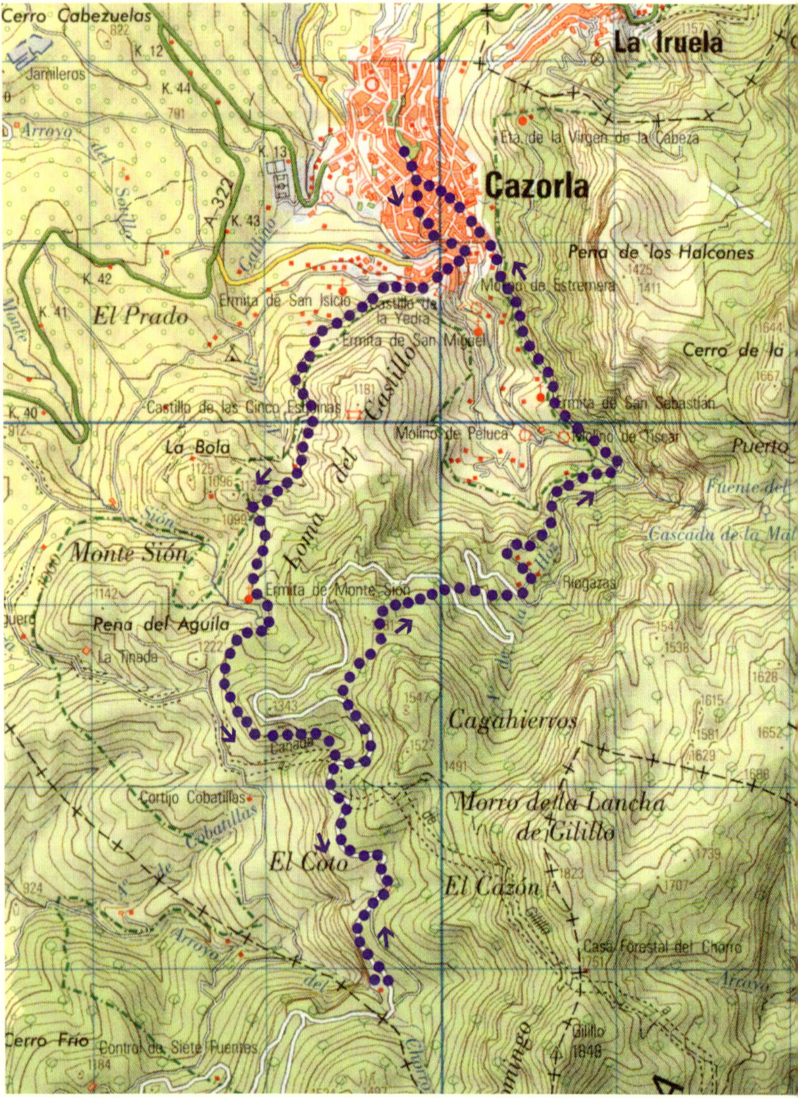

2 The Walk of Mount Sion & the Five Cornered Castle

This is a another cracking walk with a huge variety of terrain. After leaving Cazorla via its delightful Plaza de Santa María you have a steep climb via a track which loops up beneath the Castillo de las Cinco Esquinas, the Five Cornered Castle, to the beautiful Montesión monastery: at present it is manned by just one monk, Fray Antonio from Perú. This makes a great place for a first break. From here you cut up through the pine forest to the viewing point of El Chorro: from its steep cliff face the vistas are breathtaking and this is one of the best places in the Park, and in Andalusia, for the observation of griffon vultures and lammergeiers. Doubling back on a short section of the walk you angle up across the mountainside to meet with the path which leads up to El Gilillo pass. From this junction it's downhill all the way: once you're past the Riogazas control point a pretty path leads you past the NaceElRío (sic) spring then down through cultivated terraces to Cazorla.

The Route

The walk begins in front of the hotel Cuidad de Cazorla in the main square of Cazorla, the Plaza de la Corredera. 1 Cross the square and go down the street just to the left of the Banesto bank, Calle de la Nubla. At the end of this street, bear left following signs for *Casco Histórico*. Passing by a small square and then a drinking fountain head down a narrow street past a traffic light to the square of Santa María. Cross the square to the La Cueva de Don Pedro restaurant 2 then cut right up Camino de San Isicio. Soon you pass a row of willows and a spring. 3 W About 100 m past the fountain fork left 4 off the road and continue climbing. After 75m, at a park map, cut left at a sign for *Puerto El Gilillo*. The concreted road zigzags up and passes above the San Isicio chapel. Concrete gives way to dirt 5 as the track continues to loop uphill: there's P.R./G.R. waymarking. You reach a fork **(20 mins)**. 6

Here cut left and continue climbing: the five cornered castle is now above you to the left. The track levels, runs through a stand of pines, then loops right and passes above a water deposit. Careful! As the track bears once more left, branch right 7 up a steep path which climbs steeply then merges once more with the track. 8 Bearing left you pass a sign prohibiting the passage of cycles and motorbikes. You again pick up waymarking as the terrain becomes more denuded of trees. Shortly, where the track loops left, go straight ahead along a footpath to a wooden sign for *El Gilillo*. 9 Next to it a pannel explains the history of the Montesión monastery which is now just to your right **(55 mins)**.

After a break and visiting Montesión, ignoring the sign for *El Gilillo*, continue along the monastery's periphery fence via a broad path lined with cypress trees. Descending it soon merges with a broader forestry track. You pass a small white concrete hut then loop up into the trees along a broad, cobbled path. You again pick up waymarking and shortly pass a marker post for *El Chorro, 2 hrs 24 mins*. 10 Don't worry: it will take you half that time. The path passes through a metal gate and continues to climb. Views open out to the south and the west whilst ahead you'll now be able to spot the steep cliff face of El Chorro. You reach a junction in the path. 11

Here cut right. The path runs up to meet with a broad track 12 opposite another sign for *El Gilillo*. Here turn right and follow the track round the mountainside. Just before you reach the *Casa Forestal* cut right 13 and drop down through the trees to the picnic area at the walled edge of the El Chorro cliff face **(1 hr 45 mins)**.

After taking in the raptor activity, and gulping in the views,

retrace your footsteps back to waypoint 12. 12 From here continue along the track for 800m then cut right 14 on a broad path which immediately passes a wire slung between two metal posts. The path arcs right, runs uphill across an open tract of land then descends past a huge cairn. 15 Continue straight ahead into a thick stand of pines. The trees soon give way to more open terrain, Cazorla comes into sight, and you reach a spring and drinking troughs **(2 hrs 25 mins)**. 16 W

At a fork just beyond the troughs by a small cairn take the lower left hand option: the path to the right leads up to El Gilillo. The path descends to meet with the track that you left earlier 17 by a map of the Park. Angle right across the track and continue down the path which soon crosses the track a second time before, dropping steeply down, reaching it for a third time. 18 Here turn right. After just 75m you pass the white and green barrier of the Riogazas forestry control point. Just past the barrier cut left and drop down to the entrance gate of the Ríogazas hotel (closed for much of the year). Here cut left at a sign for *Mirador* and follow the track down to the viewing point. 19

After taking in the views continue down the track which, bearing right, passes beneath a picnic area then runs past a double-spouted spring 20 W before it loops down, crossses a bridge 21 then after passing above two houses and a water deposit runs by the spring of NaceElRío. 22 20m past the spring you reach a wooden sign post. Cut left following a sign for *Cazorla* and continue down towards the village. Soon the path widens to become a track which crosses a stone bridge then runs above the Chapel of San Sebastián.

You reach a fork by an enormous cairn. 23 Go straight ahead towards Cazorla. Soon you pass a water deposit then, descending, pass a second deposit. Just before reaching the first of the town's buildings bear sharp left and drop down to

meet Calle Paseo del Solar. Continue to descend and some 20m past a phone box swing left into Calle del Solar Bajo. Drop down steep steps and at the bottom turn right into Calle de la Torre. At the end of this street bear left then right, and right again, into Calle de Mariano Extremera. Turn left at the end of the street and then sharp right then pass by the *Agencia de la Seguridad Social*. Turn left at the end of the street, descend, then bear right into Calle Gómez Calderón. You arrive back at the Plaza de la Corredera **(1 hr 30 mins)**. 1

CAZORLA EASTERN CIRCUIT

Distance: 16/12 kms **Duration:** 6.5/7 or 5.5/6 hours **Rating:** Medium/Difficult

Map: Alpina 1:40000 Sierra de Cazorla or IGN 1:50000 Cazorla (928/21-37)

Ⓦ **Water:** spring by drinking troughs @ approx 1 hr 40 mins

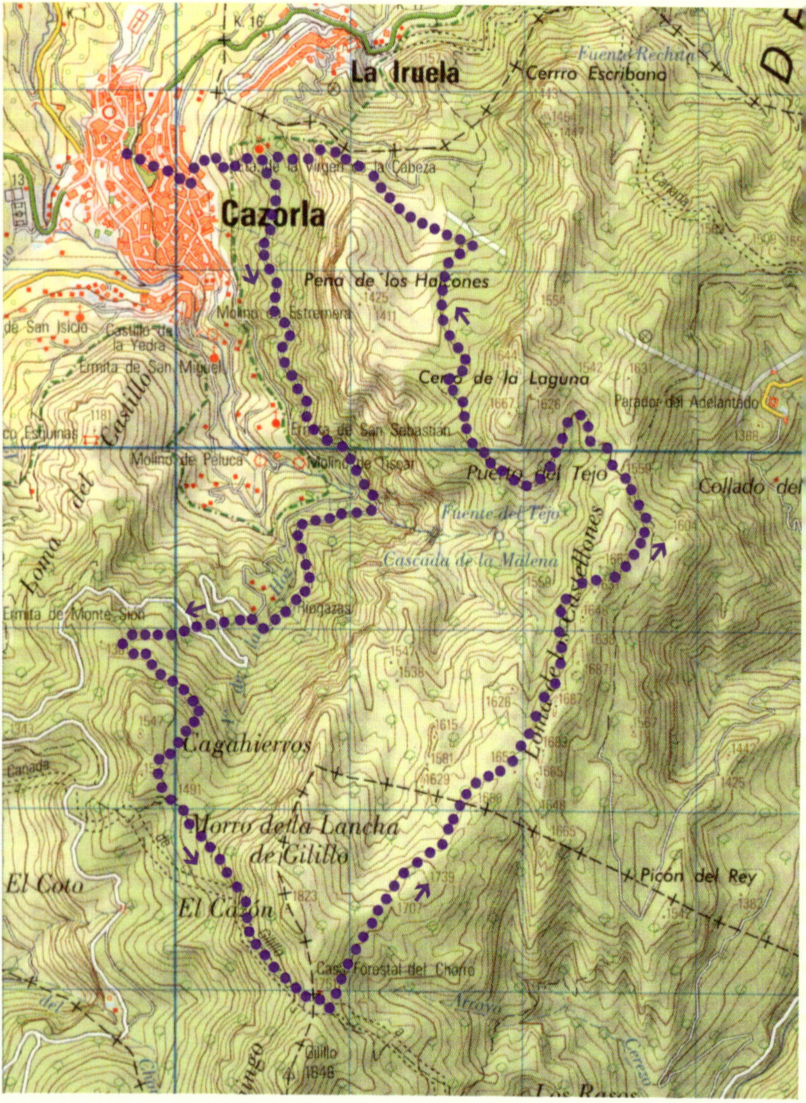

3 The Walk of the High Sierra

This circular walk from Cazorla, mostly along high mountain trails, is one of the Sierra's classic itineraries and well deserves its reputation. A long climb of nearly 900m up from the village takes you to a high pass from where the peak of El Gilillo (1848m) is easily climbed. On a clear day you are treated to amazing views of the distant Sierra Nevada, the mountains close to Antequera and all the way to the Sierra de las Nieves in the province of Málaga. From the Gilillo pass a beautiful high mountain trail brings you back to Cazorla in a long, lazy loop: it's a wonderful reward for your efforts earlier in the day. If you find the long climb intimidating you can avoid the initial 3km of mountain road above Cazorla by taking a taxi to the barrier by the Hotel Ríogazas. In spring, autumn and winter be prepared for cold conditions on the higher, often windy section of this walk. And if climbing Gilillo add an hour to the timings below.

The Route

The walk begins in in front of the hotel Cuidad de Cazorla in the main square of Cazorla, the Plaza de la Corredera. 1 Turn left along the top of the square and take the first left up Calle del Carmen. Climb steeply and opposite a church, La Iglesia del Carmen, turn right into Calle de Mercedes Gómez. Pass the *Juzgados* (courts) and at the end of the road swing left, climb, then bear sharp left again into Calle del Herrón. Follow this street up. Soon it bears right, left, then right. It narrows to become a path that climbs past a G.R.7 marker post 2 as you leave the last of the village's houses behind.

When you reach a concrete water pipe bear left and head up through the pines following white and red G.R. waymarking to a viewing platform. 3 Here you meet with the road that runs all the way round the bowl of the valley **(25 mins)**. Turn right onto the road. Soon you'll have good views of Cazorla down to the right. Ignore a waymarked G.R. cross telling you're on the wrong route. On the other side of the valley, the Castillo de Cinco Esquinas *(The Castle of the Five Corners)* is clearly visible on its bare, hill-top perch. Continue round the bowl of the valley and cross the Ríogazas River. Passing two beige concrete huts you arrive at a white hut, a *Stop* sign and a barrier **(1 hr 5 mins)**. 4

Continue past the barrier for 70m to a sign to the left of the track for *Ríogazas.* Here swing left away from the track on to a footpath and begin climbing. At first the path is indistinct but after just a few metres it improves. You wind up through pines to meet the track again. Go straight over and continue on up the path which angles sharply to the right. Soon you meet the track a second time at a point where there's a large sign with a map of the park. Angle across the track and pick up the path once again following the direction of a sign pointing to *Puerto El Gilillo*. Zigzagging up you reach more open terrain then arrive at a row of three feeding troughs and a spring where the path divides. 5 W Here angle left (there's a cairn) and climb on up into the pine forest.

The path passes beneath a cliff face where you cross sections of loose scree before bearing sharply right and climbing again. Cairns mark the path and soon you pass another sign for *El Gilillo, 1 hr*. 6 To your right, on a clear day, you will see the distant Sierra Nevada and, much closer to you, the plateau of El Chorro. The vegetation becomes sparser and the path looser underfoot as you climb on to the top of the Puerto Gilillo pass (1740m) **(2 hrs 30 mins)**. 7

(Here you could bear off to the right and climb Gilillo (1848m). If doing so cut right and when you reach an open area, angle across to its left end. Cutting right once more you climb past a

rocky outcrop then pick up an indistinct path that leads up the peak's northwest face to the summit. You'll need to use your hands as well as feet on a couple of occasions. 8 Allow 45 minutes to get up and down from the Puerto Gilillo).

At the top of the pass head straight down the far side for 20m then cut left towards a square stone hut. Just above it you pick up a narrow footpath that runs just beneath the ridge of Loma de Castellones. At times it's indistinct but cairns, green arrows and a few wooden marker posts plot your course. The path climbs then crosses the ridge that has been running to your right at its far end **(3 hrs)**. 9

20m after crossing the ridge you pass by three huge cairns where you'll see a marker post for *Ermita, 2 hrs 30 mins*. 10 Carry straight on through a mixed stand of pine and juniper. You soon pass two large cairns to the left of the path. After descending for a short distance you climb once again along a beautiful section of path. At a large cairn 11 the path swings right and descends. After reaching another stand of pines it runs across a more open area.

Follow cairns across this flatter area past a marker post 12 where a jagged outcrop of limestone juts vertically upwards: this could be a beautiful picnic spot. The path cuts through the jagged line of rocks then, bearing left, merges with a track. It soon narrows once again, now descending slightly. There is yellow and white P.R. waymarking. Soon you'll see the red roof of the Parador down to your right. Fencing runs to either side of the path as you reach El Puerto del Tejo **(3 hrs 30 mins)**. 13

Here the path divides. Ignore the path that swings right towards the Parador but rather turn left, following a green arrow and P.R. waymarking. Beyond the pass the path descends then describes a huge loop round to the left then, cutting right, climbs for a short distance then once more descends through the pine

forest. Eventually you drop steeply down, pass beneath power lines, and arrive at the abandoned farm of Prado Redondo **(4 hrs 20 mins)**. 14

Just metres before you reach the farm swing left and pass above the farm's threshing circle. You now pick up a path that arcs right into the pine forest: at first it is indistinct but it soon improves and there's G.R. waymarking. Soon the path runs past some tumbledown pens before bearing right. White and red G.R. waymarking reappears. After passing through more pines the landscape again opens out as you head towards a pylon. Here the path angles right, runs along a (dry) water course then passes beneath the electrical lines. 15

A final steep, stony section brings you to the Ermita de La Virgen de la Cabeza where you pass a sign telling of its troubled history. Pass the spring by the chapel's entrance 16 W then head for the metal cross to the left of the chapel and pick up a steep path which drops down to a road which, in turn, runs down to meet the road you followed at the start of the walk. Cross the road to the *mirador* (glossary) then retrace your steps back down to the main square **(5 hrs 30 mins)**. 1

LA IRUELA CIRCUIT

Distance: 16 kms **Duration:** 5.5/6 **Rating:** Medium

Map: Alpina 1:400000 Sierra de Cazorla or IGN 1:50000 Cazorla 928

Ⓦ **Water:** at Parador @ 1 hr 50 mins & Fuente del Oso @ 2 hrs 20 mins

4 The Walk of the Thirsty Bear

This tremendously varied walk makes for a great full day excursion. Leaving the pretty village of La Iruela you first climb up past the Alberquilla spring before contouring round the northern flank of the Escribano. You then cut up and over a high pass before descending through pine forest down to the Parador. You could break here for coffee or a snack: as a walker you'll be as well received as if you were wearing a suit. From here you have a short section of tarmac to negotiate but there are great views as you descend and you'll see virtually no traffic. Once you arrive at La Fuente del Oso you once again climb along a wonderful mountain trail that cuts up from the Guadalquivir valley to a high pass. You are first treated to wonderful views up the Guadalquivir Valley and then, beyond the pass, out across the sea of olive groves that stretches west from Cazorla. The last part of the walk takes you along the path you followed earlier in the day, leading you steeply back down to La Iruela and its spectacular Templar's castle.

The Route

The walk begins in La Iruela at the base of the castle by a pedestrian crossing 1 on the road leading from Cazorla up into the park. There's plenty of parking space for cars. Heading north away from Cazorla you soon come to a double-spouted spring and, just beyond, a wafer-bricked building. Here cut right away from the road and climb up a flight of narrow steps. They lead to a narrow path which, climbing, cuts in front of a steep rock face. There are great views back to the castle of La Iruela. At first the path runs more or less parallel with the road down to your left.

The path climbs up into a stand of pines. After cutting sharply

to the right it meets another path where you should bear 2 right and continue climbing. Soon you reach a junction with a broader path. Turn left 3 and, continuing along the path, you pass by a spring, La Fuente de la Alberquilla **(17 mins)**. It is sometimes dry. 4 Soon the path comes to a fork. 5 Ignore the lower option but rather bear right and upwards, following G.R. waymarking **(35 mins)**. After climbing steeply you reach a point where the path divides **(1 hr)**. 6

Here turn right and continue climbing. The path zigzags up and crosses an open ridge 7 where it passes by a huge cairn and eventually leads you to the top of the pass **(1 hr 25 mins)**. 8 The path, having arched right then left, crosses a more open area then begins to descend. It widens to become a track and

shortly divides. 9 Don't take the right branch which leads up to El Puerto del Tejo but rather cut left and continue your descent along a broad forestry track. The track leads down to a stone building where there's a map of the park. Just beyond this building bear hard left. After descending for 50m you reach a road that cuts in right to the Parador **(1 hr 50 mins)**. 10 W

You could head right for refreshments at the Parador. Otherwise bear left along the tarmac road, still descending. There are great views across the valley to the rugged massif of the eastern flank of the Guadalquivir valley. Having passed a group of forestry buildings and a picnic area you reach the Fuente del Oso, 'The Spring of the Bear' **(2 hrs 20 mins)**. 11 W

Just 25m past the spring, where the road arcs right, cut left at a G.R. post onto a path which climbs steeply upwards into the forest. Soon you pass a green pylon with a metal sign for *Alta Tensión*. At first you follow a line of pylons upwards. To your left is the Cerro de la Torquilla. You come to a fork at a point where another wooden posted electricity line crosses above you. 12

Here angle left and continue climbing up through the pine forest towards El Collado del Oso. Red and white G.R. waymarking reappears. This is a stunning section of path and easy to follow. The path drops down for a short distance, crosses a scree slope then resumes its ascent. There are long views up the Guadalquivir valley, over to your right. Eventually you pass through El Puerto de los Arenales (1358m) This could make a good picnic spot **(3 hrs 20 mins)**. 13 Beyond the pass the path runs level for a short distance before angling hard left then descending. Some 500m beyond the pass you reach the junction that you passed earlier in the walk. 6 From here retrace your footsteps back to your point of departure **(4 hrs 10 mins)**. 1

THE RÍO BOROSA

Distance: 21 kms **Duration:** 7/7.5 hours **Rating:** Difficult **Map:** Alpina 1:400000 Sierra de Cazorla or IGN 1:50000 Villacarillo (907/21-36), Cazorla (928/21-37), Cana de San Clemente (929/22-37) and Santiago de la Espada (908/22-36)

Ⓦ **Water:** several springs in the gorge and @ 3 hrs at the source of the Borosa

5 The Walk of the Mighty Canyon

The Sierra's best-known walk takes you along a beautiful section of the spectacular gorge of the Rio Borosa. This is a walk that gets better and better the higher you climb. After a stretch of forestry track the gorge narrows down and you follow a spectacular wooden walkway suspended above the river. Later the gorge again opens out and you reach a huge, natural ampitheatre of soaring limestone crags. From here a steep climb takes you up to a high reservoir via the course of a mill race that has been tunneled out of the mountainside. Don't worry if you think this route might be too much of a challenge: you return by the same path so the walk can be as long as you like. Bear in mind that you have a climb of 600m should you do the whole itinerary and remember, too, that this is a well-known walk so is best tackled on a weekday out of the holiday season. Take a torch for the tunnels and in the warmer months remember your swimming costume: there are lovely river pools before you climb up to the tunnels. The upper section of the walk is sometimes impassable in winter so always check with the Park rangers at Torre de Vinagre or with one of the agencies in Cazorla if walking the route when there's snow about.

The Route

The walk begins next to a map of the itinerary 1 in the car park to left the of the road, just before the trout farm *(piscifactoría)* of the río Borosa. (If arriving by car turn off the A319 by the *Centro de Interpretación Torre del Vinagre* and follow signs for *Central Eléctrica*).

Follow a broad path back to the road from the car park then, passing by the fish farm and a spring, cross a bridge and turn right. 2 Follow a track past another map of the area and head along the left bank of the river. Pass signs for *Zona de Baño* – a great spot for a swim on your return – and then a sign marking the stretch of the river where angling is permitted: *Acotado de Pesca sin Muerte*. If you tickle out a trout you'll need to put it back.

Passing by another double spouted spring, and a wooden bridge across the river, continue along the river's left bank then cross a concrete bridge and swing left 3 along the river's right bank. Soon you cross back to the left bank via a wooden bridge. At a point where the track begins to bear left and climb, branch right on path marked *Cerrada de Elias* **(35 mins)**. 4

Follow a pretty path along the left bank of the river. It crosses a footbridge and, after following the right bank of the Borosa along, crosses a second bridge back to the left bank. The Borosa's gorge begins to narrow down. Soon you cross back over the river and, passing another spring, 5 W now follow a hanging catwalk along above the river through a narrow stretch of the gorge.

The path drops down and meets with the track again by a gate and a signpost of the different species of birds which are found in the gorge. 6 Continue up the gorge, crossing back and forth over the river as the gorge, ever more spectacular, begins to open out. Up ahead the strata of La Cuerda de Las Banderillas and La Peña Plumera look like the layers of some fantastic wedding cake. You soon pass by another spring. 7 W Soon the track bears slightly right 8 and the towering massif of Castellón del Haza de Arriba (1504m) comes into sight and the pipeline which funnels the water down the left hand side of the valley to the electricty generating station *(El Central)*. Cross a bridge **(1 hr 45 mins)** 9 then follow a fence which runs to the right of the generating station and its outbuildings.

Go past a spring W then cross a narrow wooden bridge

and pick up a path at a sign pointing you towards *Laguna Valdeazores*. The path climbs steeply up the left bank of the river. Steel yourself for a steep climb of some 300m. Soon the path crosses a stream. 10 You could take a break beside a rock pool that you soon see to your right: it's possible to scramble down. Otherwise continue climbing.

To the left of you is the Picón del Haza. For much of the year a waterfall runs off its eastern flank. The path climbs up to the spectacular ampitheatre of the gorge's higher reaches: the mountains rise almost sheer up to 1500m. Soon you'll see a waterfall, *El Salto de los Órganos*, over to your right. The path swings steeply up over loose scree then bears right. 11 At a point where you see a second waterfall and the remains of a dam the path swings sharply left then climbs steeply across

another rocky scree slope. Soon it angles once more to the right at a sign for *Nacimiento de Aguas Negras/Laguna de Valdeazores*.

The path leads you into the tunnel 12 cut to bring water to the mill race: it's almost 350m long and the recent addition of a metal-posted safety rail between you and the channel means that a torch really is a help. You exit the tunnel via a metal gate then enter a second tunnel. 13 About 75m beyond the second tunnel you reach a fork. Here, cutting left, you shortly arrive at the left side of the dam of *El Embalse del Borosa*, *La Laguna de Aguas Negras* or *El Embalse de los Órganos*, depending on which map you happen to have **(2 hrs 45 mins)**. 14

Here the path divides 15 and you bear hard left. (You could also bear right, cross to the right hand side of the reservoir, then

continue for a quarter of an hour to the beautiful *Laguna de Valdeazores*. But because many 4-wheel drive excursions head for this spot my favoured option is the one described below).

Climb away from the water course along the left hand side of the reservoir then climb up the valley of the *Arroyo del Infierno* for 300m to the *Nacimiento de Aguas Negras* **(3 hrs)** where the Borosa rises from beneath the rocks. This is a great place to break for your picnic and you can replenish your water at the point where the Borosa wells up from beneath the rocks. 16 W

After allowing yourself time for a good rest, and maybe taking a dip in the reservoir, retrace your footsteps back down the Borosa gorge to arrive back at your point of departure **(5 hrs 30 mins)**. 1

SEGURA DE LA SIERRA CIRCUIT

Distance: 13.5 kms **Duration:** 5.5 hours **Rating:** Medium

Map: Alpina 1:400000 Sierra de Cazorla or IGN 1:50000 Orcera (887/22-35)

Ⓦ **Water:** spring @ Fuente dc la Tejailla @ 50 mins

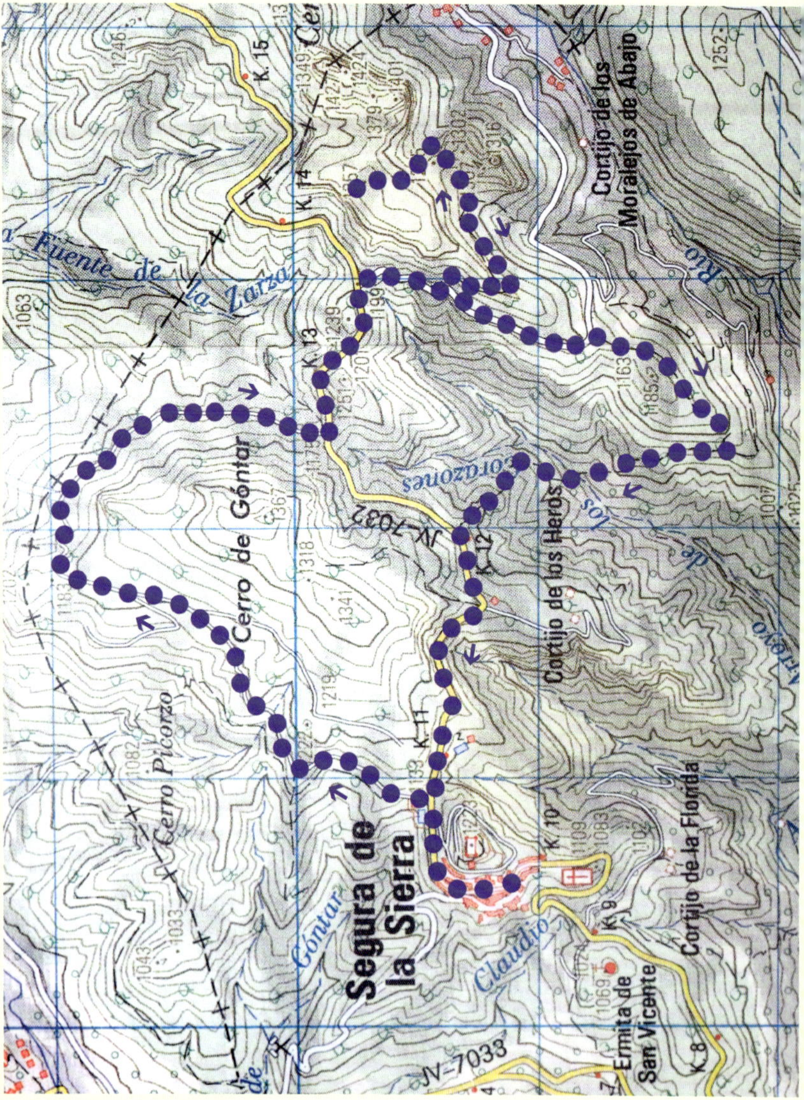

6 The Walk of Courtesan's Peak

This walk has superb views of the different mountain ranges that surround Segura de la Sierra and makes for a great half-day excursion. After contouring round Fuentecicas you have a short section of quiet road to negotiate before returning to forestry track. From here you cut up along a narrow path to the top of the Cerro de Segura La Vieja and to the heart of an amazing group of limestone peaks. This is a place where you'll be tempted to linger and makes an ideal spot for a leisuely picnic. Retracing your footsteps for just over a kilometre you return to the forest track then pick up another narrow path which drops down into the valley of the Arroyo de los Corazones before climbing 250m back up to Segura. The chances are that you won't meet with another soul on this circuit: this end of the park is only just getting focused on attracting the walking community. It would be nice to combine this walk with an overnight stay in the beautiful village of Segura: La Mesa Segureña should be your first choice.

The Route

The walk begins in the Plaza de la Encomienda, the small square in the centre of the village, opposite the church of Nuestra Señora del Collado. There are springs here if you wish to fill your bottle with pure mountain water. W 1 Facing the church turn right and head down Calle Belisa. After passing a fountain to your right you leave the last houses of the village behind. Pass a row of cypress trees to your left and just past the municipal swimming pool and tennis court bear left 2 on a track which passes above the old washhouse.

At the very first fork, swing right by a black lamp post onto a sandy track and climb up through the pines, contouring gradually round the western flank of the Picoputas (!) peak. There are wonderful views across the valley of the River Orcera to the peak of Peñalta (1412m), easily spotted because of the fire observation hut at its peak. You will see occasional white and yellow P.R. waymarking. Climbing gently upwards you soon reach an area of more recent pine plantation. A track comes in from the right to merge with yours. 3 Carry straight on and soon you pass by a goat farm, Hoya Chaspinar, to your right **(30 mins)**. 4

After passing the farm the track swings round to the right and descends through the pines. The peak of Fuentecicas towers above you to your right and, looking left, you have fine views across the valley to Navalperal. Soon you pass a spring, la Fuente de la Tejailla. 5 W The track now climbs gently upwards and you arrive at the tarmac road **(1 hr)**. 6

Swing left onto the road (you'll see P.R. waymarking) and, after just 800m, turn right at a sign for *Moralejos*. 7 Head along the track for just 250m keeping an eye open for steps which climb steeply to the left of the track. 8 Here cut left and follow a narrow path which climbs up through the pines, holly oaks and juniper. Soon it cuts left at a P.R. marker post then, running slightly down hill, reaches a fork by two small cairns. 10 Here cut left and climb on a steep footpath up through thick clumps of rosemary which, reaching a more open tract of ground, angles left and crosses a (dry) stream. Soon you pass by two drinking troughs (old bath tubs) 11 and immediately pass just to the left of an old stone wall. Head straight on up to a low coll. 12 Here, looking to your left, you'll spot P.R. waymarking and cairns which you should follow on upwards. After a steep climb the path angles hard right, then at a waymarked lonesome pine cuts left and takes you up to the top of the ridge. My favourite spot is the second highest point on the ridge where another solitary pine tree 13 provides a bit of shade: the views from here

are phenomenal. After your break, retrace your footsteps back down to the track and waypoint 8, taking care not to miss the sharp turning to the right at waypoint 10.

When you reach the bottom of the steps 8 turn left along the track. The castle above Segura soon comes into view. You reach a ridge with a line of electricity pylons at a point where the road loops sharply left. Here swing right off the road onto a track leading down towards a pylon. The Trújula gorge is down to your left. After following the ridge along the track ends: head straight on, following a narrow path which runs just to the left of the ridge through thick undergrowth. Look for cairns and stick to the clearest path. After dropping steeply downwards you reach a much clearer path. 14 Here cut right and follow the path gently uphill as it bears round to the right and contours round the Collado del Acebuche before narrowing to become a path **(1 hr 45 mins)**.

Continuing your descent through the pines you reach an olive grove. The narrow path loops down, crosses the Arroyo de los

Corazones 15 then zigzags up the other side where it widens. At this point you again pick up P.R. waymarking. The path climbs steeply upwards, crossing back and forth over a very steep track with which it later merges before once again looping away from it. Views open out across the valley as you climb on upwards, always looking for P.R. waymarking. The path crosses a more open, level swathe of ground 16 then climbs once more. Eventually it levels again, runs parallel with the road for approximately 100m, then cuts up to the tarmac. 17

Bear left and follow the road back to the village. Arriving at the outskirts of Segura 18 you reach a sign for *Castillo*. Here turn left and, climbing, you reach a junction. If you plan to the visit the castle cut left. Otherwise bear right. You pass above the unusual, square *Plaza de Toros*. At the next fork go left along Calle Castillo which descends and arrives at the Mirador de los Diestros. Here bear sharply right, then left, then right again. Bearing left once more you arrive back to your point of departure **(3 hrs)**. 1

GPS Coordinates

ARACENA

The Walk of the Virgin & the Pigs

1	29 S 714535 4197078
2	29 S 714790 4197328
3	29 S 715157 4197662
4	29 S 715349 4197727
5	29 S 715771 4198027
6	29 S 716756 4198169
7	29 S 717182 4198233
8	29 S 717745 4198116
9	29 S 718299 4197770
10	29 S 718746 4197481
11	29 S 719059 4197598
12	29 S 719035 4197671
13	29 S 718452 4197210
14	29 S 718166 4197262
15	29 S 717756 4197003
16	29 S 717680 4196988
17	29 S 716996 4197237
18	29 S 716593 4197105
19	29 S 716133 4197109
20	29 S 715708 4197056
21	29 S 715373 4196929
22	29 S 714893 4196945
23	29 S 714900 4196880

The Walk of the Bountiful Deshea

1	29 S 714531 4197071
2	29 S 714065 4196758
3	29 S 713447 4196066
4	29 S 712741 4195445
5	29 S 712178 4194974
6	29 S 712006 4194738
7	29 S 711877 4194545
8	29 S 711430 4194352
9	29 S 711074 4194533
10	29 S 709493 4195102
11	29 S 709400 4195218
12	29 S 709461 4195400
13	29 S 709950 4195809
14	29 S 710127 4195924
15	29 S 710553 4195812
16	29 S 711141 4195753
17	29 S 711763 4195912
18	29 S 712289 4195956
19	29 S 713201 4196268

The Walk of the Forgotten Hamlet

1	29 S 705428 4194657
2	29 S 705698 4194468
3	29 S 706082 4194339
4	29 S 706961 4193759
5	29 S 707459 4193925
6	29 S 707908 4194221
7	29 S 708029 4194431
8	29 S 708257 4194652
9	29 S 708257 4194652
10	29 S 709195 4195277
11	29 S 709195 4195276
12	29 S 708403 4195255
13	29 S 707149 4195418
14	29 S 706494 4195178
15	29 S 705897 4194788

The Walk of the Sensible Hippy

1	29 S 705390 4194672
2	29 S 705293 4194570
3	29 S 704647 4194172
4	29 S 704418 4194089

5	29 S 704123 4194004
6	29 S 703931 4193985
7	29 S 703829 4193782
8	29 S 703207 4193421
9	29 S 702888 4193313
10	29 S 702616 4193201
11	29 S 702407 4193248
12	29 S 701892 4193261
13	29 S 700981 4193399
14	29 S 700901 4193426
15	29 S 701148 4193746
16	29 S 701072 4194311
17	29 S 701328 4194330
18	29 S 701417 4194443
19	29 S 701726 4194568
20	29 S 701944 4195709
21	29 S 701732 4196421
22	29 S 702011 4196871
23	29 S 702078 4196896
24	29 S 702824 4196121
25	29 S 703602 4195426
26	29 S 703843 4195111
27	29 S 704043 4194875
28	29 S 704374 4194725

The Walk of the Sylvan Valley

1	29 S 701194 4200301
2	29 S 701149 4200173
3	29 S 701223 4200152
4	29 S 700978 4200003
5	29 S 700726 4199568
6	29 S 700739 4198566
7	29 S 700633 4198227
8	29 S 700605 4198131
9	29 S 700845 4197451
10	29 S 701571 4196974
11	29 S 701714 4196991
12	29 S 701831 4197131
13	29 S 701482 4198009
14	29 S 701527 4198707
15	29 S 701755 4199051
16	29 S 701774 4199360
17	29 S 701769 4199581
18	29 S 701777 4199808

The Walk of Patience & Humility

1	29 S 694694 4194128
2	29 S 694299 4194404
3	29 S 694237 4194494
4	29 S 693792 4194832
5	29 S 693276 4194929
6	29 S 692990 4195162
7	29 S 692543 4195255
8	29 S 692387 4195257
9	29 S 692338 4195316
10	29 S 692341 4195646
11	29 S 692401 4195763
12	29 S 692449 4195942
13	29 S 692897 4196206
14	29 S 693167 4196181
15	29 S 693370 4196196
16	29 S 694609 4195808
17	29 S 694674 4195801
18	29 S 694773 4195601
19	29 S 694935 4195226
20	29 S 695278 4194600
21	29 S 695196 4194497
22	29 S 695041 4194290

GRAZALEMA

The Walk of Mr Henderson's Railway

1	30 S 299448 4065656
2	30 S 299349 4065571
3	30 S 299487 4065519
4	30 S 298950 4064293
5	30 S 297935 4062337
6	30 S 296317 4060309
7	30 S 296162 4060030

The Walk of the Bandoleros

1	30 S 298721 4065915
2	30 S 298606 4065782
3	30 S 298498 4065459
4	30 S 298482 4065393
5	30 S 297706 4064539
6	30 S 297220 4064148
7	30 S 297045 4064052
8	30 S 296501 4063934
9	30 S 296389 4063796
10	30 S 295998 4063858
11	30 S 295661 4063958
12	30 S 295362 4063847
13	30 S 294974 4063400
14	30 S 293632 4062275
15	30 S 292330 4061344
16	30 S 291788 4060837
17	30 S 291468 4060040
18	30 S 291411 4058891
19	30 S 290993 4058484
20	30 S 290903 4058273
21	30 S 290718 4057749
22	30 S 290673 4057616
23	30 S 290863 4057304
24	30 S 290858 4057149
25	30 S 290645 4056441
26	30 S 290880 4056075
27	30 S 290864 4055612

The Walk of the Hidden Valley

1	30 S 299062 4067923
2	30 S 298764 4067971
3	30 S 296417 4066717
4	30 S 296251 4066658
5	30 S 295973 4066537
6	30 S 295592 4066423
7	30 S 294930 4066013
8	30 S 294332 4065779
9	30 S 293869 4065393
10	30 S 293478 4065830
11	30 S 293148 4066556
12	30 S 293509 4066906
13	30 S 293848 4067113
14	30 S 294485 4067137
15	30 S 294974 4067505
16	30 S 295520 4068226
17	30 S 295520 4068230
18	30 S 296646 4068983
19	30 S 296933 4069096
20	30 S 297303 4068570
21	30 S 297420 4068510

The Walk of the Goatherd's Leap

1	30 S 288918 4070881
2	30 S 288272 4071067
3	30 S 287951 4071214
4	30 S 286377 4070544

5	30 S 285373 4069569
6	30 S 284655 4069130
7	30 S 284017 4068448
8	30 S 283882 4068214
9	30 S 283822 4068108
10	30 S 283701 4068002
11	30 S 283562 4067782
12	30 S 283279 4067567
13	30 S 283288 4066317
14	30 S 283227 4066031
15	30 S 283502 4065733
16	30 S 283696 4064881
17	30 S 283784 4064459

The Walk of the Twin Peaks

1	30 S 288918 4070881
2	30 S 288234 4070965
3	30 S 288135 4070908
4	30 S 287742 4070298
5	30 S 287698 4070083
6	30 S 287545 4069958
7	30 S 287558 4069006
8	30 S 287267 4068694
9	30 S 287267 4068694
10	30 S 287159 4068371
11	30 S 287407 4068280
12	30 S 287847 4068283
13	30 S 287800 4068203
14	30 S 287700 4067903
15	30 S 287725 4067831
16	30 S 287671 4067682
17	30 S 287817 4067645
18	30 S 287854 4067617
19	30 S 287854 4067617
20	30 S 288605 4068117
21	30 S 288544 4069824
22	30 S 288458 4069880
23	30 S 288300 4070196
24	30 S 288278 4070481

The Walk of the Griffon Vultures

1	30 S 286933 4080054
2	30 S 286741 4080057
3	30 S 285757 4080635
4	30 S 285187 4080729
5	30 S 284943 4080506
6	30 S 283786 4080327
7	30 S 283783 4080315
8	30 S 283925 4080053
9	30 S 283958 4079825
10	30 S 283250 4079108
11	30 S 282985 4078853
12	30 S 282930 4078686
13	30 S 282522 4077877
14	30 S 283627 4078064
15	30 S 283913 4077990
16	30 S 284335 4078668
17	30 S 284255 4078403
18	30 S 285086 4078942
19	30 S 286410 4079944
20	30 S 286685 4079937

ALCORNOCALES

The Walk of the Old Mill

1	30 S 280394 4034796
2	30 S 280230 4034791
3	30 S 280262 4034397
4	30 S 279987 4033365
5	30 S 279907 4033415
6	30 S 279367 4033554
7	30 S 279113 4033458
8	30 S 279025 4033362
9	30 S 278460 4034088
10	30 S 278787 4034403
11	30 S 278946 4034452
12	30 S 279458 4034523

The Walk of the Eagle & the Kingfisher

1	30 S 280362 4034829
2	30 S 279891 4035834
3	30 S 279777 4035904
4	30 S 279554 4036211
5	30 S 279523 4036263
6	30 S 278654 4037152
7	30 S 278339 4036634
8	30 S 278389 4036560
9	30 S 278294 4036652
10	30 S 278086 4036829
11	30 S 277948 4036333
12	30 S 277833 4036230
13	30 S 278636 4035879
14	30 S 278742 4035952
15	30 S 278867 4035939
16	30 S 279132 4035810
17	30 S 279310 4035721
18	30 S 279575 4035272
19	30 S 279586 4034571

The Walk of the Queen's Bath

1	30 S 268563 4045963
2	30 S 268538 4045819
3	30 S 268313 4045479
4	30 S 268134 4045249
5	30 S 267427 4044368
6	30 S 267285 4044751
7	30 S 267075 4044777
8	30 S 266836 4044308
9	30 S 266729 4044326
10	30 S 266585 4043972
11	30 S 266550 4043916
12	30 S 266894 4043995
13	30 S 267135 4044234
14	30 S 267377 4044398

The Walk of Melanie & the Tiger

1	30 S 291879 4044333
2	30 S 292564 4044260
3	30 S 293287 4044172
4	30 S 293238 4043344
5	30 S 292808 4043248
6	30 S 292687 4043175
7	30 S 292479 4043250
8	30 S 292335 4042836
9	30 S 292321 4042717
10	30 S 292484 4042202
11	30 S 292275 4042074
12	30 S 291846 4042407
13	30 S 291633 4042719

14	30 S 291663 4042932
15	30 S 292185 4043739
16	30 S 292377 4044247

The Walk of the Cork Cutters

1	30 S 291878 4044336
2	30 S 291878 4044393
3	30 S 291454 4044356
4	30 S 291267 4044412
5	30 S 291200 4044597
6	30 S 291079 4044708
7	30 S 290659 4044801
8	30 S 290574 4044860
9	30 S 290401 4044975
10	30 S 290375 4045049
11	30 S 290298 4045176
12	30 S 290220 4045167
13	30 S 290073 4045244
14	30 S 289960 4045404
15	30 S 289865 4045606
16	30 S 290689 4046206
17	30 S 290873 4046279
18	30 S 291364 4046717
19	30 S 291746 4046040
20	30 S 292053 4045981
21	30 S 292175 4046509
22	30 S 292317 4045944
23	30 S 292366 4045801
24	30 S 292914 4044765
25	30 S 292807 4044670

The Walk of the Vizir's Garden

1	30 S 296803 4047615
2	30 S 296486 4047710
3	30 S 296449 4047738
4	30 S 297178 4047845
5	30 S 297429 4047821
6	30 S 291079 4044708
7	30 S 297604 4047661
8	30 S 290574 4044860
9	30 S 290401 4044975
10	30 S 290375 4045049
11	30 S 290298 4045176
12	30 S 290220 4045167
13	30 S 290073 4045244
14	30 S 289960 4045404
15	30 S 289865 4045606
16	30 S 290689 4046206
17	30 S 290873 4046279
18	30 S 291364 4046717
19	30 S 291746 4046040
20	30 S 292053 4045981
21	30 S 292175 4046509
22	30 S 292317 4045944
23	30 S 292366 4045801
24	30 S 292914 4044765
25	30 S 292807 4044670

LA AXARQUIA

The Walk of Chillar Canyon

1	30 S 424479 4068976
2	30 S 424382 4071312
3	30 S 424229 4072821
4	30 S 424204 4072965
5	30 S 424208 4073217
6	30 S 423860 4073211
7	30 S 423630 4073805
8	30 S 422937 4074150
9	30 S 422983 4074226
10	30 S 422569 4073943
11	30 S 422381 4073816
12	30 S 422161 4073675
13	30 S 421726 4073295
14	30 S 421525 4073367
15	30 S 421140 4073251
16	30 S 421036 4072940
17	30 S 420629 4072796
18	30 S 420427 4072331
19	30 S 420268 4072253

The Walk of the Moor & his Parrot

1	30 S 420261 4072283
2	30 S 420412 4072326
3	30 S 420621 4072788
4	30 S 421035 4072940
5	30 S 420973 4072692
6	30 S 420968 4072374
7	30 S 420951 4071671
8	30 S 420931 4071528
9	30 S 420992 4071045
10	30 S 421061 4070955
11	30 S 420789 4070635
12	30 S 420770 4070490
13	30 S 420419 4070939

The Walk of the Cool River

1	30 S 413199 4076992
2	30 S 413358 4077012
3	30 S 413504 4076960
4	30 S 413857 4076742
5	30 S 414492 4076701
6	30 S 415103 4076825
7	30 S 415605 4077870
8	30 S 415506 4077634
9	30 S 416387 4076612
10	30 S 416271 4076526
11	30 S 416063 4075238
12	30 S 415453 4075105
13	30 S 414358 4075882
14	30 S 413544 4076450

The Walk of the High Sierra

1	30 S 413199 4076992
2	30 S 413332 4077203
3	30 S 413649 4077371
4	30 S 413997 4077804
5	30 S 414314 4077832
6	30 S 415328 4078845
7	30 S 416534 4079785
8	30 S 416731 4079903

9	30 S 417379 4080615
10	30 S 417464 4080923
11	30 S 417259 4081050
12	30 S 416308 4081348
13	30 S 415775 4081354
14	30 S 415423 4081202
15	30 S 415104 4081098
16	30 S 414541 4080831
17	30 S 413652 4080472
18	30 S 413565 4079050
19	30 S 412292 4078590
20	30 S 412452 4078527
21	30 S 412713 4077823
22	30 S 412822 4077313

The Walk of the Bountiful Valley

1	30 S 409843 4073127
2	30 S 409739 4073247
3	30 S 409902 4073960
4	30 S 410238 4074591
5	30 S 409938 4075557
6	30 S 410259 4075783
7	30 S 410351 4075767
8	30 S 409702 4075690
9	30 S 409460 4075482
10	30 S 408823 4075042
11	30 S 409418 4073937
12	30 S 409324 4073765
13	30 S 409509 4073430
14	30 S 409122 4073297
15	30 S 409843 4073127

The Walk of Stepping Stones & Mountain Chapels

1	30 S 412229 4078391
2	30 S 411929 4078522
3	30 S 411770 4078609
4	30 S 411620 4079120
5	30 S 411698 4079272
6	30 S 411709 4079347
7	30 S 411798 4079635
8	30 S 411738 4079925
9	30 S 411451 4080095
10	30 S 411429 4080238
11	30 S 412176 4080488
12	30 S 411993 4079066
13	30 S 412356 4078989

ALPUJARRAS

The Walk of the Arab Baths & Ruined Mills

1	30 S 472181 4087286
2	30 S 472781 4087399
3	30 S 472832 4087389
4	30 S 473317 4087106
5	30 S 473299 4086862
6	30 S 473582 4086483
7	30 S 474450 4087010
8	30 S 473903 4088074
9	30 S 473806 4088073
10	30 S 473428 4087814
11	30 S 473219 4087422

The Walk of Saint Anthony's Spring

1	30 S 467955 4088466
2	30 S 467950 4088625
3	30 S 467932 4088835
4	30 S 467793 4089284
5	30 S 467645 4089236
6	30 S 467348 4089642
7	30 S 467257 4089806
8	30 S 467162 4090022
9	30 S 466973 4090046
10	30 S 466999 4090202
11	30 S 466961 4090280
12	30 S 466788 4090647
13	30 S 466994 4090617
14	30 S 467187 4090664
15	30 S 467628 4091467
16	30 S 467751 4091620
17	30 S 467937 4090944
18	30 S 467958 4090601
19	30 S 467667 4090362
20	30 S 468309 4089422
21	30 S 468161 4090082
22	30 S 468313 4089468
23	30 S 468309 4089422

The Walk of the Poqueira Gorge

1	30 S 468182 4090852
2	30 S 467989 4091075
3	30 S 467906 4091667
4	30 S 467802 4092037
5	30 S 468056 4092779
6	30 S 468195 4093276
7	30 S 468514 4093566
8	30 S 468880 4093993
9	30 S 468487 4092581
10	30 S 468510 4092102
11	30 S 468395 4091611
12	30 S 468158 4091062

The Walk of the High Acequias

1	30 S 468888 4093978
2	30 S 469017 4094302
3	30 S 469065 4094642
4	30 S 469080 4094845
5	30 S 469318 4095202
6	30 S 469624 4095540

7	30 S 469888 4095722
8	30 S 469923 4095886
9	30 S 470018 4096129
10	30 S 470199 4096489
11	30 S 470424 4096720
12	30 S 470509 4096971
13	30 S 470703 4097126
14	30 S 470738 4097107
15	30 S 471019 4096559
16	30 S 470840 4096192
17	30 S 470673 4095879
18	30 S 470595 4094940
19	30 S 470229 4094539
20	30 S 469813 4093407
21	30 S 469154 4092749
22	30 S 468938 4092467
23	30 S 468741 4091792
24	30 S 468610 4091660

The Walk of the Sun Mountain

1	30 S 468504 4089514
2	30 S 468771 4090000
3	30 S 468786 4090054
4	30 S 469151 4090094
5	30 S 469255 4090249
6	30 S 469552 4089700
7	30 S 469624 4089724
8	30 S 470507 4090323
9	30 S 470525 4090409
10	30 S 470584 4090535
11	30 S 471084 4091344
12	30 S 470814 4091502
13	30 S 470485 4091651
14	30 S 471420 4092252
15	30 S 471452 4092298
16	30 S 472050 4092414
17	30 S 472679 4092602
18	30 S 472794 4091933
19	30 S 473211 4092228
20	30 S 473999 4092492
21	30 S 474294 4092805
22	30 S 474276 4093382
23	30 S 474524 4094122
24	30 S 474778 4094280
25	30 S 475259 4094348
26	30 S 475779 4094998
27	30 S 475792 4095282
28	30 S 475836 4095649
29	30 S 476039 4095503
30	30 S 476553 4094999

The Walk of the 7 Lagoons

1	30 S 476257 4095376
2	30 S 476395 4095443
3	30 S 476417 4095934
4	30 S 476862 4097099
5	30 S 476439 4097589
6	30 S 476467 4098101
7	30 S 475949 4098716
8	30 S 475902 4098717
9	30 S 474855 4099704
10	30 S 474305 4100342
11	30 S 474062 4100397
12	30 S 473473 4100950

CAZORLA

The Walk of Glenn's Mill

1	30 S 499880 4196164
2	30 S 500101 4195906
3	30 S 500120 4195646
4	30 S 500322 4195601
5	30 S 500456 4195005
6	30 S 500550 4195233
7	30 S 500494 4195097
8	30 S 500628 4195089
9	30 S 500331 4195941
10	30 S 500155 4196150

The Walk of Mount Sion & the Five Cornered Castle

1	30 S 499880 4196164
2	30 S 500101 4195906
3	30 S 499830 4195766
4	30 S 499763 4195767
5	30 S 499302 4195501
6	30 S 499159 4195199
7	30 S 499063 4194656
8	30 S 498902 4194547
9	30 S 498923 4194082
10	30 S 498782 4193753
11	30 S 499491 4193298
12	30 S 499453 4193117
13	30 S 499588 4192203
14	30 S 499300 4193436
15	30 S 499297 4193439
16	30 S 499866 4193901
17	30 S 499991 4194128
18	30 S 500214 4194072
19	30 S 500387 4194335
20	30 S 500593 4194357
21	30 S 500615 4194438
22	30 S 500854 4194692
23	30 S 500155 4196150

The Walk of the High Sierra

1	30 S 499880 4196164
2	30 S 500225 4196261
3	30 S 500471 4196305
4	30 S 500431 4194054
5	30 S 499877 4193912
6	30 S 500033 4192992
7	30 S 500786 4191985
8	30 S 500645 4191529
9	30 S 501776 4193084
10	30 S 501964 4193232
11	30 S 502336 4193997
12	30 S 502610 4194270
13	30 S 502557 4194852
14	30 S 501747 4196600
15	30 S 501347 4196458
16	30 S 500480 4196679

The Walk of the Thirsty Bear

1	30 S 501077 4197227
2	30 S 501450 4197303
3	30 S 501761 4197206
4	30 S 502189 4197470
5	30 S 502968 4197129

6	30 S 503561 4196772
7	30 S 503482 4196406
8	30 S 503295 4196216
9	30 S 503257 4196105
10	30 S 503477 4195382
11	30 S 505213 4195983
12	30 S 504721 4196422
13	30 S 504346 4196202

The Walk of the Mighty Canyon

1	30 S 511964 4207695
2	30 S 512158 4207753
3	30 S 512203 4207764
4	30 S 513728 4205828
5	30 S 514453 4205400
6	30 S 514702 4205332
7	30 S 515591 4204597
8	30 S 516269 4204397
9	30 S 516300 4203756
10	30 S 516178 4203240
11	30 S 515966 4202485
12	30 S 516092 4202657
13	30 S 516320 4202279
14	30 S 516290 4202190
15	30 S 516305 4202126
16	30 S 516442 4201945

The Walk of the Courtesan's Peak

1	30 S 530540 4239192
2	30 S 530882 4239441
3	30 S 531667 4240406
4	30 S 531782 4240798
5	30 S 532235 4240835
6	30 S 532364 4239878
7	30 S 532955 4239731
8	30 S 532970 4239465
9	30 S 532937 4239122
10	30 S 533322 4239248
11	30 S 533400 4239356
12	30 S 533427 4239428
13	30 S 533259 4239639
14	30 S 532287 4238097
15	30 S 532199 4238821
16	30 S 532079 4239213
17	30 S 531920 4239299
18	30 S 530885 4239435

Andalucian Bird Checklist

LEGEND

IUCN Red List Category		Andalucía Status	
LC	Least Concern	A	Observed since 1950
NT	Near Threatened	B	Observed prior to 1950 but not since
VU	Vulnerable	C	Introduced, established breeding
EN	Endangered	D	Unknown origin
CR	Critically Endangered	E	Escape / Introduced
EX	Extinct	*	Rarity description required by ABS
DD	Data Deficient		Considered race to scare in Andalucía

The order of birds used in this list follows the IOC World Bird List 2008. English names used are those most commonly in use and therefore recognisable by the majority of birdwatchers. The list has been compiled by Peter Jones, a nature guide based close to Ronda, who leads groups and individuals throughout the province. He also leads guided tours to other parts of Spain, Morocco and many other destinations worldwide. The author can not speak too highly of Peter's birding excursions. A natural communicator, Peter has that rare ability of conveying specialist knowledge in a way that's accessible to one and all. A day in his company offers a unique insight into the extraordinarily diverse birdlife of southern Spain and would dovetail perfectly with your walks in and around Ronda and Grazalema. To contact Peter either email pr.p.jones@gmail.com or visit **www.spanishnature.com**

Andalucia Bird Society is a great resource for exchanging and or getting information on many aspects of birding here in southern Spain. If you intend visiting this area, then an open and free forum allows you to contact locals on specific site or species information. Contibute to their database and conservation efforts by submitting your vacation trip reports or sightings to the society. www.andaluciabirdsociety.org

Species List Produced and Published by Andalucia Bird Society © 2009
References: BirdLife International www.birdlife.org, IOC World Bird List 2008 version 1.7

Species	Category	Status	Seen
Red-legged Partridge *Alectoris rufa*	LC	C	
Common Quail *Coturnix coturnix*	LC	A	
Common Pheasant *Phasianus colchicus*	LC	CE	
Greylag Goose *Anser anser*	LC	A	
Mute Swan *Cygnus olor*	LC	CE	
Shelduck *Tadorna tadorna*	LC	A	
Gadwall *Anas strepera*	LC	A	
Wigeon *Anas penelope*	LC	A	
Mallard *Anas platyrhynchos*	LC	A	
Shoveler *Anas clypeata*	LC	A	
Pintail *Anas acuta*	LC	A	
Garganey *Anas querquedula*	LC	A	
Teal *Anas crecca*	LC	A	
Marbled Teal *Marmaronetta angustirostris*	VU	A	
Red-crested *Pochard Netta rufina*	LC	A	
Pochard *Aythya ferina*	LC	A	
Ferruginous Duck *Aythya nyroca*	NT	A*	
Tufted Duck *Aythya fuligula*	LC	A	
White-headed Duck *Oxyura leucocephala*	EN	A	
Little Grebe *Tachybaptus ruficollis*	LC	A	
Red-necked Grebe *Podiceps grisegena*	LC	A	
Great Crested Grebe *Podiceps cristatus*	LC	A	
Black-necked Grebe *Podiceps nigricollis*	LC	A	
Greater Flamingo *Phoenicopterus roseus*	LC	A	
Lesser Flamingo *Phoeniconaias minor*	NT	A	
Black Stork *Ciconia nigra*	LC	A	
White Stork *Ciconia ciconia*	LC	A	
Northern Bald Ibis *Geronticus eremita*	CR	E*	
Glossy Ibis *Plegadis falcinellus*	LC	A	
Spoonbill *Platalea leucorodia*	LC	A	
Little Bittern *Ixobrychus minutus*	LC	A	
Night Heron *Nycticorax nycticorax*	LC	A	
Squacco Heron *Ardeola ralloides*	LC	A	
Cattle Egret *Bubulcus ibis*	LC	A	
Grey Heron *Ardea cinerea*	LC	A	
Purple Heron *Ardea purpurea*	LC	A	
Great (White) Egret *Ardea alba*	LC	A	
Little Egret *Egretta garzetta*	LC	A	
Great Cormorant *Phalacrocorax carbo*	LC	A	
Lesser Kestrel *Falco naumanni*	VU	A	
Common Kestrel Falco tinnunculus	LC	A	

Species	Category	Status	Seen
Red-footed Falcon *Falco vespertinus*	NT	A	
Eleonora's Falcon *Falco eleonorae*	LC	A	
Merlin *Falco columbarius*	LC	A	
Eurasian Hobby *Falco subbuteo*	LC	A	
Lanner Falcon *Falco biarmicus*	LC	D*	
Peregrine Falcon *Falco peregrinus*	LC	A	
Osprey *Pandion haliaetus*	LC	A	
Honey Buzzard *Pernis apivorus*	LC	A	
Black-winged Kite *Elanus caeruleus*	LC	A	
Red Kite *Milvus milvus*	NT	A	
Black Kite *Milvus migrans*	LC	A	
Lammergeier *Gypaetus barbatus*	LC	A	
Egyptian Vulture *Neophron percnopterus*	EN	A	
Rüppell's Vulture *Gyps rueppellii*	NT	A*	
Griffon Vulture *Gyps fulvus*	LC	A	
Black Vulture *Aegypius monachus*	NT	A	
Short-toed Eagle *Circaetus gallicus*	LC	A	
Western Marsh-harrier *Circus aeruginosus*	LC	A	
Hen Harrier *Circus cyaneus*	LC	A	
Montagu's Harrier *Circus pygargus*	LC	A	
Sparrowhawk *Accipiter nisus*	LC	A	
Goshawk *Accipiter gentilis*	LC	A	
Common Buzzard *Buteo buteo*	LC	A	
Long-legged Buzzard *Buteo rufinus*	LC	A*	
Greater Spotted Eagle *Aquila clanga*	VU	A*	
Spanish Imperial Eagle *Aquila adalberti*	VU	A	
Golden Eagle *Aquila chrysaetos*	LC	A	
Bonelli's Eagle *Hieraaetus fasciatus*	LC	A	
Booted Eagle *Hieraaetus pennatus*	LC	A	
Great Bustard *Otis tarda*	VU	A	
Little Bustard *Tetrax tetrax*	NT	A	
Water Rail *Rallus aquaticus*	LC	A	
Corncrake *Crex crex*	NT	A	
Little Crake *Porzana parva*	LC	A	
Baillon's Crake *Porzana pusilla*	LC	A	
Spotted Crake *Porzana porzana*	LC	A	
Purple (Swamphen) Gallinule *Porphyrio porphyrio*	LC	A	
Moorhen *Gallinula chloropus*	LC	A	
Red-knobbed Coot *Fulica cristata*	LC	A	
Common Coot *Fulica atra*	LC	A	
Common Crane *Grus grus*	LC	A	

Species	Category	Status	Seen
Stone Curlew *Burhinus oedicnemus*	LC	A	
Oystercatcher *Haematopus ostralegus*	LC	A	
Black-winged Stilt *Himantopus himantopus*	LC	A	
Avocet *Recurvirostra avosetta*	LC	A	
Lapwing *Vanellus vanellus*	LC	A	
Golden Plover *Pluvialis apricaria*	LC	A	
Grey Plover *Pluvialis squatarola*	LC	A	
Ringed Plover *Charadrius hiaticula*	LC	A	
Little Ringed Plover *Charadrius dubius*	LC	A	
Kentish Plover *Charadrius alexandrinus*	LC	A	
Woodcock *Scolopax rusticola*	LC	A	
Jack Snipe *Lymnocryptes minimus*	LC	A	
Common Snipe *Gallinago gallinago*	LC	A	
Black-tailed Godwit *Limosa limosa*	NT	A	
Bar-tailed Godwit *Limosa lapponica*	LC	A	
Whimbrel *Numenius phaeopus*	LC	A	
Curlew *Numenius arquata*	LC	A	
Spotted Redshank *Tringa erythropus*	LC	A	
Redshank *Tringa totanus*	LC	A	
Greenshank *Tringa nebularia*	LC	A	
Green Sandpiper *Tringa ochropus*	LC	A	
Wood Sandpiper *Tringa glareola*	LC	A	
Common Sandpiper *Actitis hypoleucos*	LC	A	
Ruddy Turnstone *Arenaria interpres*	LC	A	
Knot *Calidris canutus*	LC	A	
Sanderling *Calidris alba*	LC	A	
Little Stint *Calidris minuta*	LC	A	
Temminck's Stint *Calidris temminckii*	LC	A	
Curlew Sandpiper *Calidris ferruginea*	LC	A	
Purple Sandpiper *Calidris maritima*	LC	A	
Dunlin *Calidris alpina*	LC	A	
Ruff *Philomachus pugnax*	LC	A	
Wilson's Phalarope *Steganopus tricolor*	LC	A*	
Red-necked Phalarope *Phalaropus lobatus*	LC	A	
Collared Pratincole *Glareola pratincola*	LC	A	
Common (Mew) Gull *Larus canus*	LC	A	
Audouin's Gull *Larus audouinii*	NT	A	
Yellow-legged Gull *Larus michahellis*	LC	A	
Lesser Black-backed Gull *Larus fuscus*	LC	A	
Black-headed Gull *Larus ridibundus*	LC	A	
Slender-billed Gull *Larus genei*	LC	A	

Species	Category	Status	Seen
Mediterranean Gull *Larus melanocephalus*	LC	A	
Little Gull *Larus minutus*	LC	A	
Gull-billed Tern *Sterna nilotica*	LC	A	
Caspian Tern *Sterna caspia*	LC	A	
Sandwich Tern *Sterna sandvicensis*	LC	A	
Common Tern *Sterna hirundo*	LC	A	
Arctic Tern *Sterna paradisaea*	LC	A	
Little Tern *Sterna albifrons*	LC	A	
Whiskered Tern *Chlidonias hybrida*	LC	A	
Black Tern *Chlidonias niger*	LC	A	
Pin-tailed Sandgrouse *Pterocles alchata*	LC	A	
Black-bellied Sandgrouse *Pterocles orientalis*	LC	A	
Rock Pigeon *Columba livia*	LC	A	
Feral Pigeon *Columba.l.domestica*	LC	DE	
Stock Dove *Columba oenas*	LC	A	
Wood Pigeon *Columba palumbus*	LC	A	
Turtle Dove *Streptopelia turtur*	LC	A	
Collared Dove *Streptopelia decaocto*	LC	A	
Rose-ringed Parakeet *Psittacula krameri*	LC	C	
Monk Parakeet *Myiopsitta monachus*	LC	C	
Great Spotted Cuckoo *Clamator glandarius*	LC	A	
Cuckoo *Cuculus canorus*	LC	A	
Barn Owl *Tyto alba*	LC	A	
Scops Owl *Otus scops*	LC	A	
Eagle Owl *Bubo bubo*	LC	A	
Tawny Owl *Strix aluco*	LC	A	
Little Owl *Athene noctua*	LC	A	
Long-eared Owl *Asio otus*	LC	A	
Short-eared Owl *Asio flammeus*	LC	A	
Red-necked Nightjar *Caprimulgus ruficollis*	LC	A	
Nightjar *Caprimulgus europaeus*	LC	A	
Alpine Swift *Tachymarptis melba*	LC	A	
Common Swift *Apus apus*	LC	A	
Pallid Swift *Apus pallidus*	LC	A	
Little Swift *Apus affinis*	LC	A	
White-rumped Swift *Apus caffer*	LC	A	
Roller *Coracias garrulus*	NT	A	
Kingfisher *Alcedo atthis*	LC	A	
Bee-eater *Merops apiaster*	LC	A	
Hoopoe *Upupa epops*	LC	A	
Wryneck *Jynx torquilla*	LC	A	

Species	Category	Status	Seen
Lesser Spotted Woodpecker *Dendrocopos minor*	LC	A	
Great Spotted Woodpecker *Dendrocopos major*	LC	A	
Green Woodpecker *Picus viridis*	LC	A	
Great Grey Shrike *Lanius excubitor*	LC	A	
Southern Grey Shrike *Lanius meridionalis*	LC	A	
Woodchat Shrike *Lanius senator*	LC	A	
Golden Oriole *Oriolus oriolus*	LC	A	
Jay *Garrulus glandarius*	LC	A	
Azure-winged Magpie *Cyanopica cyanus*	LC	A	
Magpie *Pica pica*	LC	A	
(Red-billed) Chough *Pyrrhocorax pyrrhocorax*	LC	A	
Jackdaw *Corvus monedula*	LC	A	
Rook *Corvus frugilegus*	LC	A	
Carrion Crow *Corvus corone*	LC	A	
Common Raven *Corvus corax*	LC	A	
Coal Tit *Periparus ater*	LC	A	
Crested Tit *Lopophanes cristatus*	LC	A	
Great Tit *Parus major*	LC	A	
Blue Tit *Cyanistes caeruleus*	LC	A	
Penduline Tit *Remiz pendulinus*	LC	A	
Sand Martin *Riparia riparia*	LC	A	
Barn Swallow *Hirundo rustica*	LC	A	
Crag Martin *Hirundo rupestris*	LC	A	
House Martin *Delichon urbicum*	LC	A	
Red-rumped Swallow *Hirundo daurica*	LC	A	
Long-tailed Tit *Aegithalos caudatus*	LC	A	
Calandra Lark *Melanocorypha calandra*	LC	A	
Short-toed Lark *Calandrella brachydactyla*	LC	A	
Lesser Short-toed Lark *Calandrella rufescens*	LC	A	
Dupont's Lark *Chersophilus duponti*	NT	A	
Crested Lark *Galerida cristata*	LC	A	
Thekla Lark *Galerida theklae*	LC	A	
Wood Lark *Lullula arborea*	LC	A	
Skylark *Alauda arvensis*	LC	A	
Zitting Cisticola *Cisticola juncidis*	LC	A	
Cetti's Warbler *Cettia cetti*	LC	A	
Grasshopper Warbler *Locustella naevia*	LC	A	
Savi's Warbler *Locustella luscinioides*	LC	A	
Great Reed Warbler *Acrocephalus arundinaceus*	LC	A	
Sedge Warbler *Acrocephalus schoenobaenus*	LC	A	
Reed Warbler *Acrocephalus scirpaceus*	LC	A	

Species	Category	Status	Seen
Western Olivaceous Warbler *Hippolais opaca*	LC	A	
Melodious Warbler *Hippolais polyglotta*	LC	A	
Willow Warbler *Phylloscopus trochilus*	LC	A	
Common Chiffchaff *Phylloscopus collybita*	LC	A	
Iberian Chiffchaff *Phylloscopus ibericus*	LC	A	
Bonelli's Warbler *Phylloscopus bonelli*	LC	A	
Blackcap *Sylvia atricapilla*	LC	A	
Garden Warbler *Sylvia borin*	LC	A	
Orphean Warbler *Sylvia hortensis*	LC	A	
Common Whitethroat *Sylvia communis*	LC	A	
Dartford Warbler *Sylvia undata*	NT	A	
Spectacled Warbler *Sylvia conspicillata*	LC	A	
Subalpine Warbler *Sylvia cantillans*	LC	A	
Sardinian Warbler *Sylvia melanocephala*	LC	A	
Bearded Reedling *Panurus biarmicus*	LC	A	
Firecrest *Regulus ignicapilla*	LC	A	
Wren *Troglodytes troglodytes*	LC	A	
Nuthatch *Sitta europaea*	LC	A	
Short-toed Treecreeper *Certhia brachydactyla*	LC	A	
Starling *Sturnus vulgaris*	LC	A	
Spotless Starling *Sturnus unicolor*	LC	A	
Ring Ouzel *Turdus torquatus*	LC	A	
Blackbird *Turdus merula*	LC	A	
Fieldfare *Turdus pilaris*	LC	A	
Redwing *Turdus iliacus*	LC	A	
Song Thrush *Turdus philomelos*	LC	A	
Mistle Thrush *Turdus viscivorus*	LC	A	
Robin *Erithacus rubecula*	LC	A	
Bluethroat *Luscinia svecica*	LC	A	
Nightingale *Luscinia megarhynchos*	LC	A	
Rufous-tailed Scrub Robin *Erythropygia galactotes*	LC	A	
Black Redstart *Phoenicurus ochruros*	LC	A	
Redstart *Phoenicurus phoenicurus*	LC	A	
Whinchat *Saxicola rubetra*	LC	A	
Stonechat *Saxicola rubicola*	LC	A	
Northern Wheatear *Oenanthe oenanthe*	LC	A	
Black-eared Wheatear *Oenanthe hispanica*	LC	A	
Black Wheatear *Oenanthe leucura*	LC	A	
(Rufous-tailed) Rock-thrush *Monticola saxatilis*	LC	A	
Blue Rock-thrush *Monticola solitarius*	LC	A	
Spotted Flycatcher *Muscicapa striata*	LC	A	

Species	Category	Status	Seen
Pied Flycatcher *Ficedula hypoleuca*	LC	A	
Dipper *Cinclus cinclus*	LC	A	
House Sparrow *Passer domesticus*	LC	A	
Spanish Sparrow *Passer hispaniolensis*	LC	A	
Tree Sparrow *Passer montanus*	LC	A	
Rock Sparrow *Petronia petronia*	LC	A	
Orange-cheeked Waxbill *Estrilda melpoda*	LC	CE	
Black-rumped Waxbill *Estrilda troglodytes*	LC	CE	
Common Waxbill *Estrilda astrild*	LC	CE	
Red Avadavat *Amandava amandava*	LC	CE	
Alpine Accentor *Prunella collaris*	LC	A	
Dunnock *Prunella modularis*	LC	A	
Blue-headed Wagtail *Motacilla flava flava*	LC	A	
Citrine Wagtail *Motacilla citreola*	LC	A*	
Grey Wagtail *Motacilla cinerea*	LC	A	
White Wagtail *Motacilla alba*	LC	A	
Tawny Pipit *Anthus campestris*	LC	A	
Meadow Pipit *Anthus pratensis*	LC	A	
Tree Pipit *Anthus trivialis*	LC	A	
Water Pipit *Anthus spinoletta*	LC	A	
Chaffinch *Fringilla coelebs*	LC	A	
Brambling *Fringilla montifringilla*	LC	A	
Serin *Serinus serinus*	LC	A	
Greenfinch *Carduelis chloris*	LC	A	
Siskin *Carduelis spinus*	LC	A	
Goldfinch *Carduelis carduelis*	LC	A	
Citril Finch *Carduelis citrinella*	LC	A	
Common Redpoll *Carduelis flammea*	LC	A*	
Linnet *Carduelis cannabina*	LC	A	
Red Crossbill *Loxia curvirostra*	LC	A	
Hawfinch *Coccothraustes coccothraustes*	LC	A	
Corn Bunting *Miliaria calandra*	LC	A	
Yellowhammer *Emberiza citrinella*	LC	A	
Rock Bunting *Emberiza cia*	LC	A	
Ortolan Bunting *Emberiza hortulana*	LC	A	
Cirl Bunting *Emberiza cirlus*	LC	A	
Reed Bunting *Emberiza schoeniclus*	LC	A	

Andalucian Flower Checklist

LIST OF SOME COMMON SPECIES OCCURING IN ANDALUCÍA
(List kindly provided by Martin Jacoby)

Plants: (reference numbers in Mediterranean Wild Flowers
by Blamey & Grey-Wilson, Harper/Collins 1993)

Species		Date	Place
0058	Birthwort *Aristolochia bætica*		
0130c	Snow in Summer *Cerastium gibraltaricum* *(boissieri)*		
0157	Bladder Campion *Silene vulgaris*		
0191c	Wood Pink *Dianthus sylvestris*		
0197c	Spanish Barberry *Berberis hispanica*		
0208	Virgin's Bower *Clematis cirrhosa*		
0243	Spiny-fruited Buttercup *Ranunculus muricatus*		
0258c	Dwarf Lark's-spur *Delphinium nanum/gracile*		
0276	Peony *Pæonia broteroi*		
0283	Corn Poppy *Papaver rhœas*		
0310c	Hedge Mustard *Sisymbrium officinale*		
0313	Sand Stock *Malcolmia littorea*		
0336	Sweet Alison *Lobularia maritima*		
0337c	Shepherd's Purse *Capsell bursa-pastoris*		
0354c	Purple Cabbage *Moricandia moricandioides*		
0354c	Wall Rocket *Diplotaxis catholica*		
0355c	Black Mustard *Brassica nigra*		
0376	Wild Mignonette *Reseda lutea*		
0377	Dyer's Rocket *Reseda luteola*		
0382	Stonecrop *Sedum sediforme*		
0396	Navelwort *Umbilicus rupestris*		
0404	Evergreen Rose *Rosa sempervirens*		
0416c	Wild Pear *Pyrus bourgæna*		
0420c	Hawthorn *Cratægus monogyna*		
0428	Bramble *Rubus sp.*		

Species		Date	Place
0431	Carob *Ceratonia siliquae*		
0446	Bean *Trefoil Anagyris foetida*		
0453	Spiny Broom *Calycotome villosa*		
0454	Hairy Broom *Cytisus villosus*		
0475	Gorse *Ulex europæus*		
0478	Yellow Broom *Retama (= Lygos) sphærocarpa*		
0480	White Broom *Retama (= Lygos) monosperma*		
0481	Spanish Broom *Spartium junceum*		
0483	Yellow Lupin *Lupinus luteus*		
0508	Pitch Trefoil *Psoralea bituminosa*		
0525	Yellow Vetch *Vicia lutea*		
0536	Tangier Pea *Lathyrus tingitanus*		
0550	Pea *Lathyrus clymenum*		
0556	Large Yellow Restharrow *Ononis natrix*		
0572	Small-flowered Melilot *Melilotus indica*		
0596	Lucerne *Medicago sativa*		
0625	Common Bird's-foot Trefoil *Lotus corniculatus*		
0640	Orange Bird's-foot *Ornithopus pinnatus*		
0642	White Clover *Trifolium repens*		
0644	Hare's-foot Clover *Trifolium arvense*		
0645	Red Clover *Trifolium pratense*		
0662	Star Clover *Trifolium stellatum*		
0682	Asparagus Pea *Tetragonobolus purpureus*		
0684	*Scorpiurus muricatus*		
0690	Kidney Vetch *Anthyllis vulneraria*		
0696	Rush-like Scorpion Vetch *Coronilla juncea*		
0708	Horseshoe Vetch *Hippocrepis multisiliquosa*		
0710	Italian Sanfoin *Hedysarum coronarium*		
0735	Bermuda Buttercup *Oxalis pes-caprae*		
0743	Round-leaved Crane's-bill *Geranium rotundifolium*		
0748	Little Robin *Geranium purpureum*		
0761	Common Stork's-bill *Erodium cicutarium*		
0763c	Ivy *Hedera helix*		
0787c	Yellow Flax *Linum tenue*		
0799	Sun Spurge *Euphorbia helioscopia*		
0813	Sea Spurge *Euphorbia paralias*		

Species		Date	Place
0820	Annual Mercury *Mercurialis annua*		
0824	Castor Oil Plant *Ricinus communis*		
0850	Common Milkwort *Polygala vugaris*		
0865	Mastic Tree *Pistacia lentiscus*		
0885	Mediterranean Buckthorn *Rhamnus alaternus*		
0893c	Spanish Mallow *Malva hispanica*		
0897	Small-flowered Mallow *Malva parviflora*		
0910	Small Tree Mallow *Lavatera cretica*		
0917	*Stegia (= Lavatera) trimestris*		
0936	Mediterranean Mezereon *Daphne gnidium*		
0953	Perfoliate St John's-wort *Hypericum perfoliatum*		
0961	Grey-leaved Cistus *Cistus albidus*		
0971	Gum Cistus *Cistus ladanifer*		
0975	*Halimium halimifolium*		
1017	French Tamarisk *Tamarix gallica*		
1032	Squirting Cucumber *Ecballium elaterium*		
1033	White Bryony *Bryonia cretica*		
1052	Myrtle *Myrtus communis*		
1073	Sea Holly *Eryngium maritimum*		
1074	Eryngo *Eryngium aquifolium*		
1087	Alexanders *Smyrnium olosatrum*		
1097	Shepherd's Needle *Scandix pecten-veneris*		
1101	Rock Samphire *Crithmum maritimum*		
1105	Water Dropwort *Oenanthe fistulosa*		
1108	Fennel *Fœniculum vulgare*		
1134	Corn Caraway *Rhidolfia segetum*		
1136	False Bishop's Weed *Ammi visnaga*		
1141	Giant Fennel *Ferula communis*		
1161	Spreading Hedge Parsley *Torilis arvensis*		
1168	Wild Carrot *Daucus carota*		
1176	Strawberry Tree *Arbutus unedo*		
1178	Tree Heath *Erica arborea*		
1198	Scarlet Pimpernel *Anagallis arvensis*		
1245c	Narrow-leaved Ash *Fraxinus angustifolia*		
1248	Olive *Olea europæa*		
1251	Common Centaury *Centaurium erythræa*		

Species		Date	Place
1256	Oleander *Nerium oleander*		
1289c	Cleavers *Galium aparine*		
1305	Wild Madder *Rubia peregrina*		
1305c	Field Madder *Sherardia arvensis*		
1316	Bindweed *Calystegia sepium*		
1331	Mallow-leaved Bindweed *Convolvulus althæoides*		
1338	Dwarf Convolvulus *Convolvulus tricolor*		
1341	Heliotrope *Heliotropium europæum*		
1355c	Gromwell *Lithodora prostrata*		
1367	Honeywort *Cerinthe major*		
1383	Purple Viper's Buglos *Echium plantagineum*		
1395	Borage *Borago officinalis*		
1429	Tree Germander *Teucrium fruticans*		
1445	White Horehound *Marrubium vulgare*		
1465	Jerusalem Sage *Phlomis purpurea*		
1469c	Horehound *Ballota hirsuta*		
1485c	Woundwort *Stachys ocymastrum*		
1499c	Wood Calamint *Calamintha sylvatica*		
1524	Pennyroyal *Menta puligeum*		
1526	Rosemary *Rosmarinus officinalis*		
1528	French Lavender *Lavandula stœchas*		
1545	Wild Clary *Salvia verbenaca*		
1563	Black Nightshade *Solanum nigrum*		
1573	Mandrake *Mandragora autumnalis*		
1589	French Figwort *Scrophularia canina*		
1601	Mullein *Verbascum sinuatum*		
1609	Snapdragon *Antirrhinum majus*		
1626c	Sad Toadflax *Linaria tristis*		
1636	Woolly Fluellen *Kickxia lanigera*		
1645	Ivy-leaved Speedwell *Veronica hederifolia*		
1646	Pale Speedwell *Veronica cymbalaria*		
1651	Yellow Bartsia *Parentucellia viscosa*		
1655	Branched Broomrape *Orobanche ramosa*		
1693	Greater Plantain *Plantago major*		
1706	Plantain *Plantago afra*		
1711	Laurustinus *Viburnum tinus*		

Species		Date	Place
1713c	Honeysuckle *Lonicera periclymenum*		
1720	Fedia *Fedia cornucopiae*		
1725	Red Valerian *Centranthus calcitrapa*		
1732	Wild Teasel *Dipsacus fullonum*		
1749c	Drumstick Scabious *Scabiosa simplex*		
1759	Rampion Bellflower *Campanula rapunculus*		
1783	Throatwort *Trachelium cæruleum*		
1793	Southern Daisy *Bellis sylvatica*		
1824	Everlasting Flower *Helichrysum stœchas*		
1842	Aromatic Inula *Dittrichia (= Inula) viscosa*		
1843	Common Fleabane *Pulicaria dysenterica*		
1848	Yellow Sea Aster *Asteriscus maritimus*		
1858	Corn Chamomile *Anthemis arvensis*		
1879	Yellow Milfoil *Achillea ageratum*		
1890	Anacyclus *Anacyclus radiatus*		
1894	Corn Marigold *Chrysanthemum segetum*		
1895	Crown Daisy *Chrysanthemum coronarium*		
1908	Corn Marigold *Calendula arvensis*		
1916	Common Groundsel *Senecio vulgaris*		
1920	Flat-topped Carline Thistle *Carlina corymbosa*		
1935c	Globe Thistle *Echinops strigosus*		
1960	Giant Thistle *Cirsium scabrum*		
1960c	Stemless Thistle *Cirsium acaule*		
1966	Syrian Thistle *Notobasis syriaca*		
1970	Spanish Thistle *Chamæpeuce (=Ptilostemon) hispanica*		
1971	Galactites *Galactites tomentosa*		
1979c	Humble Artichoke *Cynara humilis*		
1982	Milk Thistle *Silybum marianum*		
1988	Mantisalca *Mantisalca salmantica*		
1990	Red Star-thistle *Centaurea calcitrapa*		
2006	Knapweed *Centaurea pullata*		
2020	Spanish Oyster Plant *Scolymus hispanicus*		
2023	Chicory *Cichorium intybus*		
2030	Bearded Tolpis *Tolpis barbata*		
2032	False Dandelion *Hyoseris radiata*		
2046	Ox-tongue *Picris echioides*		

Species		Date	Place
2059	Meadow Goat's Beard *Tragopogon pratensis*		
2067c	Hawk's-beard *Crepis vesicaria*		
2073	Sow-thistle *Sonchus tenerrimus*		
2076	Prickly Lettuce *Lactuca serriola*		
2081	Rabbit's Bread *Andryala integrifolia*		
2090	Branched Asphodel *Asphodelus ramosus agg.*		
2096	Blue Leafless Lily *Aphyllanthes monspeliensis*		
2113c	Autumn Crocus *Colchicum lusitanum*		
2163	Sea Squill *Urginea maritima*		
2171c	Star of Bethlehem *Ornithogallum orthophyllum*		
2183	Peruvian Squill *Scilla peruviana*		
2191	Spanish Bluebell *Hyacinthoides hispanica*		
2201	Tassel Hyacinth *Muscari comosum*		
2215	Leafless Asparagus *Asparagus aphyllus*		
2222	Smilax *Smilax aspera*		
2224	Rosy Garlic *Allium roseum*		
2229	Three-cornered Leek *Allium triquetrum*		
2265	Hair-leaved Snowflake *Leucojum trichophyllum*		
2270	Sea Daffodil *Pancratium maritimum*		
2278	Paper-white Narcissus *Narcissus papyraceus*		
2282	Black Bryony *Tamus communis*		
2290	Yellow Flag *Iris pseudacorus*		
2305	Barbary Nut *Gynandiris sisyrinchium*		
2307	Field Gladiolus *Gladiolus italicus (= segetum)*		
2314	Romulea *Romulea bulbocodium*		
2357	Dwarf Fan Palm *Chamærops humilis*		
2361	Large Cuckoo Pint *Arum italicum*		
2378	Friar's Cowl *Arisarum simorrhinum*		
2380	Broad-leaved Helleborine *Epipactis helleborine*		
2397	Heath Spotted Orchid *Dactylorhiza maculata*		
2416	Early Purple Orchid *Orchis mascula ssp. olbiensis*		
2422	Mirror Orchid *Ophrys ciliatum (= speculum)*		
2423	Yellow Bee Orchid *Ophrys lutea*		
2442	Sawfly Orchid *Ophrys tenthredinifera*		
2444	Bumblebee Orchid *Ophrys bombyliflora*		
2451	Tongue Orchid *Serapias lingua*		

Glossary

acequia	a man-made irrigation channel. Many of those in Andalucía date from the Moorish period
alcornoques	cork oaks
almiñar	minaret
arroyo	stream
ayuntamiento	town hall
barranco	gorge or canyon of the type found in the Alpujarras
cairn	small pile of rocks/stones serving as way-marker
calera	pit where lime was made by firing limestone.
canuto	steep sided gorge where a warm, humid climate fosters extraordinarily diverse flora
capilla	chapel
cerro	peak or mountain
choza	simple hut or dwelling, often with thatched roof
cortijo	farm, from a few to several thousand acres large
coto (de caza)	hunting reserve
dehesa	forest which has been partially cleared to leave selected species eg evergreen and cork oak.
era	threshing area, often circular
guiri	foreigner (slang)
G.R.	abbreviation for Gran Recorrido or Long Distance Footpath
huerta	small patch of cultivated land
humilladero	small mountain shrine

karst	type of limestone
laja	jagged ridge formed when limestone strata run vertically upwards
mirador	viewing point
puerto	mountain pass
P.R.	abbreviation for Pequeño Recorrido or Short Distance Footpath
rejas	window grills
romería	procession and picnic, often involving an open-air mass at a chapel or shrine
sierra	range of mountains
secadero	flat platforms used in the Aaxrquía for laying out grapes in the sunshine
tinao	roof spanning a village street in the Alpujarras

Hoja de pedido de mapas
Maps Order Form

Atención de: *To:* ....

Email/Fax: ....

De Parte de: *From:* ....

Email/Fax: ....

Fecha: *Date:* ....

Estimados Señores/Señoras,

Dear Sir/Madam,

Les ruego mandarme los siguientes mapas, contra reembolso:

Please send me the following maps, to be paid on receipt of order:

No(s) de Mapa(s): Map reference(s):

....

....

....

....

....

El pedido va en nombre de: *Please send order in the name of:*

....

A esta dirección: *To this address:*

....

....

....

....

Les agradezco su amable cooperación

Many thanks for your help

Also by Guy Hunter-Watts

The Andalucían Coast to Coast Walk

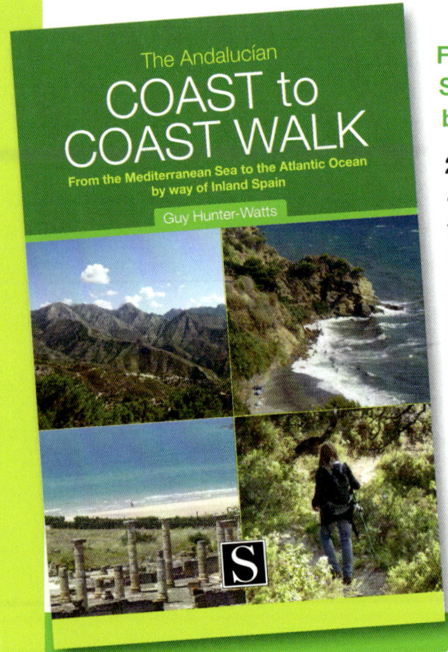

From the Mediterranean Sea to the Atlantic Ocean by way of Inland Spain

21 days of walking, 430 kilometres of trail through pristine Natural Parks and ancient hilltop villages.

This extraordinary on-foot odyssey takes you from the Mediterranean Sea to the Atlantic Ocean through southern Spain's most beautiful tract of mountain terrain.

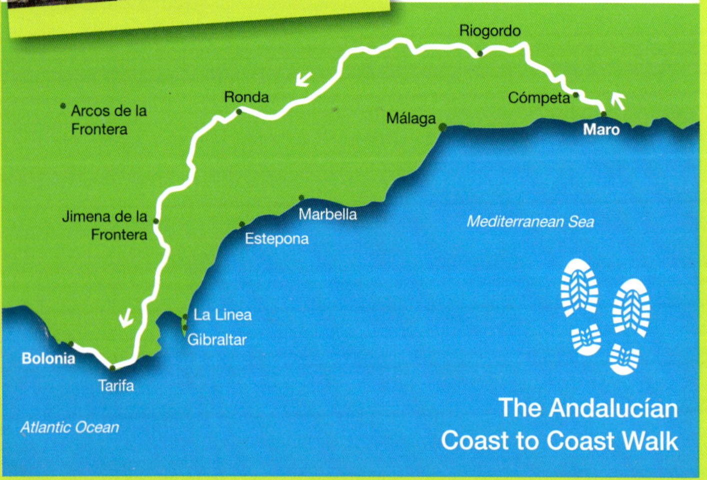

ISBN: 978-84-89954-89-2 Buy online at: www.santanabooks.com